The Book of Numbers

THE BOOK OF NUMBERS

A Critique of Genesis

Calum Carmichael

Yale
UNIVERSITY
PRESS
New Haven & London

Copyright © 2012 by Yale University.
All rights reserved.
This book may not be reproduced, in whole or in part, including illustrations, in any form (beyond that copying permitted by Sections 107 and 108 of the U.S. Copyright Law and except by reviewers for the public press), without written permission from the publishers.

Yale University Press books may be purchased in quantity for educational, business, or promotional use. For information, please e-mail sales.press@yale.edu (U.S. office) or sales@yaleup.co.uk (U.K. office).

Set in Postscript Electra type by Westchester Book Group.
Printed in the United States of America.

Library of Congress Cataloging-in-Publication Data
Carmichael, Calum M.
The book of Numbers : a critique of Genesis / Calum Carmichael.
  p.   cm.
Includes bibliographical references and index.
ISBN 978-0-300-17918-7 (alk. paper)
1. Bible. O.T. Numbers—Commentaries.   2. Bible. O.T. Genesis—Commentaries.   I. Title.
BS1265.53.C37 2012
222'.1406—dc23   2011044949

A catalogue record for this book is available from the British Library.

This paper meets the requirements of ANSI/NISO Z39.48–1992 (Permanence of Paper).

10 9 8 7 6 5 4 3 2 1

Contents

Preface   vii

ONE   Genesis Extended   1

TWO   Pharaoh and Yahweh as God-Kings (Numbers 1–4)   15

THREE   The Suspected Adulteress and the Nazirite (Numbers 5 and 6)   26

FOUR   A Test Case for the Study of Biblical Law
(Lev 6:2–7 [5:20–26] and Num 5:6–10)   44

FIVE   Joseph and Moses as Sources of Discord (Numbers 7–14)   54

SIX   Joseph's Dreams and the Laws of Numbers 15   68

SEVEN   The Status of Firstborn (Numbers 16–18)   90

EIGHT   The Ritual of the Red Heifer (Numbers 19)   103

NINE   Speech Acts (Numbers 20–24)   120

TEN   Sexual and Religious Seduction (Numbers 25–31)   135

ELEVEN   Reuben's Legacy (Numbers 32–36)   159

List of Abbreviations   179

Notes   181

Index of References   195

Subject Index   205

Preface

The Book of Numbers, the least researched of the books that make up the Pentateuch, presents a puzzling combination of law and narrative. Seemingly haphazard sequences of rules interrupt an ongoing story about Israel's wanderings in the wilderness. Some of these rules are often analyzed (the suspected adulteress, the daughters of Zelophehad, and the Sabbath stick-gatherer), and some have proved elusive (the Red Heifer and the nazirite). With this book I continue a process of discovery that, in the beginning, I did not know I was undertaking: to demonstrate how each law in the Pentateuch is a response to a problem arising in a narrative incident. Events in the Book of Genesis prove to be the springboard for every rule in Numbers. At the same time, I show that the same thinking is at work for the narratives in Numbers. They present episodes parallel in Genesis in order to counter disturbing developments that occurred among the fathers of the nation. I propose a new way of thinking about how the Pentateuch came into being, a perspective that opposes the long-standing Graf-Wellhausen, JEDP hypothesis about different sources (Jahwistic, Elohistic, Deuteronomistic, and Priestly).

This book's primary aim is to transform our understanding of Numbers. Noting that stories in Genesis are so written as to anticipate future events like the sojourn and enslavement in Egypt and the acquisition of the land of Canaan, I argue that the migratory account of Jacob-Israel and his sons in Canaan and Egypt, the beginnings of the nation's history in Genesis 25–50, furnishes issues on which Numbers, in both story and law, renders judgment. Numbers also thinks ahead to life beyond Israel's wilderness wanderings between Egypt and Canaan in the era of Moses. Opposing what occurred among the fathers of the nation and among the wilderness generation, Numbers holds out higher standards to which later Israelites are to adhere.

In quoting biblical texts I have relied upon the King James Authorized Version (AV) of 1611, but I have made changes where these were called for. I have used the AV because it is almost always a more literal rendering of the Hebrew original than any other translation. It also serves to remind the reader that biblical literature is a product of the past and hence of a different culture from our own.

I thank Ryan O'Dowd, Cornell University, and Blaire French, University of Virginia, Charlottesville, for their helpful comments on some chapters. Most of all, I am indebted to my wife, Debbie, for her critical comments and close attention to every facet of the manuscript.

1

Genesis Extended

The Book of Numbers is an integral part of a narrative that runs from Genesis through 2 Kings: the Primary History, as it has come to be called.[1] Numbers might be viewed as a study in secular and sacred leadership—with a twist. Moses represents more the secular side and Aaron the sacred. The twist is that their decisions and actions often oppose the ways of the ancestors in the Book of Genesis, particularly the conduct of Jacob, Judah, and Joseph. Before proceeding to an analysis of Numbers (in chapter 2), some comments are in order to introduce the role of Numbers in Genesis–2 Kings.

The Primary History depicts life from the creation of the world through the creation of Israel as a nation to its end in exile in Babylon. In the epic we have the unfolding of the history of the generations. There is among scholars, most welcome in my view, increasing recognition of and detailed argumentation from a nonreligious perspective for the unified character of Genesis–2 Kings. Much recent work has paid attention to the connections between one narrative and another, with Moshe Garsiel one of many critics pointing to the numerous links: for instance, the marriages of David and Jacob in 1 Samuel 18 and Genesis 29, respectively, which involve two sisters, noncommercial bride-prices, devious fathers-in-law, and the flight from them, which requires a wife (Michal, Rachel) to make use of household gods (*teraphim*) in order to escape the hostile fathers (Saul, Laban). I have long argued that the fable about the proposed marriage between the son of the thistle and the daughter of the cedar in 2 Kgs 14:1–14, puzzlingly relayed to curb the saber-rattling of King Amaziah, owes a great deal to the story in Genesis 34 about the slaughter of all the males of Hamor's clan by the two sons of Jacob, Simeon and Levi. They took up arms against the proposed marital alliance between the son of the ass (Hamor) and the daughter of the ox (Jacob). A major aim of this book is to bring out a plethora of hitherto unrecognized links between the narratives and laws in Numbers and the contents of Genesis. Greifenhagen's claim that "Joseph is essentially bypassed" and forgotten after his story has been relayed at the end of Genesis could not be further from the truth, as is Thomas Römer's claim that the Joseph story is virtually an appendage to the Pentateuch in its final form.[2]

Bodies of rules, law codes in some sense—for instance, Exodus 21–23 and Deuteronomy 12–26—are part of the narrative history of Genesis–2 Kings. Numbers does not have a comparable body of rules that might conveniently be called a code of laws but we do find, interspersed among its narratives, different sequences of rules. The joint presentation of storytelling and laws, not just in Numbers but to a lesser extent in Leviticus too, immediately invites puzzlement because the recitation of a series of rules that every so often interrupts a continuous narrative history seems anomalous. Equally awkward is the impression that there often appears to be neither rhyme nor reason why one law follows another. This mode of literary arrangement wherein it appears that narrative flow is interrupted by legal text is present throughout the Pentateuch. Because Numbers is a continuation of Leviticus I shall focus in this chapter on some laws in Leviticus to set the stage for my analysis of Numbers, for what is true of Leviticus is also true of Numbers.

Consider, then, one example from Leviticus that serves well to indicate the problem of sequence. Lev 19:11–12 has a seemingly haphazard succession of rules—theft, false dealing, lying, swearing falsely by Yahweh's name, and profaning God's name: "Ye shall not steal, neither deal falsely, neither lie one to another. And ye shall not swear by my name falsely, neither shalt thou profane the name of thy God: I am Yahweh." If we consider this particular instance of the problem of sequence, the issues that arise are worth unpacking because the example serves to lay out clearly the difference between the long-standing Wellhausen, JEDP, scholarly approach and my argument about the highly integrated character of Genesis–2 Kings.

A recent book by Christophe Nihan brings out the gulf in the respective positions. His book is a model of its kind: very well researched in terms of the Wellhausian approach he favors and faithful to scholars who strongly adhere to the method in question. His aim is "to reassess the difficult question of the formation history of the book of Leviticus, in relationship to the composition of the Torah as a whole and to the history of the early Second Temple period, during which this book was written."[3] He makes the common claim that, despite appearances, Leviticus was not composed as a coherent narrative at a certain historical moment but incorporates a considerable number of additions over time.

Almost all the added extras he identifies he detects by exercising sensitivity to language and syntax; and also by inferring historical developments behind literary texts. One problem, however, is that different scholars exhibit different sensitivities to language and syntax, providing many variations in parsing texts, and, from my perspective, producing quite bewildering arrays of propositions about editorial additions and the dating thereof. While Nihan details the many scholars and their views, he does not address the implicit but never questioned assumption that differences in the texts must necessarily indicate differences in the period of time they were produced. My approach is fundamentally at odds with their attribution of historical development, so carefully yet so variably parsed from the texts and unquestioningly based by these scholars on that bulwark of received opinion, the JEDP hypothesis. Moreover, working on the same historical critical assumptions, on the same material in the Pentateuch (the Patriarchal stories in Genesis and the account of the Exodus from Egypt), scholars such as Römer and John Van Seters come to results quite at odds with each other. For the latter JE is the primary redactor, for the former it is P.[4]

One of Nihan's conclusions is a typical tour de force of contemporary neo-Wellhausian scholarship: "Later [after Lev 1–3 has used an alleged earlier document], Lev 1–3 was included into P's narrative by means of Lev 8–9, building an inclusion with Ex 25–29, as well as by various additional redactional devices, such as the envelope created by the motif of Moses' [actually non-] admission into the sanctuary in Ex 40:35 and [admission with Aaron] Lev 9:23." For Nihan, these additions are spread over many periods of time and the dates guessed at. The final form of Leviticus is dated to the Second Temple period and for Nihan constitutes a window into the life and institutions of the state Yehud (Judea after the return from exile). But the complaint of Montesquieu from over two hundred years ago about those who construct history still applies: "They don't make a system after reading history; they begin with the system and then search for proofs. And there are so many facts over a long history, so many different ways of thinking about it, its origins are ordinarily so obscure, that one always finds materials to validate all sorts of opinions."[5]

If we wish to gain insight into the substance of the rules in Leviticus, Nihan has us consider similar rules in law codes that allegedly predate Leviticus: the Decalogue, the Covenant Code, and the Deuteronomic Code. He then cites the succession of rules in Lev 19:11–12 (quoted above), which he claims belong to a separate Holiness Code (H), a fifth main source which Wellhausen's scholarly heirs have added to the Priestly Code of Leviticus 1–15. The Leviticus rule about theft completes the prohibition ... in Ex 20:15; Deut 5:19 [against stealing] with two others concerning deception of a fellow Israelite ... not found in the other codes. V. 12 [about misusing God's name] takes up Ex 20:7; Deut 5:11 [not to use Yahweh's name in vain], but restates it emphasizing the specific aspect of the prohibition on swearing a false oath ... in Yahweh's name (instead of the more general prohibition on misusing the name in the Decalogue), and adds a different rationale: the fear of desecrating Yahweh's [text has God's] name. This rationale betrays a characteristic feature of H which introduces for the first time in the Torah the notion that not only Yahweh but also his [text has God's] *name* are holy and thereby liable to be desecrated.

In Nihan's view, it is all about additions, with the last one supposedly revealing the final editor's contribution to Israelite legal history and Israelite religion.[6]

Plainly, Nihan pursues the form of literary analysis associated with Graf-Wellhausen, dividing the Pentateuch into different sources and assuming that these sources reflect historical development. But it is possible to pursue less complicated means of understanding the text so that, as in mathematics where the simpler solution is usually the more convincing one, the more convoluted one then becomes precarious. For example, when considering the series of laws in Lev 19:11–12, I too assume a narrator-lawgiver (or scribe or school of scribes) who is familiar with other parts of the biblical corpus. But whatever the sources of his knowledge for the diverse contents of this corpus might have been originally, he set down the rules' disparate subject matter in response, not to existing laws in other codes of law in order to update them but to a disturbing event in the life of the nation's founding father, Jacob-Israel (Genesis 27).

Isaac had asked Esau to bring him a game dish that he enjoyed with a view to conferring the blessing of the firstborn on Esau. But in collusion with his mother, Jacob set about stealing Esau's birthright. To this end, the two of them prepared a meat dish from one of their domestic animals. Jacob disguised himself as his hairy brother and presented the dish. Isaac, who was blind, identified the bringer of the meat as Esau by feel and expressed surprise at how quickly he had brought the food. Asked who he was, Jacob lied by saying that he was Esau. We have in this story a clear succession: an intention to steal involving false dealing, followed by a blatant lie. It is the same order as in the prohibitions in Lev 19:11: "Ye shall not steal, neither deal falsely, neither lie one to another." When asked by Isaac about the speed with which he had brought the dish, Jacob, invoking God, swore falsely by audaciously saying, "Yahweh your God made it come before me" (Gen 27:20). In the prohibition in Yahweh's own words against false swearing in Lev 19:12 both names are used—as in Gen 27:20: "Ye shall not swear by my name falsely, neither shalt thou profane the name of thy God: I am Yahweh."[7]

Instead of comprehending this cluster of rules as a product of a bewildering process of redaction involving different and even hypothetical documents and inferred time periods, we can view the medley as formulated in reaction to issues raised when Jacob cheated Esau. Not only do particulars in the episode carry over into details in the rules; by unraveling this thought process a more natural and certainly more engaging method of composition emerges. Did the scribe of Leviticus have before him a written text? I think we should envision the narratives and the laws as being written down simultaneously and being in conversation with each other, rather than one serving as background material to the other. At some seat of learning and training it may have been realized, generally, that to derive the full benefit of several sources of information it was essential to keep them several. Like similar laws probing different aspects of a narrative incident, similar narratives probe different aspects of some basic situation (for example, the suffering of the people in the wilderness because of lack of water). The uncovering of legal, ethical, and religious ideas by a full and thorough integration of the narrative and legal materials has driven the complex composition of Genesis through 2 Kings. It is vain, I think, to try to separate out behind-the-scene sources and impose our historical knowledge on them. Historical inquiry should focus primarily on the narrator's own interest in history, his going back and forth between the generations as recorded in Genesis–2 Kings. The narrator is aware of historical development, and it is his sense of past and future we should heed, not scholarly speculations about the dating of different bodies of material.

While I do not set aside the achievements of the Wellhausian methodology—even if judgments about different strands of material might be off the mark, much illumination is often forthcoming—it is possible to so view the unity of the material as to cast serious doubts on many of the method's results. Even the major distinctions among the inferred sources, P, H, and D, turn out to be decidedly shaky because, in my view, all the material in Genesis–2 Kings is a product of the same process of composition. Critics who have pursued and continue to pursue the source-critical approach are, in my view, like alchemists who attempt to make gold out of disparate elements without suspecting that they stand beside a goldmine.[8]

In concluding a chapter entitled "Genesis as Part of a Larger Unity" that deals with the harmonious character of Genesis–Kings, Tom Brodie states, "There is significant evidence not only that Genesis is unified but that the same is true of the larger body of the Primary History. Many problems within the Primary History remain unresolved, but as with Genesis, the weight of evidence is shifting, and the idea of literary unity is gaining plausibility. It is the simplest hypothesis that accounts for the data."[9] I take Brodie's point further to claim that the laws are an integral part of the larger literary unit of Genesis–2 Kings. Enabling us to discern many more of the interconnections than have been shown to date, my results prove compatible with this developing trend.

My hypothesis that the laws took up issues in the narratives and not, at least not directly, societal problems in the lawgiver's time came long after I noted links between an increasing number of laws and narrative incidents in Genesis–2 Kings. The first time I broke through to what has become my primary hypothesis was when considering the rule against plowing with an ox and an ass together in Deut 22:10. I thought that the rule may not have a literal meaning but, like the rule about illegitimacy in early English law "Whoso bulleth the cow, the calf is yours," be coded communication expressed as a proverb that criticized Jacob's lackadaisical attitude to Shechem's treatment of Dinah.[10] Jacob's moderate approach to Dinah's contact with the Hivite people is depicted in Genesis 34. Jacob seemed not to care overmuch that the house of Israel would enter into a marriage alliance with the Hivite (Canaanite) house of Hamor (Ass). The rule against plowing with an ox and an ass together portrays the idea that Shechem, the son of the ass Hamor, plowed in a sexual sense Dinah, the daughter of the ox—Jacob refers to his house as that of the ox in his comment on the incident in Gen 49:6. The prohibition is directed against intermarriage with the Hivites, an injunction actually spelled out in Deut 7:1–3. One reason for the law's cryptic expression is that it attacks the founding father of the nation, Jacob.

I assume that the narrator-lawgiver's knowledge of legal lore in his time was brought to bear on the nation's traditions and that he used that knowledge to formulate the laws he set down in the text. In this light, although rules come before narratives, the rules set down in the biblical text, having reacted to what is going on in the narratives, reformulate preexisting ones. Because biblical rules are the earliest written version of that early law, we have no way of knowing the legal lore and practices that existed before they were formulated and that the lawgiver was surely steeped in. I do not exclude the possibility that rules found in other Near Eastern writings may have been known to biblical authors, but the evidence remains elusive.[11] When we observe how the procedure is from narrative to legal formulation, not the reverse, strange sequences of rules, oddities in their language, and puzzling features of their contents time and again make sense.

The writing down of a biblical command often meant the spelling out of the rule implicit in the narrative incident in light of how the lawgiver understood the rule in his time. That is, he *formulated* the rule in response to the incident. A good example is the injunction about menstruation in Lev 15:19–24. When Rachel's father, Laban, pursues and catches up with the fleeing Jacob and his family, Rachel hides her father's household gods, which she has stolen from his home. Laban searches for them, but Rachel prevents him from coming upon them by claiming to be unclean because of her menstrual flow of blood. She tells her father that she cannot arise from the camel's saddle on which she sits (Gen 31:34). Implicit in her statement is the notion that he should touch neither her nor the object on which she sits because each is off-limits on account of menstrual blood. It is precisely such a narrative occurrence that typically triggers the lawgiver's interest in any implicit rule that might be at stake, in this instance the one underlying Rachel's attitude to her menstrual discharge. Thus he formulates a rule: "And if a woman have an issue and her issue in her flesh be blood, she shall be apart seven days: and whosoever toucheth her shall be unclean until the even. And every thing that she lieth upon in her separation shall be unclean: every thing also that she sitteth upon shall be unclean" (Lev 15:19, 20).[12]

I have tested almost all of the Pentateuchal rules in light of what takes place in the narratives of Genesis through 2 Kings and find the same relationship at play. I had not, until writing this book, tested the laws in the Book of Numbers against narrative incidents but do so now. With its completion, the tally comes to over four hundred laws since I first began the exercise with the rule against plowing with the ox and the ass. In this book, but confined to Numbers, I also examine an idea I have not considered before in any large-scale manner. Just as a great many laws in Exodus, Deuteronomy, and Leviticus relate to issues in Genesis, so do many of the narratives contained in Exodus–2 Kings, for example, the one about Saul's daughter that Garsiel pointed out. The narratives in Numbers relay the history of Israel's migration from Egypt through the wilderness to the border of Canaan. The write-up of this epic reflects at every turn, I shall argue, the influence of the previous migratory history in Genesis 25–50 when Jacob and his family migrated from Mesopotamia to Canaan and then to Egypt. Past experiences in Canaan and Egypt in the time of the fathers of the nation as depicted in Genesis are the focus of so many of the narratives and the accompanying laws in Numbers.

The recognition that both the narratives and the laws in Numbers consistently return to events in the Book of Genesis is crucial for comprehending in a quite new way Numbers' diverse contents. Balaam's confrontation with an angel, which ensures Israel's deliverance from the king of Moab's enmity, emulates Jacob's confrontation with an angel, which delivers him from a previously hostile Esau (Numbers 22–24; Genesis 32). The five daughters of Zelophehad find that when their sonless father dies they are excluded from inheriting his estate. Moses, however, corrects the existing law of inheritance and permits daughters in the absence of sons to inherit after Israel conquers Canaan (Numbers 27). The topic is taken up because of a dramatic example of potential loss of inheritance in a Genesis episode. Jacob feared that Simeon's and Levi's slaughter of the fathers and sons of the Hivites put the entire house of Jacob at risk of retribution. It would face similar loss of fathers and sons: "And Jacob said to Simeon and Levi, Ye have troubled me to make me to stink among the inhabitants of the land, among the Canaanites and the Perizzites: and I being few in number, they shall gather themselves together against me, and slay me; and I shall be destroyed, I and my house" (Gen 34:30).

The rules about a woman's vow and oath in Num 30:2–17 have a quite specific background in the Genesis account of Jacob's vow to God at Bethel and his oath to Laban on returning to Bethel about the household gods that each man does not know are in the possession of Jacob's wife, Rachel—she is also Laban's daughter—as they flee from her father's house (Gen 28:20–22; 31:32, 35:7, 14, 15). The rules referred to in Num 30:16 about female vows and oaths—"These are the statutes, which Yahweh commanded Moses, *between a man and his wife, between the father and his daughter*, being yet in her youth in her father's house"—come from considering the implications of Jacob's vow at Bethel and his oath to Laban in regard to Rachel (see chapter 10). The supposed ill-fitting material in Numbers 28 and 29, which precedes the section about vows and oaths and which lays out the requirements for cultic life (including some about vows), is also informed by reflection on Jacob's vow at the very beginning of Israel's cultic life, the worship of El-Elohe-Israel in Genesis 32.

Genesis presents the prehistory of Israel's origin as a nation. Numbers, in turn, reviews the period after the Exodus from Egypt when Israel actually becomes a nation and takes up time and again issues in Genesis. The organized cult that we come upon in Exodus, Leviticus, Numbers, and Deuteronomy did not exist during patriarchal times. After the nation with its established cult comes into existence, its founding fathers are not forgotten, and we have assessment of issues touching on the sacred that arose among them. The aim is to ensure that priests properly handle equivalent issues that might turn up in later national life.

To appreciate the composition of Numbers it is crucial to take stock of a mode of history writing that is common at all times. In a justly renowned lecture at St. Paul's Cathedral in London in October 1966, David Daube began by saying, "All history-writing transfers features of one event or one great personage to another, and, indeed, much history-acting is in imitation of previous occurrences. Whoever nowadays writes about Napoleon is likely to lend him some traits of Caesar, and Napoleon himself—not to mention de Gaulle—would on occasion look to that example."[13] The phenomenon of history writing incorporating previous history writing, especially by viewing the present as like the past in order to counter developments in the earlier period, *imitation par opposition*, is a major characteristic of Numbers in relation to Genesis.

In other biblical material the role of imitation par opposition is well recognized. Fate or providence or history has a disguised Joseph pay back his brothers in mirroring fashion to remind them of their evil treatment of him. When they come to Egypt to buy food to relieve the famine back in their own country of Canaan, Joseph is vizier in Egypt. The brothers' acts of hatred against him are recalled—like Moses after him, Joseph is depicted as knowing the past and the future—and there is retaliation in kind. The brothers had concealed the true nature of his fate by having their father believe what his eyes told him, namely, that Joseph's blood-stained coat meant that he had been killed by a wild beast. By way of reprisal, so the narrator slants his story, Joseph falsely accuses the brothers of wrongful looking: they are spies who have come to Egypt to view "the nakedness of the land" (Gen 42:12). A false claim made by the brothers, which involves sight, is paid back by Joseph's false accusation of their wrongful looking. Later, Joseph, once his father's favorite child, has Benjamin, the son who has replaced him in his father's affections, brought to Egypt to remind the brothers of what they did to him. Another instance of imitation par opposition within the Joseph story is worked out in response to the fact that the brothers sought but did not in fact receive money for selling Joseph as a slave.[14] Recall that Joseph had angered his brothers because in a dream he saw himself as a sheaf of grain to which they, as sheaves of grain, would bow down as ruled to ruler or, more to the point, as we shall see in chapter 6, worshipers to a divine being. In Egypt, Joseph torments the brothers by surreptitiously slipping money into their sacks of grain after they have already paid for it. The additional money placed inside the sacks is not a generous act but a retaliatory one representing the payment they never received for attempting to sell Joseph, the exalted "sheaf of grain." When they received the grain from Joseph in Egypt they had indeed bowed down to him, exactly as Joseph's dream predicted (Gen 42:6).

Imitation par opposition frequently shows up in the relationship between one narrative and another. A story often echoes a previous one in order to affirm that justice comes in many forms; that, even if a particular wrong cannot be righted, there is some measure of retribution at work. The second story might not originally even be related to the first. The narrative about Jacob's marriages to the daughters of Laban illustrates the position well. The unwanted elder daughter Leah is slipped into the wedding tent in place of the desired younger daughter Rachel. The story is so recorded that we are meant to see it in relation to Jacob's acquisition of the birthright when he, the younger brother, cheated the elder brother Esau out of the blessing of the firstborn. The narrator does not alert the hearer-reader to the connection, but it is to be picked up nonetheless.

The links between the narratives and the rules in Numbers and the narratives in Genesis about Jacob, Judah, and Joseph are precisely of this implicit kind. I assume that the original recipients of the material, let us say in a scribal school, readily recognized the connections. In any event, the formation of Numbers cannot be understood without awareness of two features: imitating in order to oppose and, in the mode of communication extolled by Heraclitus of Ephesus, "neither telling, nor concealing, but indicating."[15] To be sure, in the literary convention adopted by the scribes when they have Moses turn to incidents in his own lifetime in order to pronounce judgments on them, he is made to cite the event. When, however, they have Moses render judgments on incidents in Genesis, which occurred long before he lived, he is not made to cite events outright, but he is not made to cover over either; instead, he provides indication for those immersed in the nation's lore.

There is, then, a pattern to the presentation of all of the material in Numbers. The past is corrected, particularly unacceptable tendencies that the patriarchs exhibited. Their conduct needed to be judged, even if excused up to a point, because of the milieu in which they operated (in Egypt, for example). If there is a formula at work in the writing up of the history in Numbers, it is repetition with change—in a later generation heading to the new land and for the better because the earlier unacceptable conduct was not to be replicated. The program that emerges takes under particular cognizance the results of Joseph's life and policies in Egypt. An example in Leviticus 25 anticipates the pattern in Numbers: the Jubilee Year that is institutionalized for the Israelites stands in opposition to what Joseph institutionalized for the Egyptians at the end of their famine. The Sabbatical cycle in Leviticus 25, with its climactic Year of Jubilee, relates back to the developments in Egypt. The policy adopted because of Joseph's counsel to Pharaoh is the key to how the Israelite institution came to be formulated. In Genesis 37–50, seven years of plentiful harvests in Egypt are followed by seven years of famine, but Joseph's policy enables everyone to be fed. In a climactic year of the famine, every Egyptian is enslaved and each gives over his ancestral property to Pharaoh. In Lev 25:2–13, seven Sabbatical Years of no harvests interspersed over a period of forty-nine years leads to a climactic fiftieth year when there is again no harvest, but during the fallow years everyone continues to be fed. The seven Sabbatical Years mimic the seven years of famine in Egypt. In the fiftieth year, every enslaved Israelite is freed and every Israelite who has sold ancestral property returns to it—the opposite of what happened to the Egyptians under Joseph.[16]

The literary process I am focusing on shows up in the Book of Genesis. The past is mended by having it repeated but revised in order to oppose its unacceptable tendencies. To justify the attainment of the coveted position of firstborn son, Isaac has to undergo a life-threatening encounter at the hands of his father, Abraham. Isaac's experience mimics his elder brother Ishmael's. Most unfairly, Ishmael underwent a near-death experience after Abraham sent him away into the desert with his mother, Hagar (Genesis 21). God's intervention to prevent intercourse between Sarah and Abimelech in Genesis 20 is intended to communicate, among other matters, a negative reaction to Sarah's sexual defilement by Pharaoh as initiated by Abram in Genesis 12. The narrator (or scribe or school of scribes) responsible for setting out both stories does not remove one and keep the other. After all, the dubiousness of Abraham's and Sarah's ploy is still very much in the fore in Genesis 20. The aim is not to sanitize tradition about Abraham and Sarah but to present the later development by way of furthering ethical reflection on the conduct of the actors in a previously told story, where cultural milieu determines the patriarch's action.

Concentration on patriarchal conduct in Genesis with a view to avoiding its repetition in later Israelite life is a major feature of the narratives and rules recounted in Numbers. The narrative in Numbers 25 and the related one in Numbers 31 depict Israelite antagonism to any dealings with Moabite or Midianite women. The two stories are so written as to counter Israelite idolatrous tendencies by invoking and strengthening the spirit of opposition that Simeon and Levi exhibited when dealing with the Hivites in Genesis 34 and 35. The incipient nation's first sexual and religious encounter with a foreign group, the Hivites, raises the equivalent and more intense concern about encountering the later Moabites and Midianites. Numbers draws out the potential problem of idolatry in the Genesis incident with a view to countering it (see chapter 10). This process of judgment occurs throughout the Book of Numbers. Another instance is how the loss of Joseph to his family in Genesis 37 brings to the attention of the Numbers lawgiver the loss of inheritance to some of Joseph's descendants in Numbers 27 and 36 (see chapters 10 and 11). Arrangements are set out to prevent any loss.

The placement of collections of laws at different points in Genesis through 2 Kings reveals an intense interest in beginnings in line with the major role of Genesis as a document about origins. The deity's rules about killing animals and humans appear at the fresh beginning of the world after the Flood (Gen 9:3–6). The Decalogue, the Book of the Covenant in Exodus 21–23, and the succeeding rules about the institution of the cult make their appearance at the start of the nation after the exodus from Egypt. The laws of Leviticus regulating the priesthood are put immediately after the setting up of the Tabernacle on the first day of the first month in the second year after leaving Egypt, and the laws of Deuteronomy 12–26 are set down in anticipation of the Israelites starting a new life in the land of Canaan. The spotlight is primarily on seminal events as they are depicted in Genesis–2 Kings, and because Genesis contains so many of these its role in Numbers too is substantial.

The primary feature of biblical lawmaking is, I repeat, that the laws take up issues arising in the nation's history, especially at its beginnings, with the laws incorporated into a coherent narrative that begins in Genesis and concludes in 2 Kings. It should seem obvious that if bodies of laws are incorporated into an ongoing narrative at certain points, there will be a significant connection between one and the other. This is indeed the case. When scholars attempt to make sense of the rules by choosing instead to reconstruct actual life in ancient Israel, they have been missing this fundamental feature of all of the laws. The cases the laws take up and render judgment on come not primarily from the world of experience (although there must have been some link to issues in the scribes' own time), but from a narrative history as recorded in Genesis through 2 Kings.

Karl Llewellyn urged law students when first handling cases to knock their ethics into temporary anesthesia and immerse themselves in the cases: "Dig beneath the surface, bring out the story, and you have dramatic tales that stir, that make the cases stick, that weld your law into the whole of culture." When we deal with biblical law, the dramatic tales served up in the biblical texts provide the cases, and digging beneath their surface does indeed furnish the issues the laws take up. Something of a parallel in a quite different ancient culture is how, inspired by the rise of legal advocacy in his time, Sophocles in *Oedipus the King* and *Oedipus at Colonus* explores with consummate literary sensitivity legal and ethical issues in the Greek myths about origins. Recognizing the nature of the biblical integration of law and narrative provides us with a literary representation of ancient Israelite culture. Assnat Bartor's recent book highlights the remarkable literary character of the biblical laws themselves.[17]

The recovery of what the law might have been in real life is not my aim, nor do I think it is a plausible one because of the lack of reliable historical records. My position is the opposite of one expressed by Charles Foster Kent in 1906 and still standard in scholarly circles. Frustrated by the "confusing labyrinth" of the laws, Kent argued that "before [they] can be intelligently read . . . they must be systematically codified, (1) logically, according to subject matter, and (2) chronologically, within each group, so that the enactments and usages of successive periods can be studied in their true historical order." In other words, as Austin Blum points out, "Kent believes that historical knowledge permits scholars to understand the biblical laws better than the lawgivers themselves did. Kent performed this feat of perception through the presumption that the actual placement of the laws in the text was of no importance. For him, the laws gain meaning only when they are organized chronologically, which allows Kent to see how they developed in response to what he and other scholars conjecture to be the changing social conditions of ancient Israelite society, and by subject matter, presumably through Kent's own common law perspective."[18] I could not disagree more with Kent's position and will set out to oppose the long-standing consensus that he articulated so clearly over one hundred years ago. My thesis opposes the conventional, rather disparaging view that "the compilations of laws and customs [come] from different sources, all brought together without any real attempt at editing or correlation."[19] In contrast to views such as Kent's, I believe that the sequence and placement of laws—the very elements they find not even confounding but irrelevant—are vital keys to their meaning.

A clear instance where I differ markedly from other critics is the assessment of similar rules in the different codes of law. They wrongly, in my view, see two similar rules reflecting different historical periods in the life of the nation. The first thing to be said about their approach is that it is highly speculative because we simply do not know the history of ancient Israel outside of the biblical record, which I consider to be often fictional or mythical or pseudohistorical. It is not that I am denying some historical reality to the rules. Their contents may well mirror actual practices and be based on rules known to the compiler(s) of the biblical rules when he committed them to writing. The rules are, in fact, even more interesting than any assumptions about the historical realities of ancient Israel might suggest. Once we view them as arising from reflection on the mythical and legendary history in Genesis–2 Kings, we can pinpoint exactly why the rules take up the problems they do and we can appreciate how deeply the biblical authors thought about things.

The assumption that goes into my hypothesis can be examined; the standard historical-critical cannot because there are no sources external to the text to back up ideas about how Israelite society really operated. I repeat that I am not dismissing the possibility, even the likelihood, that what the biblical lawgivers do was also geared to making an impact on their own time and place. It is just that I know no way of accessing that purpose or the impact it may have had. In any event, the standard view that one law belongs to this source and time and another similar law to a different source and a different time can be countered with a plausible alternative. A case in point, the narrative in Genesis 34 about Shechem's seduction of Dinah, explains why two similar rules about seduction exist and why they also differ markedly from each other (Exod 22:16, 17 and Deut 22:28, 29). The contents of each rule differ because divergent judgments can arise depending on what aspect of the narrative tradition is under review: the refusal of the daughter in the Exodus rule corresponds to the refusal of Dinah to the foreigner Shechem in the story; the fixed bride-price for an Israelite seducer in the Deuteronomic law opposes Shechem's negotiating a bride-price for Dinah.

2

Pharaoh and Yahweh as God-Kings (Numbers 1–4)

I begin the analysis of Numbers by emphasizing and extending the recognition that as Numbers is part of the larger body of material Genesis through 2 Kings, its contents continue where the Book of Leviticus leaves off. Num 3:4 refers to the incident in Leviticus 10 about the deaths of Aaron's two sons, Nadab and Abihu, so plainly here is evidence that Numbers is a continuation of Leviticus. In keeping with the character of biblical history writing, the past is constantly reworked (and future events in Joshua through 2 Kings anticipated too).[1] Before concentrating on Numbers, I will comment about Leviticus, with a glance at Exodus also, to underscore how fundamental the Book of Genesis is to the make-up of so much of the material that follows.

GENESIS AND LEVITICUS

An operative principle in Leviticus, one that will very much continue in Numbers, is that the Israelites should pursue a contrasting program to the one Joseph devised when he was governor in Egypt. Yahweh's rule is to prevail in the new land to which Israel is headed. In that Yahweh is not a ruler with worldly power in the mold of Pharaoh and Joseph, an equivalent but contrasting authority is set up. The inspiration for the model is resistance to Egyptian ways that focuses on the role of Moses as someone standing in a relationship to his deity like Joseph in relation to the pharaoh. The principle is *imitation par opposition* in line with Lev 18:3: "After the doings of the land of Egypt, wherein ye dwelt, shall ye not do . . . neither shall ye walk in their ordinances." The Egyptians had ordinances, so Moses will lay down ordinances for the Israelites. These statutes may be comparable but will fundamentally oppose what are imagined to be Egyptian statutes. In the incest rule in Lev 18:14, Moses, for example, prohibits the very union that his parents had contracted in Egypt (Exod 6:16, 20; Num 26:59): "Thou shalt not uncover the nakedness of thy father's brother, thou shalt not approach to his wife: she is thine aunt."

The concluding part of Leviticus (Leviticus 25–27) opposes Joseph's policy on behalf of Pharaoh in Egypt when the Egyptians became slaves at the time of the famine. After the famine, Pharaoh provided them with seed to sow in fields that were again productive (Gen 47:23–26). In Leviticus, it is Yahweh rather than an earthly ruler who acts to keep famine away and provide the Israelites (if they prove to be obedient subjects) the goods of the earth: "If ye walk in my statutes, and keep my commandments, and do them; Then I will give you rain in due season, and the land shall yield her increase, and the trees of the field shall yield their fruit. And your threshing shall reach unto the vintage, and the vintage shall reach unto the sowing time; and ye shall eat your bread to the full, and dwell in your land safely" (Lev 26:3–5).[2]

For the Leviticus lawgiver (as for the narrator in the Book of Exodus) the figure of Yahweh corresponds to the figure of the pharaoh. Greifenhagen notes that "the narrative [in Exodus] portrays YHWH and Pharaoh in parallel fashion: the prophetic formula 'Thus says YHWH' (Exod. 5.1) corresponds with 'Thus says Pharaoh' (5.10), YHWH threatens with the sword (5.3) as does Pharaoh (5.21), and both YHWH and Pharaoh are accused of causing evil (5.22–23)." Greifenhagen, however, leaves to a footnote the observation, "Of course, the fact that Pharaoh was considered divine or semi-divine in Egyptian belief further makes him a worthy opponent for YHWH." Carl Keil had already noted that the relationship between the Israelites and Yahweh, their God-King, resembled the relationship between the Egyptians and their king.[3] However, the relationship between Yahweh and the Israelites is markedly different from the relationship between Pharaoh and his people, as illustrated in the following example.

After the famine, the Egyptians have no fields or houses or animals that they might choose to give over to the pharaoh because he has already acquired them, nor might they choose to give over their persons or acquire persons for themselves because all persons already belong to the pharaoh. The one transaction the Egyptians are able to enter into with the pharaoh concerns the production of food. He gives them seed to sow the fields with. They keep four-fifths of the yield for themselves and give the remaining fifth to the government (Gen 47:23–26). For the Israelites, in turn, a different but related regimen prevails, as emerges in Leviticus 27. Unlike an Egyptian under the pharaoh, the Israelite is not coerced but, out of devotion to his deity, is in a position to freely hand over fields, houses, animals, and persons to Yahweh and to acquire them back. The Israelite might dedicate a house or a field to Yahweh, in effect putting it under priestly control. He can take either back, but an act of redemption is necessary. If he chooses to redeem, there is an additional cost to the transaction. He has to pay a one-fifth premium over and above the value that the receiving priest on behalf of Yahweh originally placed on the gift. This premium is the same as the one-fifth value of the harvest that the Egyptian serf has to pay to his lord and master, the pharaoh, for the initial seed he has given to him.

Revealingly, when an Israelite redeems a field he pays the extra premium according to the seed that is sown in his field (Lev 27:16, 19). Jacob Milgrom states, "One is inclined to associate the institution of the one-fifth with the 20 per-cent levied by Joseph on all Egyptian produce (Gen 47:24)," but Milgrom gives no indication why he is so inclined and what to make of the common element.[4] He focuses on a small observation that both situations involve a 20 per-cent levy, but he derives no meaning and provides no context. My thesis does: even though the Israelite situation is different from the Egyptian, the agricultural assessment for the Egyptians in Gen 47:24 directly influences the agricultural assessment for the Israelites in Lev 27:16, 19.

Whatever connection to actual practices in ancient Israel there might be in the background to those biblical injunctions in Leviticus, we should read them as hypothetical constructions. Their chief aim is to render judgment on issues taken up from traditions embodied in the narratives. We cannot therefore read biblical rules as directly reflecting historical realities, although in some respects they must have. In commenting on the existence of any legal constitution, John Griffith opts for a down-to-earth, realistic position and states that it is "no more and no less than what happens." In this light it is unwise to speak of a biblical constitution because we do not find rules that come from everyday life in ancient Israel. Bruce Wells is also skeptical about making judgments about the realities of Israel's judicial system. He asks, "What is the relationship between the laws in the Pentateuchal codes and the laws of ancient Israel and Judah? To say they are the same is highly problematic." He further expresses the view that "it is difficult to say anything with certainty concerning the laws of ancient Israel and Judah because scholars simply do not know what they were. Perhaps the Pentateuchal laws yield some insight into the legal systems of ancient Israel and Judah, but is this really so?"[5]

GENESIS AND EXODUS

The Book of Exodus in relation to the Book of Genesis also yields results similar to Leviticus in relation to Genesis (and, as we shall see, Numbers in relation to Genesis). An operative principle in Leviticus, we saw, is that the Israelites should pursue a contrasting program to the one that Joseph devised when he was governor in Egypt. Along these lines, Matthew Rindge has recently drawn attention to how the depiction of Joseph in Genesis 37–50 inspired the depiction of Moses as a counter-Joseph in Exodus: "In terms of relation to foreign rule, Moses is the antitype of Joseph." T. E. Fretheim has drawn close links between the plague narratives in Exodus and the details of the story of creation in Genesis 1 such that the plagues in Egypt are the obverse of the created order in Genesis 1. Greifenhagen similarly pursues the link: "Deliberate connections with Genesis seem to be forged repeatedly in the first two chapters of Exodus. The narrative intention seems for the macroscopic or universal events in Genesis (creation, flood) to foreshadow the microscopic or particular events in Exodus (creation and salvation of Israel)." David Cotter notes that the departure of the Israelites from Egypt in Exodus is written up in line with Jacob and his family's escape from their servitude with Laban, just as David Daube had previously articulated the striking similarity between the two stories. I too have argued that the writer of Exodus takes stock of many of Joseph's actions and adopts an ethical stance that often reveals a negative judgment on Joseph.[6]

GENESIS AND NUMBERS

As Genesis does in Exodus and Leviticus, so the narratives in Genesis continue to play an influential role in Numbers. They provide not just the issues that are taken up in the Numbers laws, but also the topics that turn up in the Numbers narratives about Israel's experiences after the Exodus from Egypt. Not only, then, does Numbers continue where Leviticus leaves off, but, as in Leviticus, precise links with Genesis show up in Numbers as well. Some of these have long been recognized; for example in Num 3:1 the formula providing genealogical information, "these are the generations of . . . ," is the same one that divides Genesis into different family histories.[7]

Mary Douglas argues for a connection between Genesis and Numbers and thinks that the reference to Jacob and his twelve sons at the beginning of Numbers introduces a series of interconnections between the two bodies of material. Indeed, she has a heading "Numbers' Commentary on Genesis" and under it lists a number of links. She draws one, for example, between Genesis 19, the seduction of Lot by his daughters when Amnon and Moab came into existence, and the seduction of the Israelite men by the daughters of Moab in Numbers 25. She writes, "The beginning of Numbers starts with the end of Genesis and the ending of Numbers arrives by an inverted parallel at the beginning of Genesis.

Thus in Gen 50:24 the dying Joseph's last words were an oath saying that God will visit the sons of Israel and bring them to the land which he has sworn to give to Abraham, Isaac, and Jacob."[8] However, Douglas does not, in fact, note all that many links, nor is she quite accurate in claiming that "the beginning of Numbers starts with the end of Genesis," and her link between the daughters of Lot and the daughters of Moab is not, in my view, the important one between Genesis and Numbers. I will argue that the links are far more extensive and much more precise than she realized. Some have been noted by other scholars.

Gordon Wenham draws attention to Num 13:2, 22: the Israelite spies at Hebron "search the land of Canaan, which I [Yahweh] give unto the sons of Israel." The statement relates back to Gen 13:14–18 when God first promised Abraham near Hebron that he would inherit the land (cp. on Hebron and environs Gen 14:13–24, 23, 25:9, 35:27–29, 50:13). Wenham comments, "The narrator knew these traditions, and he assumes the spies did and that the reader does. It is essential that they be borne in mind." Devora Steinmetz notes that Num 35:33—"The land cannot be cleansed of the blood that is shed therein, but by the blood of him that shed it"—is an echo of God's words to Noah and his sons after the flood: "Whoso sheddeth man's blood, by man shall his blood be shed" (Gen 9:6). Adriane Leveen, accurately in my view, sees Numbers as "an integral part of the larger Torah, referring to, and even at times replicating, earlier scenes or episodes and anticipating later ones, such as the death of Moses at the end of Deuteronomy." Jon Levenson points out that in Gen 50:1–13 the itinerary starting in Egypt for the journey of Jacob's body to Canaan foreshadows the route Israel takes in Num 33:1–49 after they came out of Egypt and entered Canaan from Transjordan.[9] There are also in Numbers frequent references to episodes in Exodus, especially the enslavement in Egypt. After all, chronologically and geographically, Israel has just come out of Egypt, so the backward glance at the Egyptian experience is wholly understandable. Nonetheless, I view the relationship between Numbers and Genesis as more detailed than the relationship between Numbers and Exodus, reading the whole of the Book of Numbers as a reworking and reiteration of key episodes in the Book of Genesis.

Having substantial interest in sacerdotal matters, Numbers especially takes up from the Genesis traditions those instances in which the role of the sacred comes into play. The following is a list of examples: Numbers 15, with its five rules, focuses on the idolatrous and religious features of Joseph's dreams (Genesis 37); Numbers 19, with its institution of a ritual using ash from a burnt Red Heifer to counter the presence of death, has its inspiration in the story about how Jacob attained the right of the firstborn from Esau by giving him the "red, red" food so that Esau could fend off death (Gen 25:21–23); Numbers 21, when

Israel makes a vow at Arad, links up with Jacob's vow at Bethel (Genesis 28); Numbers 30, which concerns vows and oaths, especially a woman's, also links up with Jacob's vow at Bethel and, additionally, with Jacob's oath about the household gods in his wife Rachel's possession as they return to Bethel (Gen 31:32, 35:1); Numbers 22–24, when Balak hires the diviner Balaam, who in the end is physically opposed by an angel, replicates Jacob's physical encounter with the divine being in Genesis 32; Numbers 25 and 31, with their fierce hostility to any Israelite involvement with Moabite or Midianite women, stand as a condemnation of the potential for idolatry in Genesis 34 and 35 when the Hivite women were incorporated into Jacob-Israel's house; the calendar of public sacrifices and feasts in Numbers 28 and 29 links up with Jacob's erection of one altar when settling in Hivite territory and then a second one after he has the Hivite women give up their gods (Gen 33:20, 35:7); Jacob's altars declare a commitment to the Israelite god and to Israel's future worship, the subject matter of so many narratives and laws in Numbers.

More precisely, in regard to both sacred and nonsacred matters, the history recounted in the Book of Numbers covers not only what it outwardly records, the events in the wilderness. The history also takes in the nation's beginning, the births of Esau and Jacob in Genesis 25, and subsequent events in Genesis 25–50. The range is briefly alluded to in Num 20:14–16 when Moses requests from the king of Edom permission for his people to pass through Edomite territory. Moses begins by saying to the king, "Thus saith thy brother Israel, Thou knowest all the travail that befell us." Moses is referring to the fraught relations beginning at their births between the ancestors, the brothers Jacob and Esau (Genesis 25), and continuing until Esau's descendants, the Edomites, settled in the hill country of Seir (Genesis 36). Moses in Num 20:14–16 next recounts to the king his people's history after Edom took up permanent residence in Seir: "Then our fathers went down into Egypt, and we dwelt in [Joseph's] Egypt a long time; and then the Egyptians [under the pharaoh 'who knew not Joseph' (Exod 1:8)] vexed us, and our fathers. And when we cried unto Yahweh, he heard our voice, and sent an angel, and hath brought us forth out of Egypt [their current location at Edom's border]." What we have in Num 20:14–16 is a line drawn from Jacob-Israel's history as depicted in Genesis, through the incipient nation's experience in Exodus with the oppressive pharaoh, and on to the time in the wilderness that Numbers depicts.

Another example of how the Numbers narrator takes up from Genesis (as well as from Exodus) centers on his major concern that the Israelites should not return to Egypt because of the better food they had there (Numbers 11). This is an appeal to the living experience of the audience Moses is portrayed as addressing.

Not only, however, is the narrator, through the voice of Moses, intent on avoiding a return to Egypt for the food there, he is also concerned, I shall argue, throughout his composition that there should be no return to the problems of the patriarchal period, those of Jacob's relations with his brother Esau and Joseph's with his brothers. The troubles in each instance very much involved matters of food: the "red, red" dish for a starving Esau, a game dish for their father, Isaac, and the relief of famine for Joseph's brothers. Leveen rightly underscores the role of past events in the writing up of Numbers. She comments about Moses' request to the king of Edom in Num 20:14–16: "Moses' recourse to prior events as a prologue to present exigencies is a fine example of the persistent turn to the past in biblical narrative. What happens there, or, more precisely, what one remembers to have happened there, repeatedly impacts the present. Current actions and requests can be understood, so our example argues, only in a context provided by the past." She also writes that "Egypt functions as a sieve through which narrative time is organized."[10] I will be intent on pointing out that the patriarchal period beginning with Jacob likewise acts as a filter and a guideline.

I proceed by outlining the initial contents of Numbers in its relation to Genesis. The following table gives an overview of common elements:

Genesis 41–47	Numbers 1–4
Divine ruler, a surrogate, and priests Pharaoh is the God-King of the Egyptians with Joseph as his surrogate. The priests in Egypt stand in a special relationship to Pharaoh.	*Divine ruler, a surrogate, and priests* Yahweh is the God-King of the Israelites with Moses as his surrogate. The Israelite priests stand in a special relationship to Yahweh. They are his firstborn sons.

In Numbers, the contrast continues to show up between Pharaoh as a god with his stand-in Joseph—who is spoken of as "even as Pharaoh" (Gen 44:18)—and Yahweh with his representative Moses. Yahweh is Israel's supreme ruler, their God-King, as expressed in Num 9:23: "They [the Israelites] kept the charge of Yahweh at the commandment of Yahweh by the hand of Moses." Moses' role as representing that highest authority immediately emerges in Numbers 1: from each tribe he has a census compiled to serve the military purpose of overcoming the Canaanites, the enemy the Israelites are about to encounter after their escape from the Egyptian oppression.

The tribe of Levi (of which Moses is a member) stands separate from the other tribes. They constitute an exceptional body in that they have a special duty to attend to the needs and functioning of the sanctuary. The Levites emerge in Num 1:47–53, 3, 4, and 8 as having a unique relationship to Yahweh. They resemble the priests in Egypt in relation to Pharaoh (Gen 47:22): "Only the land of the priests bought he [Joseph] not; for the priests had a portion assigned them of Pharaoh, and did eat their portion which Pharaoh gave them." The Levites similarly receive their food from their God-King Yahweh. They are given so much more attention than the Egyptian priests in the Joseph story because Yahweh as Israel's ruler also functions through them as a group. The idea of their representing God before the people continues to show up in later rabbinic sources (*b. Yom.* 19a; *b. Kidd.* 23b; *b. Ned.* 35b).

It is important to note for my purposes that not just in Numbers 1 but throughout Numbers the founding fathers of the tribes, Reuben, Simeon, Gad, Judah, Joseph, etc., are frequently cited. The fact that they are suggests that the Numbers narrator is aware of and incorporates into his narration their histories as we find them recounted in the Book of Genesis.

Numbers 2 lays out the plan of the camp in the wilderness according to the tribal arrangements as traced through the Genesis patriarchs, the sons of Jacob. The Levites are left out of this particular military arrangement because of a special status to which Num 1:47–53 has introduced us and Numbers 3 spells out fully. That status is of utmost importance. The tribe of Levi is appointed as controller of the sanctuary, its members as rulers in the sphere of the sacred. Leveen is content simply to point out that, in contrast to the omission of the tribe of Levi in the genealogy of Jacob in Numbers 1, the tribe is singled out in Num 1:47–53.[11] The major reason for concentration on the Levites, I would emphasize, is that their role—the role of priests and a priestly class within Israel—did not yet exist at Jacob's death (Genesis 50) and hence separate attention is given to them in Num 1:47–53 and Numbers 3 and 4. Within the tribe of Levi, Moses and Aaron enjoy an even higher position (Num 3:1–10, Numbers 4). Moses has untouchable authority at this time because of his role as the deity's supreme representative, and his brother Aaron and his family have the highest function in the sanctuary, namely, the priestly office that is exercised in the inner part of it. The further distinction in rank even within a distinguished tribe is a matter that is central to Numbers 16–18 (see chapter 6).

Numbers 3 also introduces us to a topic that reappears throughout the entire book. Interest in firstborn sons and their history going back to Jacob's acquisition of primogeniture from Esau (Genesis 25), to which Numbers 19 will return in a major way, is a topic that turns up time and again in Numbers. Numbers 3 brings up the topic of primogeniture for the first time, an important reference to past history in Egypt, to the Book of Exodus in this instance: "And I [Yahweh], behold,

I have taken the Levites from among the sons of Israel instead of all the firstborn that openeth the matrix among the children of Israel: therefore the Levites shall be mine. Because all the firstborn are mine; for on the day that I smote all the firstborn in the land of Egypt I hallowed unto me all the firstborn in Israel, both man and beast: mine shall they be: I am Yahweh" (Num 3:11–13). Serving as Yahweh's firstborn and belonging to Yahweh at the sanctuary, the Levites have a perpetual living there (recalling the Egyptian priests with Pharaoh). Num 3:40–51 draws out the importance of the topic by describing how all firstborn males of the Israelites must be counted because Yahweh has a claim on their lives. Action on the claim is set aside, however, in that the Levites substitute, man for man, for each firstborn Israelite counted. For those Israelites who are in excess of the number of Levites, five shekels have to be paid to the sanctuary to redeem them. To repeat: an interest in the status of the firstborn is major throughout Numbers.

Numbers 4 delineates the Levites' duties at the sanctuary. Different families of Levites do different tasks. Particular Levite families are excluded, however, on pain of death, from working in the inner part of the sanctuary. That area is for the sons of Aaron alone to serve. Thus Num 4:17–20 inform us that on account of their particular proximity to the inner part of the sanctuary, the Kohathites, a Levite family, are especially vulnerable if they approach the holy things. Distinctions among groups of Levites have no parallel in Genesis. (It is probably a stretch to suggest that Joseph is seen as having priestly powers too. However, with his divine status, Pharaoh certainly did give him special powers, and Joseph himself attributes his capacity to interpret dreams to God [Gen 41:16]. Joseph also married a daughter of an Egyptian priest: "And Pharaoh called Joseph's name Zaphnath-paaneah; and he gave him to wife Asenath the daughter of Poti-pherah priest of On" [Gen 41:45]).

The concerns so far laid out in Numbers 1–4 should be viewed as largely a reaction to the equivalent arrangements to the ones we find in Pharaoh's Egypt when the Israelites were in residence there and when the Egyptians already had a class of priests and the sons of Jacob-Israel had no such thing. In Numbers, Yahweh is the King of the Israelites and, like Pharaoh over his subjects, he has claims on them because they belong to him. As in Gen 47:22, where the Egyptian priests have a special standing in relation to the pharaoh, so in Numbers 1–4 the Levites have a unique relationship to Yahweh. Like the Egyptian priests vis-à-vis the pharaoh (Gen 47:22), the Levites receive a corresponding permanent living from Yahweh.

Before moving to a full analysis of Numbers 5 and 6 in the next chapter, I ask at this point why the rules there—exclusion from the camp of those in an unclean bodily state, a breach of trust in some matter, a suspected adulteress, and a temporary male or female nazirite—follow after the focus in Numbers 3 and 4 on the Levites. I start by puzzling over the sequence of the laws in Numbers 5 and 6, a problem that has certainly perplexed critics. Gray goes so far as to state that these rules "have as little relation to the preceding and following chapters (7. 8. 9 or 10) as they have to one another."[12] The placement of the first rule about the removal of the unclean from the camp in the wilderness—one with a skin ailment, one with a genital discharge, and one who has been in contact with the dead—is, as Gray notes, perhaps less puzzling. After all, the wilderness camp has been the subject of previous interest in Numbers 2, and its sanctity has been a focus of concern.

Another factor has to be noted, however, one which is especially relevant to understanding why the following rules about breach of trust, suspected adultery, and the temporary dedicated office of a nazirite, are set down. Uncleanness of the bodily kind in focus can be lethal because it occurs within the sacred camp. As Milgrom states, "Impurity [*tum'a*] is the realm of death."[13] Within the camp's precincts, death directly coming from God is an ever-present danger, as I just noted for those Levite families who approach too closely an especially sacred area: "And Yahweh spake unto Moses and unto Aaron, saying, Cut ye not off the tribe of the families of the Kohathites from among the Levites: But thus do unto them, that they may live, and not die, when they approach unto the most holy things . . . they shall not go in to see when the holy things are covered, lest they die" (Num 4:17–20). The deity's direct meting out of death is what we must give attention to in assessing the next rules about breach of trust, suspected adultery, and the nazirite. These three rules are indeed the ones that invite most puzzlement. A single Genesis narrative is crucial, I will argue, for understanding each of them. Thus three interrelated issues in the story of Judah and Tamar in Genesis 38 account for the presentation of the three rules: Judah fails to keep a promise to give Shelah to Tamar so that she can conceive by him (a breach of trust); Tamar appears to commit adultery in order to become pregnant (a suspected adulteress); but what she does is in a sacred cause (a nazirite). Each of these three rules in Numbers 5 and 6, then, refers back to a particular problem of Judah, a son of Jacob-Israel, in producing a firstborn son.

Why, however, should there be a focus on the narrative in Genesis 38 about Judah, especially after so much attention has been given to the Levites in Numbers 3 and 4? The explanation is that a consistent tendency of the narrator-lawgiver of Genesis–2 Kings is to seek out the first instance of a problem in the nation's history (or prehistory). As it happens, Judah provides the earliest example in the history of the incipient nation of the loss of a firstborn son whose life is directly taken by God. This is a matter of much moment in Numbers because its narrator has a persistent interest in a topic that flows from the profound idea that Israel is God's firstborn, even to the extent that concrete expression of the idea is given in the sacred role of the Levites. They are in some special sense Yahweh's firstborn who, substituting for all the other Israelite firstborn, save their lives from being taken directly by God (Num 3:44–4:49). In Genesis 38 Judah's firstborn, Er, dies, and then shortly after that Onan dies because he refuses to produce a firstborn on behalf of the childless Er. Onan's is an offense against the sacred order. The contents of the Genesis narrative center on the convoluted ways by which the loss is overcome, and the rules in Num 5:5–6:27 address the issues involved. The drama of the story is the threatened loss to Judah of any son to carry on his lineage because of God's direct action.

God removes Er and Onan from Judah's family without any human involvement in their deaths. Such direct action by the deity is, I repeat, the cue for the compiler of Numbers to look to the future life of the nation and have the priests participate in comparable issues affecting the sacred sphere. Israelite priests did not exist in Judah's time. In Numbers they play the role that God did in Genesis. This is true for the three rules under consideration. The priests take over the deity's role and Judah's role in dealing with Tamar's pregnancy because the offenses in question very much touch on sacred matters.

The narrative about Judah, then, acutely raises matters concerning the topic of the firstborn, a topic that is essentially about issues of inheritance—perpetuity of a line and testamentary right of succession. These issues recur throughout Numbers, just as an interest in the topic of firstborn status has already shown up in Numbers 3 in regard to the Levites. Genesis 38 relays, it is well recognized, the origin of the Judahite clans.[14] Num 26:19–22 expands on this history: "The sons of Judah were Er and Onan: and Er and Onan died in the land of Canaan. And the sons of Judah after their families were; of Shelah, the family of the Shelanites: of Pharez, the family of the Pharzites: of Zerah, the family of the Zarhites. And the sons of Pharez were; of Hezron, the family of the Hezronites: of Hamul, the family of the Hamulites. These are the families of Judah according to those that were numbered of them, threescore and sixteen thousand and five hundred."

3

THE SUSPECTED ADULTERESS AND THE NAZIRITE (NUMBERS 5 AND 6)

The two laws about the suspected adulteress and the nazirite—one follows the other but only minor links in language and structure between them have been observed—have long proved notoriously difficult to interpret. The Near Eastern parallels that critics have produced for proceedings against the suspected adulteress are rather thin, one expert bluntly stating, "This ordeal of bitter waters has no analogy in the ancient East."[1] As for the vocation of the nazirite, we are equally lacking much illumination from Near Eastern sources. It points to "a fascinating, albeit elusive, aspect of Israelite religion."[2] In any event, Near Eastern sources contribute nothing to explaining the juxtaposition of the two rules in Numbers 5 and 6. Little or no light, moreover, has been forthcoming to account for what prompted the lawgiver to present the law of the suspected adulteress in the first place and why he set it down at the point he does. It appears just after a rule about a man or a woman who breaks a promise in some matter, offending against a fellow human and God too, doubtless on account of the sacred character of the promise made (Num 5:5–10). It comes just before a rule about a man or a woman who takes on the vocation of a nazirite, that is, when the person chooses for a limited period of time to set himself or herself apart for a sacred task (Num 6:2–21). We noted in the previous chapter that George Buchanan Gray, who is particularly alert to puzzling over why one rule might follow another and where they fit into the narrative context in Numbers, is quite at a loss to cast light on the problem.[3]

From the perspective of comparative law it is of some interest to find a rule in CH 131 in which a husband accuses his wife of adultery but lacks evidence. She swears an oath to clear herself. In CH 132 someone else accuses the man's wife, and in this instance she is subject to an ordeal somewhat comparable to the biblical procedure: she is cast into a river to determine her guilt (if she drowns) or her innocence (if she survives).[4] In Numbers 5 water also plays a role. In this instance, however, the woman is not cast into a river but has to drink a concoction that is part water, part dry earth taken from the floor of the sanctuary, and part an inky residue from a parchment inscribed with a curse. The imprecation is to the effect that if she is guilty of adultery her belly will swell and her thigh will rot, referring, almost certainly, to her uterus and genital area.[5] By and large, critics and translators assume, rightly in my view, that she is pregnant and that the effect of the curse is to cause a miscarriage in the guilty. Num 5:28 is explicitly about the innocent: "She shall be free, and retain seed," that is, her conscience being clear, she will carry her child to term.[6]

I will argue that the rule about the suspected adulteress in Numbers 5 can be illumined by relating it to Judah's dealings with Tamar in Genesis 38. She is the only example in biblical narrative of a wife suspected of adultery by her husband, or, to put it more circumspectly, by the man who effectively is her husband.[7] Her position is highly unusual but it is characteristic of storytelling at all times to take up the strange and the exceptional. As David Daube states, "It is a point to be observed in all literatures at all times that those departments of legal commerce the regulation of which is controversial are popular providers of subjects for saga, drama, novel and the like."[8] A highlight of the Tamar story is her suspected adultery, and it certainly provides much drama. In Numbers, we are to imagine Moses setting out rules and procedures for the Israelites in their forthcoming occupation of the land of Canaan. He turns to problems in the history of his people, especially the first instance of one, and produces judgments for comparable problems likely to arise in the future.

The narrative in Genesis 38 about Tamar's union with Judah is vital not only for understanding why the rule about the suspected adulteress is set down in Numbers 5, but also for comprehending the following institution in Numbers 6, which has baffled interpreters, namely, the temporary vocation of a male and, somewhat surprisingly, a female nazirite. In suggesting that the two rules in Numbers 5 and 6 should be viewed against the background of the problems in the Judah–Tamar story in Genesis 38, I would point out that a two-way process is at work. Just as there is a backward look at previous history on the part of Numbers, so stories in Genesis often point to significant developments in the future (the acquisition of the land of Canaan in Gen 12:1–3; the sojourn and enslavement in Egypt in Gen 15:13; and the continuation of Judah's line in Gen 38:29, 30). The Tamar story also proves crucial for interpreting the topic of a breach of trust which precedes the law of the suspected adulteress in Numbers 5. These three laws (a breach of promise, the suspected adulteress, and the nazirite) might appear unrelated, but the sequence becomes fully intelligible in light of the Tamar narrative.

Genesis 38	Numbers 5–6
Problems producing a firstborn Judah faces loss of a firstborn. He compounds the problem by breaking a promise to give Shelah to Tamar. She appears to commit adultery, but her action is in a sacred cause.	*Problems producing a firstborn* Three rules take up issues arising from Judah's problems in producing a firstborn: breach of promise; suspected adultery; and commitment to a sacred cause.

SUSPECTED ADULTERESS

The rule reads as follows:

12 If any man's wife go aside, and commit a trespass against him, 13 And a man lie with her carnally, and it be hid from the eyes of her husband, and be kept close, and she be defiled, and there be no witness against her, neither she be taken with the manner; 14 And the spirit of jealousy come upon him, and he be jealous of his wife, and she be defiled: or if the spirit of jealousy come upon him, and he be jealous of his wife, and she be not defiled: 15 Then shall the man bring his wife unto the priest, and he shall bring her offering for her, the tenth part of an ephah of barley meal; he shall pour no oil upon it, nor put frankincense thereon; for it is an offering of jealousy, an offering of memorial, bringing iniquity to remembrance. 16 And the priest shall bring her near, and set her before Yahweh: 17 And the priest shall take holy water in an earthen vessel; and of the dry earth that is on the floor of the tabernacle shall the priest take, and put it into the water: 18 And the priest shall set the woman before Yahweh, and uncover the woman's head, and put the offering of memorial in her hands, which is the jealousy offering: and the priest shall have in his hand the bitter water that causeth the curse: 19 And the priest shall charge her by an oath, and say unto the woman, If no man hast lain with thee, and if thou hast not gone aside to uncleanness with another instead of thy husband, be thou free from this bitter water that causeth the curse. 20 But if thou hast gone aside to another instead of thy husband, and if thou be defiled, and some man have lain with thee beside thine husband: 21 Then the priest shall charge the woman with an oath of cursing, and the priest shall say unto the woman, Yahweh make thee a curse and an oath among thy people, when Yahweh doth make thy thigh to rot, and thy belly to

swell; 22 And this water that causeth the curse shall go into thy bowels, to make thy belly to swell, and thy thigh to rot: And the woman shall say, Amen, amen. 23 And the priest shall write these curses in a book, and he shall blot them out with [into] the bitter water: 24 And he shall cause the woman to drink the bitter water that causeth the curse: and the water that causeth the curse shall enter into her, and become bitter. 25 Then the priest shall take the jealousy offering . . . 27 And when he hath made her to drink the water, then it shall come to pass that, if she be defiled, and have done trespass against her husband, that the water that causeth the curse shall enter into her, and become bitter, and her belly shall swell, and her thigh shall rot: and the woman shall be a curse among her people. 28 And if the woman be not defiled, but be clean; then she shall be free, and retain seed. 29 This is the law of jealousies, when a wife goeth aside to another instead of her husband, and is defiled; 30 Or when the spirit of jealousy cometh upon him, and he be jealous over his wife, and shall set the woman before Yahweh, and the priest shall execute upon her all this law. 31 Then shall the man be guiltless from iniquity, and this woman shall bear her iniquity. (Num 5:12–31)

In what way does Tamar provide an example of a suspected adulteress? In the narrative, in order to fulfill the levirate custom Judah promises to give his son Shelah to the widowed and childless Tamar so that she can conceive a child. Judah, however, fails to deliver on the promise. This is the breach of faith underlying the law that precedes the one about the suspected adulteress in Numbers 5. (I shall reserve particular discussion of its contents for the next chapter.) The effect of Judah's broken promise is that Tamar traps Judah, not Shelah, into becoming her levirate husband. Judah is not aware of what she is doing because she disguises herself as a prostitute in order to obtain seed from him. When the facts about the situation become known to him, Judah acknowledges the legitimacy of Tamar's actions. Before he does so, however, because Tamar had disguised herself in order to seduce him, Judah accuses her of adultery when he discovers her pregnancy. As the levirate custom requires, she had been betrothed to a member of his family, and Judah is sure that she is pregnant by someone outside the family. Betrothal, from the perspective of Judah, is a form of inchoate marriage in keeping with what we know from Deut 22:23–27. Judah orders Tamar to be burned, perhaps on the grounds that she deserves a mirroring punishment: she is presumed to have burnt with passion and hence, because the offense of adultery merits death, burning is the appropriate penalty. Yet on further inquiry Judah finds that he is the one who made her pregnant. However bizarrely—it is the exceptionalism that characterizes storytelling—Judah himself turns out to be a husband, in the levirate sense, who suspects a wife of adultery, subjects her to a death sentence, but discovers that she is not in the wrong. When he says that Tamar "has been more righteous than I because I gave her not to Shelah my son" (Gen 38:26), he openly acknowledges his culpability in withholding the levirate husband and by extension the justifiability of Tamar's ruse to make him the levir. She is therefore not guilty of adultery. (Esther Menn wondered whether in light of the Numbers rule, because Tamar proved herself innocent and went on to conceive twins, she could be viewed as a suspected adulteress. Menn also discusses the legitimacy of Judah fulfilling the role of the levirate husband as father-in-law and cites Near Eastern examples of fathers-in-law as levirs.)[9]

The issues in the narrative turn up in the Numbers rule. The rule uses two verbs, not one (*ne'elam* and *nisterah*), about a woman concealing her adultery. It was crucial that Tamar disguise herself thoroughly in her transaction with Judah. She had to hide from him in two ways. She had to conceal that she was having intercourse with someone other than Shelah (because in Judah's mind the only person Tamar could legitimately have sex with is Shelah, the next in line to fulfill the levirate custom). Also, she had to conceal the fact that it was Judah, her father-in-law, with whom she was having intercourse (thereby breaking an incest taboo). The need for Tamar to ensure that she cannot be recognized by Judah explains the puzzle that Assnat Bartor articulates: "Why does the lawgiver choose to describe an aspect of her behavior that is so self-explanatory and obvious? Do we not understand that hiding is integral to the act of adultery?"[10]

As was Tamar in the story, the suspected adulteress is threatened with a gruesome punishment that mirrors the nature of her offense. That part of her body with which she might have offended, her thigh region, will rot should she confess her guilt.[11] The means of getting her to confess is for her husband to present at the sanctuary "a grain offering of remembrance," serving to "bring iniquity to remembrance." Memory played a crucial role in establishing Tamar's innocence in the far-from-innocuous event in Genesis 38: she produced for Judah the two objects he had given her as a pledge to pay for the service she rendered, his seal-and-cord and his staff, tangible reminders of his participation. The objects constituted proof as good as a wife might ever produce that her husband is the father of the child she carries. In the ordinary way of things, it is almost impossible for a wife to prove that her husband is the one who impregnated her months back in time. Tamar arranged matters well, knowing exactly what she was doing when she asked Judah for items of his that he would later recognize. Without them she knew she would face a fearful reckoning. The proceedings in the Numbers rule can do no more than appeal to the woman's conscience to trigger confession of her wrongdoing—as Tamar appealed to

Judah's memory and conscience; hence the psychological impact in a sacred setting of the grain offering of remembrance.

In the rule, the priest additionally gives the woman a drink that has been concocted from water in an earthen vessel to which earth from the floor of the sanctuary is added. A curse written on parchment is also dipped into it so that the water somehow retains the execration. The aim is again to elicit confession of a past deed. The curse washed into the water may play a role similar to the role that Judah's seal plays in the story. His seal was apparently of a kind attached to a cord and usually worn around the neck: "Rolled over documents incised in clay, it would be the means of affixing a kind of self-notarized signature."[12] Seal and drink concoction, respectively, serve to vindicate or to condemn. Without the seal Tamar was condemned, which means that her body and its fetus would burn, but when she produced it she was innocent. In the law, the married woman, imbibing the water with the curse, has to recall her past sexual activity and, having done so, confess either guilt, which will cause gruesome bodily harm, or innocence, which will leave her body unharmed. The ritual might be viewed as devised to mirror the turning point in the narrative when Tamar, already condemned and thus cursed, produced the seal identifying Judah as the father of the child. In the law, before the woman drinks the water she is already laboring under her husband's accusation of adultery and she too seeks vindication. She is not subject to questioning, and no utterance comes from her other than her assent, "amen, amen," to accepting the effects of the bitter water. In the story Tamar utters no words between obtaining the pledge from Judah and producing it to establish her innocence.[13]

The woman's hair is unbound in the rule, and this action may also be designed to incorporate a particular facet of the story. Tamar's covered head concealed her identity in a public place in order to engage in a deception. Ordinarily, a covered head seems to indicate a woman of modesty, but Tamar had to hide who she was.[14] Tamar's situation was an inevitably topsy-turvy one: with her covered face the betrothed Tamar's vulnerable position was seeming sexual wrongdoing, breaking the law of adultery (and incest). The reason she covered her face, however, was to conceal her legitimate intent on following out Judah's unfulfilled commitment to a religious duty, the execution of the levirate custom. Once Judah upheld her intent, Tamar's covered head actually communicated her legitimacy as an honorable kinswoman, not one of loose morals. The law focuses on a less complicated situation: the woman accused of a deception has her hair unbound to be shamed in a public setting while facing up to her alleged adulterous act. The hair and the head are, then, signs of guilt or innocence in the law and the narrative.

Perhaps the most telling detail in the rule that links to the Tamar story is the surprising statement that the husband is free of iniquity even if he has been wrong to suspect his wife of adultery in the first place (Num 5:30, 31). Why does the rule bother to declare him free of guilt? After all, the rule is entirely taken up with her offense. In the story Judah had good reason to suspect Tamar of an adulterous relationship. She was bound by a legal tie to Judah's family and had been sent back to her father's home to await summons from Judah to receive Shelah. But Shelah in fact was not given to her. Her pregnant state had all the appearance of indicating a wrongful liaison. However, at the conclusion of the trial held in Judah's household, she produced reliable evidence proving Judah to be the father of the children in her womb. Tamar, in effect, turned her trial around to becoming a trial of Judah, who confessed his involvement with her. In most instances, as I indicated, solid evidence that a husband has in fact been the one who impregnated his wife would be lacking. It is this uncertain situation that invites recourse to a test of the kind we find in Numbers 5 in which the guilt or innocence of both the husband and the wife comes into reckoning. Judah could not have expected to encounter Tamar disguised as a prostitute. His later justified suspicion of her conduct is pertinent to the surprising, seemingly unnecessary declaration in the law's concluding statement: an accusing husband whose allegation turns out to be wrong is declared to be free of guilt himself.[15]

The law considers how a woman may have committed an act of betrayal against her husband, and the expression used, *limʿol maʿal* ("act unfaithfully"), has sacred overtones (Num 5:12). Notably, its use here is the only instance in biblical legal sources where the inherent sacred character of the marriage bond emerges, precisely because trust, being central to the institution of marriage, is the overriding consideration when the issue of unfaithfulness arises. Trust is a private matter, legislation can have no impact, and only God can be invoked so as to appeal to a sacred, if second best, sphere of influence.[16] In the story in Genesis 38 the idea of the sacred is central to the marital union Tamar seeks. Tamar's act with Judah went against the incest taboo, but Judah says she was correct to pursue conception within his family. He thought the offense was adultery, but it was even worse: father-in-law incest (Lev 18:15, 16, 20:12, 21). Her act was deemed to be in order because the levirate custom was a profound and vital duty whose obligation was so sacred that it even superseded the incest taboo. On account of the uniqueness of Tamar's situation, the idea of a sacred union powerfully emerges—hence the appropriateness of the language with its sacred overtones about acting unfaithfully (*limʿol maʿal*).

THE NAZIRITE

The rule reads as follows:

2 When either man or woman shall separate themselves to vow a vow of a nazirite, to separate themselves unto Yahweh. 3 He shall separate himself from wine and strong drink, and shall drink no vinegar of wine, or vinegar of strong drink, neither shall he drink any liquor of grapes, nor eat moist grapes, or dried. 4 All the days of his separation shall he eat nothing that is made of the vine tree, from the kernels even to the husk. 5 All the days of the vow of his separation there shall no razor come upon his head: until the days be fulfilled, in the which he separateth himself unto Yahweh, he shall be holy, and shall let the locks of the hair of his head grow. 6 All the days that he separateth himself unto Yahweh he shall come at no dead body. 7 He shall not make himself unclean for his father, or for his mother, for his brother, or for his sister, when they die: because the consecration of his God is upon his head. 8 All the days of his separation he is holy unto Yahweh. 9 And if any man die very suddenly by him, and he hath defiled the head of his consecration; then he shall shave his head in the day of his cleansing, on the seventh day shall he shave it. 10 And on the eighth day he shall bring . . . 11 And the priest shall offer . . . and make an atonement for him, for that he sinned by the dead, and shall hallow his head that same day. 12 And he shall consecrate unto Yahweh the days of his separation, and shall bring a lamb of the first year for a trespass offering: but the days that were before shall be lost, because his separation was defiled. 13 And this is the law of the nazirite, when the days of his separation are fulfilled: he shall be brought unto the door of the tabernacle of the congregation: 14 And he shall offer his offering unto Yahweh. . . . 18 And the nazirite shall shave the head of his separation at the door of the tabernacle . . . and shall take the hair of the head of his separation, and put it in the fire. . . . 19 And the priest shall take . . . and shall put them [offerings] upon the hands of the nazirite, after the hair of his separation is shaven: 20 And the priest shall wave them . . . and after that the nazirite may drink wine. 21 This is the law of the nazirite who hath vowed, and of his offering unto Yahweh for his separation, beside that that his hand shall get: according to the vow which he vowed, so he must do after the law of his separation. (Num 6:2–21)

Just as Tamar's boldness in obtaining a child for her dead husband is the inspiration for the law of the suspected adulteress, so too is her action the model for the institution of the nazirite. A major aspect of the Genesis narrative is the tenacity with which she commits herself to acquiring a child for her dead husband in fulfillment of a sacred custom. The males in the family who should have done the duty failed to act: Onan had greedily sought to acquire his dead brother's share of the estate by withdrawing from intercourse with Tamar; Judah, in turn, presumably feared that Shelah, like two sons before him, would die if sent to her. Tamar overcomes the opposition to her conceiving a child by dedicating herself to obtaining conception, that is, by becoming a *qedešah* ("a consecrated woman"), even if the text does not have Tamar declare herself as such. It is Tamar's sacred vocation that accounts for commentators seeking some divine figure bound up in the role of Tamar (Ishtar, the mother of Adonis, Smyrna, or a goddess in general). Menn thinks there may be reason for attributing "an uncanny, almost superhuman power to Tamar, in that she performs the role reserved for God in the stories containing the barren wife motif."[17] The sacred task to which Tamar committed herself for a brief period has its analogue in the temporary dedication of the nazirite in the law in Numbers 6. In fact, Tamar's adventure provides all of the building blocks for the institution of the impermanent nazirite. We can readily note the correspondences between story and law but, first, we might pose the following questions.

Why are both genders included? Baruch Levine points out that the "formulation *'iš 'o 'iššah* [man or woman] is actually quite rare in biblical law." Karel Van Der Toorn further notes, "In a context that usually speaks of men only, this detail [reference to a woman also] is striking indeed." We might thus expect that there is good reason why a woman should be cited in the rule. Why is there so much focus at the law's outset on refraining from wine and any product associated with the grape? To date, the despairing judgment is that "it is not possible to recapture the rationale behind the prohibition of grape products." Why does the rule confine itself to a temporary state of consecration? The two nazirites we encounter elsewhere in biblical sources, Samson in Judg 13:1–7 and Samuel in 1 Sam 1:1–11, are lifelong dedicatees. Why should the person's head signify his or her separated state? Why also is contact with the dead the only medium of uncleanness that disrupts that person's state? Jacob Milgrom wonders why other types of uncleanness, such as skin ailments, sexual disease, or a female nazirite's menstrual blood, do not disrupt the nazirite's state.[18] Why is a wife or a husband not included in the close family members for whom the nazirite might become unclean if they die? All of these questions may receive an answer when we look at what is undoubtedly Tamar's heroic act and read the law in light of her fraught experience. For example, to answer the first about why the nazirite in the law is female or male (Num 6:2): Tamar made sure she acquired Judah's outward identifying symbols, his seal-and-cord and staff, because they turn out to be the evidence establishing that he has been drawn into fulfilling the levirate custom. Judah had a sacred duty under it.

BAN ON WINE

In overturning the injustice done to her by her father-in-law, Tamar seized the opportunity of a sheep-shearing festival to waylay Judah at a place called Enaim as he was journeying to the event. Drinking is very much associated with such a festival: "Sheepshearing was the occasion for elaborate festivities, with abundant food and drink."[19] As I shall shortly note, Jacob alludes to Judah's inebriation in his farewell address to his sons in Genesis 49, and the later *Testament of Judah* (12:3) spells it out and makes much of it. Judah himself was also under a sacred duty to see to it that the levirate custom was fulfilled. The part of the rule opposing products of the grape reacts against the licentious character of how Tamar conceived by Judah. The Numbers lawgiver would be opposed both to the stratagem Tamar adopted to become pregnant and to Judah's drunken liaison with a prostitute. We should read the rule as countering features in the story to which objection is taken. Why does it even ban the consumption of dried products derived from grapes? The explanation is probably that, as other biblical texts indicate, these products can be associated with lovemaking. The Levirate is not a union to be linked with sexual pleasure or the kind of merriment brought about by drink—it is a weighty obligation.

Much in the law connects with the story, if we bear in mind the lawgiver's priestly concerns. The emphasis in the Numbers law on how the nazirite must refrain from any association with the vine evokes features of the seduction at the place ʿ*enayim* (Enaim, Gen 38:21). In Jacob's farewell comments to his son in Gen 49:12, he alludes to Judah's drunkenness at Enaim (ʿ*enayim*) in a play on words so characteristic of these sayings: "Dull were the eyes [ʿ*enayim*] from wine."[20] The rare word *ḥaklili* in reference to dullness or redness of eyes from drinking occurs only in Gen 49:12 about Judah and Prov 23:29 about drinking and lovemaking. Prov 23:29 also refers to inebriated males who fall for harlots. It is a combination also made much of in Hos 4:11: "Whoredom and wine and new wine take away the heart." As we find with Tamar, the context in Hosea reveals the same switching back and forth between actual harlotry and religious attachment: Yahweh will not punish daughters and spouses who play the harlot—actual harlotry—because the men are unfaithful to him in a manner involving the libertinism of heathen fertility cults—religious harlotry.

The Hosea passage is quite extraordinary. It holds out the example of women who, breaking sexual rules, are not held accountable for the offenses—just like Tamar in the end was not punished for her offense. The women in Hosea are not penalized because of the bad behavior of the men who are involved in foreign worship—again like Judah's bad behavior in withholding the levirate seed and attending a licentious Canaanite festival. Judah, moreover, thought Tamar was a Canaanite sacred prostitute, that is, he was not averse to whoring after foreign gods by lying with her, just as Hosea claims about the Israelites in his time.

Both Gray and Levine draw attention to the text in Amos 2:11–12 with its reference to nazirites and drinking. In the same context (Amos 2:7, 9) we also have a reference to the Canaanites and to a father and son going into the same woman, exactly the situation in Genesis 38.[21]

The nazirite is not permitted even to eat food made from grapes and raisins (Num 6:3). The rule appears to be referring to grape or raisin cakes of the kind cited in Hos 3:1 that an adulteress enjoys receiving from her paramour. In Hosea they symbolize the seductive attractions of idolatry (adultery), and in Jer 7:18; 44:19 (cf. Isa 16:7) they are offered to a Canaanite goddess. In Cant 2:5 the lovesick maiden yearns for her lover's raisins.[22] Wine and the enjoyment of sex provide heightened states of temporary attachment. The lawgiver judges that the consecrated person in a temporary state of devotion to a sacred cause must avoid, not sexual relations—involvement in them may be the intent of the sacred task at hand—but any products of the vine. The opposition to them represents a negative reaction to Judah's enjoyment of Tamar with its striking combination of worldly, foreign, and sacred features. In the Mishnah mention is made of a man becoming a nazirite for the purpose of producing a son (*Nazir* 2:7). A daughter does not count, a fact reminiscent of the levirate custom requiring a son to be born.

In the second-century BCE *Testament of Judah*, the patriarch recounts how he encountered Tamar on his way to shear his sheep; how she was adorned in bridal array and was sitting "in the city Enaim by the gate." "For," Judah adds, "it was a law of the Amorites, that she who was about to marry [possibly regular marriage, not levirate] should sit in fornication seven days by the gate. Therefore, being drunk from wine, I did not recognize her; and her beauty deceived me, through the fashion of her adorning" (12:2, 3).[23] I find it interesting that, in this later interpretation, Tamar awaits marriage with someone when Judah ends up having intercourse with her. In Genesis 38 Tamar awaits Shelah in marriage, but it is Judah who ends up having intercourse with her, the act being interpreted as valid for levirate marriage. As the two other biblical references to it testify, sheep shearing was indeed an occasion of merriment and licentiousness (1 Samuel 25; 2 Sam 13:23–

28). Tamar's situation has a revealing reference in Ruth 4:12: "And let thy house [Boaz's] be like the house of Pharez, whom Tamar bare unto Judah, of the seed which Yahweh shall give thee of this young woman [Ruth]." Each woman, childless and in need of the remedy provided by the levirate custom, conceives by a man belonging to the previous generation, each is sexually experienced, and each in the boldest of ways seeks out the man to impregnate her. In a way similar to Tamar's ploy, Ruth waits until Boaz is merry from wine before making a seductive approach to him at midnight on his threshing floor (Ruth 4:7).

In sum: the rule in Numbers 6 prohibits anything associated with the vine during the period of a nazirite's vow because the Numbers lawgiver does not like that Tamar had to face the obstacle she did in fulfilling a sacred duty. The nazirite institution incorporates features from the story in order to oppose them. Wine is one way to overcome a male's unwillingness to provide his sexual services (Judah's—he would not have had sex with Tamar in a sober state), but when the duty is a sacred one no such assistance should play a role—hence the prohibition about the wine and any products of the grape. The rule curiously concludes—it seems unnecessary—with permission for the nazirite to drink wine again after the period of dedication is over. Why should attention be given to this aspect of the postnazirite state? Judah's conduct may be in focus. Before going to his festival he should have soberly committed himself to making sure that the levirate custom had been fulfilled by sending Shelah to Tamar. Once he had done his duty, he could then have gone to the festival and become merry with wine.

THE NAZIRITE'S HEAD COVERING

Tamar concealed, of necessity, her identity from Judah. She put off her widow's clothes, wrapped herself in other clothes, and put on a veil. Judah, we learn, "thought her to be a harlot for she had covered her face." The Numbers rule defines the identity of the nazirite by her uncut hair—symbolically imitating, I suggest, Tamar's covering of her face. The rule again imitates in order to oppose. In keeping with Tamar's mission, the licentious feature in the narrative is transformed into a sacred act. This link between narrative and law needs to be expanded.

In the narrative Tamar acts the part of a prostitute, a profession that advertises itself by some external mark. In Gen 38:15 Tamar's sign that she is a harlot relates to her head: she covers it with a veil ("When Judah saw her, he thought her to be an harlot; because she had covered her face"). In the law in Num 6:5 an external mark signals the dedicated state of the nazirite: long, loose, untrimmed hair is obligatory. According to Milgrom, "The Nazirite could always be recognized by his [her] appearance and it is no wonder that the term for Nazirite can also refer to his [her] hair." Levine rightly states that "throughout the present legislation, 'head' is a way of referring to 'hair.'"[24] Tamar's covered head signifies that she is in reality a *qedešah*, a special kind of "holy woman" seeking sexual intercourse. In contrast to Tamar's apparent intent of servicing a client but comparable to her true intent of performing a religious duty, the nazirite sanctifies her or his head (Num 6:11). Carl Keil is perhaps overstating the case but is basically correct when he declares that the role of hair in the law is a sign that the nazirite's sanctified head is "an ornament in which his [her] whole strength and fullness of vitality were exhibited, and which the Nazirite wore in honor of the Lord."[25] The female figure of Wisdom in Proverbs 9 provides a parallel: a beguiling woman whose stance imitates and opposes the seductiveness of a loose woman.

The unloosening of the suspected adulteress's hair by removing her headdress in the preceding rule in Num 5:18 and the withholding of a razor from the nazirite's head so that her hair continues to grow in the nazirite rule in Num 6:5 is not just a coincidental link between the two laws. Critics see the connection only in terms of how one law has come to be set down after what is to them a quite unrelated law.[26] In the narrative, the significance of Tamar's covered head relates both to the concern with her harlotry, for which Judah intends to burn her, and to her dedicated state for the purpose of fulfilling the levirate duty, for which Judah proceeds to commend her. Both these aspects emerge in the two laws.

In the law of the suspected adulteress, unbinding the woman's hair is an integral part of the ordeal determining whether she has played the harlot, and in the law of the nazirite, growing the hair long indicates a dedicated state. Levine points out that all usages of the verb *paraʿ* "somehow connote dishevelment or disarray, but the phenomenology of the *nazir* differs from that pertaining to mourning or shaming."[27] This is not quite accurate. The loose hair in the law of the suspected adulteress relates to the shameful role of Tamar as a prostitute, and the uncut hair in the nazirite law relates to the other aspect of Tamar's covered head as an honorable woman bent upon a sacred task. In these two matters of the hair, the two laws take up facets of Tamar's seemingly licentious activity in order to oppose the role they play in the narrative. When the nazirite's hair requires cutting because of contact with a corpse or because the period of dedication has come to an end, the hair is burnt. Burning in the narrative (Tamar is to be burnt for her offense) and in the law creates a boundary between the sacred and the profane. Another link between the two laws is the placement of sacrificial materials in the palms of the suspected adulteress in Num 5:18 and in the palms of the nazirite in Num 6:19. The context in the former is the woman having her head unbound to reveal her hair and in the latter the nazirite having her or his hair shaven off.

The description of the "holy or consecrated woman" Tamar is the inspiration for the focus on the hair and head of the nazirite. Tamar's covered face signifies her intent to bring forth new life in the form of a child, and, as both Gray and Levine emphasize, the nazirite's uncut hair communicates vitality. Tamar can be viewed as a *qedešah* for the duration of her task just as the term *qadoš* in the law signifies the nazirite's holiness for the duration of her or his sacred commitment (Num 6:5). On the basis of Assyrian texts, Joan Westenholz notes that "Tamar could have been considered by the Canaanite inhabitants [of Enaim] as a veiled, married *qadištu*-woman." It has not been established what exactly a *qadištu*-woman is, but in Old Babylonian texts and her equivalent in the earlier Sumerian texts she is peculiarly linked with childbirth.[28]

A NAZIRITE'S CONTACT WITH THE DEAD

Deaths in Judah's family drive the narrative. Tamar's husband dies with no heir born to him. Onan next dies in avoiding the duty to impregnate when he withdraws from intercourse. Judah's own wife is next to die. He mourns her and then goes to the sheep-shearing festival and has his sexual encounter with Tamar.

Death also plays a major role in the nazirite vow. If a close member of the dedicatee's family dies she must not come into contact with the dead body. So long as she avoids it, her consecrated state is not affected. If, however, "someone dies very suddenly upon her," the vow is terminated. She has to purify herself and start the period of separation over again. Why the interest in two different kinds of death with a sudden death affecting the execution of the vow? Presumably, the sudden death means that the person could not avoid contact with the victim. This aspect of the institution has in focus, I suggest, the fact that Onan died struck down in the close presence of Tamar while avoiding full intercourse with her. His misdeed offended against the levirate custom and therefore made a mockery of a sacred commitment. The rule's concern with the interruption of a nazirite's vow because of a sudden death is intended to recall Onan's demise and Tamar's unavoidable proximity at the moment of death. The ritual, in turn, serves both to recall a problematic event in the past and to undo the negative development by an action that imitates the original wrong.

Tamar was an essential player in fulfilling the levirate custom. After Onan's death she had to return to her own family and await Shelah's coming of age.

When, however, Judah holds back the now-mature Shelah, Tamar takes the initiative in resuming the quest for a son. That is, she resumes her sacred cause. We have, then, in both story and rule, the interruption of a sacred commitment and its resumption following a pause.

As I have indicated, Milgrom is puzzled why other types of uncleanness—skin ailments, sexual disease, and a female nazirite's menstrual blood—do not interfere with the nazirite's state. He accounts for the sole interest in corpse contamination by claiming that there exists in the law a residual hint of ancestor worship for the purpose of exorcising the fear of corpses. Why this concern should exclude the other manifestations of uncleanness is not clear. Again, however, the focus on the Judah–Tamar story is so much closer to the lawgiver's concerns. There is, to be sure, the recall of an ancestor, namely, Onan, but certainly not with the aim of worshiping him.

The law does not spell out what kind of vow it has in view, but it may be the specific one of producing a child (as with the births of the nazirites Samson and Samuel), just as the preceding law about the suspected adulteress probably centers on the woman's pregnant condition. The notice about close family members who die does not, puzzlingly, include the person's spouse, an indication perhaps that the law has in view a levirate situation of the kind depicted in Genesis 38.

After Tamar obtains seed from Judah she changes out of the garments that signaled her sacred state as a *qedešah*. She puts her widow's clothes back on and casts aside her veil. The change in her appearance signals the completion of her sacred commitment. The law, in turn, has the nazirite shave her head—an analogous, dramatic change in appearance to signal the end of her temporary consecrated state.

After the nazirite has accomplished her vow, she is brought to the sanctuary and made to fulfill certain ritual instructions so that she can resume normal life. What is odd is that she is brought before the religious authorities and does not voluntarily present herself to them. One critic states, "Why the Nazirite should need to be brought instead of coming by himself [herself] it is not easy to see."[29] I would point out that the pregnant Tamar was brought before Judah's household jurisdiction. She did not come of her own volition. In the end, Judah's judgment on her affirmed that her cause was right. During the preceding three months she was not in fact covering up her harlotry but was indeed devoting herself to the task of producing a child for her dead husband. The narrative thus acknowledges her commitment to a dedicated task, and from the viewpoint of the law in Numbers 6 she provides the earliest example of a temporary nazirite. Overall, the ritual can be viewed as invented tradition to record the narrator's judgment on a crucial but decidedly questionable event at the nation's beginning.

SAMSON AND SAMUEL

There are two biblical narratives in which the nazirite appears, the births of Samson and Samuel. Each contains features that take on added significance once we observe the hitherto unrecognized link between the Judah–Tamar narrative and the Numbers nazirite law. As in the law, each episode shares a focus on both male and female commitment to a sacred task and on the role of wine. As in the Judah–Tamar story, each shares a focus on the woman's conception of a firstborn child and on prostitution.

A barren mother, Manoah's wife, is told that she will conceive a son who will be a nazirite. In the meantime she has not to consume wine or strong drink (Judg 13:2–5). When her son Samson is born and goes on to live the life of a nazirite he involves himself with a prostitute (Judg 16:1). No doubt the account is geared to showing the disorderly nature of the times: "In these days there was no king in Israel: every man did that which was right in his own eyes" (Judg 17:6; 18:1; 21:25). It is also the case, however, that Samson's involvement with the prostitute has a positive outcome because, however precarious his situation, it enables Yahweh to visit death upon Israel's enemies and decrease their numbers. We recall that in the most unruly way Judah's involvement with a prostitute enables his future line to receive Yahweh's blessing of offspring.

In the other episode, Samuel's mother, Hannah, promises that if she conceives she will dedicate her son as a nazirite to the sanctuary (1 Sam 1:11, especially emphasized in the Septuagint). She makes her vow at the sanctuary in Shiloh, where the priest Eli falsely accuses her of drunkenness and, equally interesting, views her as a loose woman of the kind that Eli's own sons promiscuously engaged with at the sanctuary (1 Sam 1:11, 13, 15, 16). Like Tamar, she has in fact dedicated herself to a sacred task, and, appearances to the contrary, she too is no prostitute.

In sum, the topics of prostitution and drinking in both the Samson and Samuel stories become more significant in light of Tamar's role as a prostitute on the occasion of Judah's trip to a festival. That the topics turn up in each story is not accidental but typical of biblical narrative because aspects of what occurs in one generation are seen to repeat themselves in another.

AARON'S BENEDICTION

The climax to the three laws in Num 5:5–6:27 is the celebrated blessing upon the sons of Israel: "Yahweh bless thee, and keep thee: Yahweh make his face shine upon thee, and be gracious unto thee: Yahweh lift up his countenance upon thee, and give thee peace. And they [Aaron and his sons] shall put my name upon the sons of Israel; and I will bless them" (Num 6:24–27). Critics invariably see no connection between this blessing and the preceding rule about the nazirite. They have long expressed bafflement as to why it comes at this point in the Book of Numbers. A. H. McNeile states, "This fragment of priestly tradition has no connexion with what precedes or follows it."[30] If, however, the preceding rules have been formulated against the backdrop of the troubles faced by Judah, a son of the original Israel, then the benediction is most apt. Both rules involve the role of the sanctuary where Aaron exercises his priestly function.

The highlighting of Yahweh's face as communicating a favorable disposition is reminiscent of the role that the face plays in both Tamar's attempt to fulfill a sacred duty and the covering of the nazirite's face to indicate a dedicated state. The covering of the face of the consecrated person is done with a view to receiving divine favor.

As for the need for divine favor, Judah's troubles included strife (on account of Joseph) among the first sons of Israel, infertility, loss of posterity and possessions (Er's inheritance), and the potential disappearance of Judah's name (the threat of no offspring to perpetuate his line). The potential fate of this son of Israel runs counter to the standard positive content of biblical blessings for the collective sons of Israel. Coming after the laws in Numbers 5 and 6 that address salient issues among the members of the first generation of Israelites, the benediction wishes for future sons of Israel a destiny different from the one Judah faced. His very name was threatened with extinction because the continuity of his line was at risk owing to his marriage to a Canaanite woman. In the saga, Yahweh's task was a destructive one, causing the deaths of two of Judah's half-Canaanite sons (Er and Onan) with the third (Shelah) losing his role in perpetuating Judah's name as a son of Jacob-Israel. Unlike the curse that came upon the three sons of Judah (death to two of them, denial of a role in perpetuating the Israelite family name for the other), three times the benediction in Num 6:24–27 repeats the divine name over the sons of Israel. Its climactic statement expresses the wish that Yahweh's name remain on them: "And they [Aaron and his sons] shall put my name upon the sons of Israel; and I will bless them." Upholding the name of the Israelite god preserves the purity of an Israelite's line of descent from Canaanite infusion of the kind that almost wiped out Judah's. Acknowledging Yahweh's name also guarantees future blessings on each generation of Israelites.

What occurs in the Judah–Tamar story understandably evoked much interest because it is about the genealogical history of King David (Gen 38:29 and Ruth 4:18–22). David's story plays a major role in Genesis through 2 Kings. As has become increasingly recognized, many links are forged between Genesis–Deuteronomy and the Books of Samuel and Kings. Milgrom notes how the

Balaam story in Numbers 22–24 anticipates accounts in Samuel and Kings about later monarchical times. He observes that the predictions in Num 24:7, 8 about the Amalekite king Agag and about Israel's victories over its enemies anticipate the crushing of these enemies in the time of Kings Saul and David (1 Samuel 15:8; 2 Sam 8:12, 12:31).[31]

4

A TEST CASE FOR THE STUDY OF BIBLICAL LAW
(LEV 6:2–7 [5:20–26] AND NUM 5:6–10)

I have reserved a detailed discussion of the rule about a breach of trust in Num 5:6–10 until now because scholars invariably relate it back to the rule in Lev 6:2–7 (5:20–26) about dissembling in a transaction. They view the Numbers rule as an addition or supplement to the Leviticus rule. The treatment of the two rules serves to demonstrate the irreconcilable difference between my understanding of biblical law and that of scholars committed to the long-standing historical-critical approach. Aside from contesting their views, I particularly wish to demonstrate that the distinction scholars make between the two sources P and H cannot (certainly in this favorite illustration of it) be sustained.

It has been an axiom of biblical criticism that similar rules in the biblical codes are to be explained by developments over time—revisions of supposedly earlier rules with additions made to meet changing societal circumstances. Considerable claims are made as a consequence of this entrenched view. We are to think of different authors living at different times who update the rules. The rule in Num 5:5–10 (breach of trust) is viewed as a supplement to the one in Lev 6:2–7 (5:20–26) (dissembling in a transaction). Each involves an offense against Yahweh. On account of the similarities and differences between the two rules, Jacob Milgrom makes the boldest of claims: "That this law [in Num 5:5–10] assumes and supplements the law of Lev. 5:20–26 [6:2–7] bears momentous weight in determining the redaction of the Book of Numbers. The fact that the redactor could not merely attach this supplement to the main body of the law on Leviticus can only mean that, for him at least, the text of Leviticus was already fixed. Thus, if this supplement was incorporated into the Book of Numbers, the only possible conclusion is that it was assembled after the Book of Leviticus had achieved its final form." He assigns Lev 6:2–7 [5:20–26] to P and Num 5:5–10 to H.[1]

Disagreeing, I contend that the rules are similar not because there has been updating but because each is a response to two different issues arising on two separate occasions recounted in Genesis 37–50. To be sure, the two issues involve similar matters. Whether different authors living at different times are involved in articulating these rules I have no way of knowing. Certainly, the differences between one law and the other do not constitute prima facie evidence for the conventional view, which proves easy to set aside as an assured result once we see a plausible alternative way of interpreting the two rules in question. The fundamental (but not necessarily exclusive) link is between law and narrative tradition, not between law and changing societal problems. The extant laws a lawgiver brought to bear when formulating his rules in response to narrative issues we also cannot know. He certainly must have been highly familiar with legal lore in his time, but we have no direct access to what he knew.

DISSEMBLING IN A TRANSACTION: LEV 6:2–7 [5:20–26]

The rule in Lev 6:2–7 [5:20–26] prohibits swearing (by God's name) in furthering a deceptive action. The rule states,

> 2 If a soul sin, and commit a trespass [*ma'al*] against Yahweh by dissembling to [*kiḥeš*] his fellow in that which was delivered unto him to keep [deposit, *piqqadon*], or in the placement of one's hand [*teśumet yad*], or through robbery [*gazel*], or through withholding ['*ašaq*] his fellow; 3 Or finding something lost and dissembling about [*kiḥeš*] it, and sweareth falsely in any of all these that a man doeth, sinning therein: 4 Then it shall be, because he hath sinned, and is guilty, that he shall restore that which he robbed, or that which he withheld, or that which was deposited with him, or the lost thing that he found, 5 Or all that about which he hath sworn falsely; he shall even restore it, and shall add the fifth part more thereto, and give it unto him to whom it appertaineth, in the day of his trespass offering. 6 And he shall bring his trespass offering unto Yahweh . . . 7 And the priest shall make an atonement for him before Yahweh: and it shall be forgiven him for any thing of all that he hath done in trespassing therein.

The rule responds to an incident in the Joseph story. Long-recognized problems in translating some of the words in the rule and in understanding the deceptions listed become immediately soluble once we see them in light of this incident. When the brothers of Joseph go to Egypt to buy grain, Joseph instructs his steward to slip the money they paid for it back into their bags. Joseph has already tormented them by withholding Simeon in Egypt in order to compel the brothers to return to Egypt with Benjamin. On their journey back to Canaan the brothers come upon the money, and the discovery causes consternation among them. Jacob too is greatly perplexed by the developments. Eventually, but with the utmost reluctance, Jacob permits Benjamin to accompany the brothers back to Egypt to buy more grain, and he has them take double the money they paid the first time. Jacob says to them, "May God Almighty give you mercy before the man, that he may send away your other brother, and Benjamin" (Gen 43:14).

In the rule in Leviticus the word *piqqadon* does not mean a deposit in the commercial sense invariably favored by translators and interpreters but refers to a deposit of money about which the seller deceives the purchaser, as Joseph did with his brothers. The term is found only one other time, in Gen 41:36, where it refers to the deposited grain that Joseph set aside from the seven years of plentiful harvests ("store to the land," in AV and "reserve for the land" in JSB) to provide relief from future starvation. It is from this set-aside grain that the brothers receive their allotment. Although critics note in passing that the term *piqqadon* occurs only in Gen 41:36 and in Lev 6:2 [5:21], they have made nothing of the ideas behind the common usage. They have chosen to read the term as referring not to money for a reserve of grain that a buyer is then deceived about by the seller, but to a deposit whereby a person commits to another some object for safekeeping and the custodian of the thing is viewed as the deceiver in the relationship. All interpretations of the rule are involved in this error. Thus Z. W. Falk states, "According to Lev. v 20f., a person alleged to have misappropriated a deposit . . . was required to take an oath." The rule, in fact, states no such requirement about an oath. More recently and more circumspectly, Bruce Wells writes, "Apparently, these defendants have been accused of having in their possession some item that actually belongs to another person, probably the person bringing the claim."[2] For these scholars the receiver of goods is the offender, but this interpretation is wrong. It is the person receiving the goods who is subject to deception. To be sure, as Wells's caution indicates, it is not obvious from the text who exactly is the deceiver. We can comprehend the rule only in light of knowing the case in question, namely, the brothers' purchasing of grain from a deceptive Joseph. The Numbers rule about a breach of trust is not the source of the Leviticus rule.

The next term in the rule for a deception is an expression that occurs nowhere else: *teśumet yad*, literally, "the putting of the hand." Translators try various meanings: a pledge (RSV), an investment (JSB), fellowship (AV, taking up the Septuagint's *koinonia*), a contract (NEB), and partnership (Philo in *De Spec. Leg.* 4.31). The reference, I submit, is to the deception about the money put back in the brothers' sacks of grain. A simple act of buying grain for money became a convoluted transaction because of the placement of the money in the sacks. In

Gen 43:22, after returning to Egypt, the brothers in much distress say to Joseph's steward, "We cannot tell who put [*śum*] our money in our sacks," and the steward replies, "Fear not: your God, and the God of your father, hath given you treasure in your sacks: your money came to me." Acting on behalf of Joseph, the steward did receive their money—only to slip it back into their luggage. The steward attributes the placement of money in the sacks to God instead of admitting his responsibility. In the rule, "the placement of the hand" conveys the deception of placing the money in the sacks of grain by the hand of the steward. The rule goes on to cite how the person "sweareth falsely" in the matter, as did the steward. The false swearing adds to the wrongful action and has nothing to do with defendants in a court of law denying what they have done under oath. No wonder those critics who introduce this line of reasoning have difficulty understanding why a court does not penalize severely such a false oath.[3]

The rule next refers to a deception having to do with robbery. The reference takes up from the story about how the returning brothers, after being ushered into Joseph's house, feared they would receive not hospitality but rough treatment, enslavement, and seizure of their donkeys: "And the men were afraid, because they were brought into Joseph's house; and they said, Because of the money put back in our sacks the first time we were brought here; he wants to overpower us and seize us, and take us for bondmen, and our asses" (Gen 43:18). If this fate had befallen them, it would have been an act of pillage against these foreigners. The rule in Leviticus refers to *gazel*, robbery, a term used precisely for this kind of action.

In the rule, the next deception after robbery is about an act of withholding under the guise of the law. The term ʿ*ašaq*, as Milgrom points out, refers to acts of withholding something or someone, land, farm animals, and persons, ostensibly for legal reasons.[4] The reference is, I think, to the withholding of Simeon in Egypt on the trumped-up charge of spying (Gen 43:9). In the rule, the offense is coupled with robbery because when the steward allays the brothers' fears and assures them that he received their money, he has the withheld Simeon brought to them. That is, the fraud of withholding a person comes in the same context as the brothers' fear of being victims of an act of robbery.

The final deception cited in the rule is when someone finds something that had been lost but dissembles over its discovery. A development in the story is again relevant: the brothers return the money in their sacks to the steward, who dissembles by saying that he had already received their money. By putting the money back in the brothers' sacks, the steward both had the money and did not have it. The deception turns on his pressing overliteral meaning, on privileging letter over spirit, *verba* over *voluntas*. An example from a different sphere comes from the fourth-century bishop of Alexandria, Athanasius. In one version of the story, he was fleeing from would-be assassins who overtook him and challenged him as to his identity. "Keep running," he replied, "you are quite close to Athanasius."[5] The steward's claim that he had their money is a distortion, and the further claim that it was God's doing is a misuse of the divine name: "Peace be to you, fear not: your God, and the God of your father, hath given you treasure in your sacks: I had your money" (Gen 43:23).

In sum, the deceitful actions in the rule in Lev 6:2–7 (5:20–26) are highly detailed and various, yet we can link each of them to the Joseph story. The rule in consequence displays a coherent character that is otherwise difficult to detect. It constitutes commentary on an aspect of the story. My reading differs in a major way from other interpretations, which rely heavily on reading the rule as reflecting problems in the society of the lawgiver's time. Thus Erhard Gerstenberger writes, "The priestly tradents of the Leviticus text appropriated into their collections numerous norms associated with the social aspects of life and were thus by no means oriented toward purely spiritual concerns." Gerstenberger asks why there is no mention of other wrongs, such as "bodily harm, violations against marriage and family order, or legal misrepresentation," and suggests that the wrongs cited serve for other examples also.[6]

It is indeed common for critics, when puzzling over the variety of wrongs cited, to speak of additions to the rule over time.[7] The details of Joseph's wrongdoing, however, make such claims unnecessary. Moreover, the offenses in the rule are serious ones (for example, withholding a person, robbery), yet the punishment (restoration of the goods plus a fifth part added) is not commensurate in burden. On this account alone we should pick up that the rule is not meant to convey actual social sanction for serious wrongdoing. If the rule were indeed to extend to the egregious wrongs cited by Gerstenberger, would not the punishment go beyond a rather mild form of compensation and invite severe penalty? Moreover, why should we assume that the offenses noted in the rule represent but a selection of a larger body of offenses? And if perchance the offenses cited extended to other offenses, why particularly the ones Gerstenberger mentions? why not more or other offenses? His reasoning opens the door to this kind of speculation. If viewed independently of the story, the rule is decidedly odd for reasons adduced above. Only when we read the rule as focused on the incident in the Joseph story can we avoid the difficulties that arise when critics assume that biblical rules respond to pressing problems in the society at large. The strangeness of the rule disappears because every aspect of it makes sense when set against the peculiar elements in the narrative.

Even the calculation of the compensation for the victim of deception reflects back on the story. The wronged person receives an extra fifth part of whatever was handed over originally. How has this figure been arrived at? The one-fifth is the same as the amount an Egyptian serf during Joseph's governance of Egypt had to pay after harvesting the initial seed allotted to him (Gen 47:24). That allocation is similar to the one Joseph gave his brothers. The amount was payable in grain. Doubtless, Joseph saw such a tax as equitable. Just so, if the rule in Leviticus is focused on the grain bought by the brothers, then the lawgiver's judgment is that, in light of the dishonesty when the allotment of grain was made, an extra fifth part should be added to the original amount when a deception of this kind is discovered.

In the story there is no such discovery. The proposal that there should be compensation is a hypothetical construction on the part of the lawgiver. When the brothers in Egypt went off with the grain plus the money in their sacks they had in reality gotten the grain for nothing. Nevertheless, the lawgiver zeroes in on the wrongdoing done to the brothers by Joseph and his steward. Because Joseph was up to no good in the transaction, the lawgiver sees that a just outcome might be that the brothers return the money, keep the grain, and have a compensatory fifth added to the grain because of the deception practiced on them.

BREACH OF TRUST: NUM 5:6–10

As I have noted, critics commonly view the rule about breach of trust as updating that about dissembling in a transaction in Lev 6:2–7 [5:20–26]. But this is the kind of assumption about historical development which I reject if both rules are to be comprehended. The Numbers law concerns a man or a woman who breaks faith (*ma'al*) in some matter. The rule reads as follows:

> 6 When a man or a woman commits sins against humankind thereby engaging in an act of betrayal [*ma'al*] against Yahweh, and that person feels guilty; 7 Then they shall confess their sin which they have done: and shall recompense the trespass with the sum thereof, and add unto it the fifth part thereof, and give it to whoever has been trespassed against. 8 And if that person has no kinsman to recompense the trespass unto, let the trespass be recompensed unto Yahweh, even to the priest; beside the ram of the sin-offering whereby a sin-offering shall be made for him. 9 And every offering of all the holy things of the sons of Israel, which they bring unto the priest, shall be his. 10 And every man's hallowed things shall be his: whatsoever any man giveth the priest, it shall be his.

Rather than updating the Leviticus rule, this rule constitutes, as I have indicated (see chapter 3), commentary on a different narrative, the Judah–Tamar story in Genesis 38. At least three features of the story are readily seen to be taken up by the Numbers law. First, Judah explicitly confesses that he failed to keep his promise to give Shelah to Tamar—"Then said Judah to Tamar his daughter in law, Remain a widow at thy father's house, till Shelah my son be grown" (Gen 38:11)—for the purpose of producing an heir for her dead husband: "And Judah acknowledged them [his seal, cord, and staff], and said, She hath been more righteous than I; because that I gave her not to Shelah my son" (Gen 38:26). Anticipating life in the land of Canaan, the rule concerns an Israelite man or woman who breaks a promise. Should the person acknowledge guilt, he or she is to confess the offense, make good the promise, and pay a fifth part penalty. The rule in Num 5:5–10, but not the rule in Lev 6:2–7 [5:20–26], calls for the offender to confess his offense. Milgrom sees the confession in Numbers as a distinctive feature of the alleged source H. The matter is simpler. Confession is a feature of the Judah–Tamar narrative that influences the Numbers rule, but it is not a feature of the Joseph incident, which underlies the Leviticus rule.[8] There is no need to posit a document H over against a document P.

Second, and quite remarkably, when we are told that there is no kinsman to receive the compensation we realize that the wronged person is dead. Thus the rule, having called for compensation to be paid to the offended party, then immediately states, "If that person has no kinsman to recompense the trespass" (Num 5:8). How puzzling that a sensible, seemingly straightforward rule about compensating a wrong should involve someone who is dead and yet not openly cite this fact! It is certainly an odd situation. It accurately reflects, however, the situation in the Judah–Tamar story, in which Er is dead and the postmortem failure to provide him with a child wrongs him. The wrong is being done to his dead person. Commenting on the Numbers rule, critics explain away the problem. G. B. Gray states, "Provision is now made that if the rightful owner be dead, and there also be no next-of-kin (*goel*) to whom the property can be restored, it is to become the priest's."[9] Gray's statement "Provision is *now* made that if the rightful owner be dead . . ." is a rationalization because the text does not mention any passage of time but simply goes from a statement about the liability owing to the wronged party to the lack of any kinsman to receive the compensation in his place. Timothy Ashley openly rationalizes when he states that the section of the rule about the lack of a kinsman has been added because we can assume that the primary party owed compensation has died in the interim and there is no kinsman to act as a redeemer.[10]

Why must we assume that a section has been added to a rule? Just because an idea does not appear to follow logically does not necessarily mean it was added at a later time. It is possible to work out an underlying logic without the use of an explanation about a "later addition." If, then, we are not dealing with an addition to the rule, how do we account for the most unusual situation where *no* kinsman exists to substitute for the dead man?[11] Even more to the point, why does the rule pass over in silence the death of the primary party, especially if it is to be assumed (wrongly in my view) that he has died in the interim period between offense and reparation for it? We have to assume, I submit, that the rule is a direct response to the case at hand, the already dead Er and the issue of what to do with his patrimony.

If we turn to Judah's conduct with Er's widow, Tamar, we find, taking into account the uniqueness of the situation, parallels that prove most illuminating. Judah leads Tamar to believe that he will send his youngest son, Shelah, to give her seed to fulfill the duty of continuing the line of her dead husband, Er. Thereby Er would acquire the benefit of a son and heir (Gen 38:11). In material terms the benefit is the reinstatement of his line and the continued enjoyment by his heirs of his share of the family estate. The sum (*roʾš*) referred to in Num 5:7 about recompensing the trespass equals the part of the estate belonging to Er. But Judah breaks faith in the matter by failing to send Shelah to Tamar and hence, just as in the law where the wronged person is dead, so the dead kinsman, Judah's own son Er, is wronged. The verb in the law, *maʿal*, although used in regard to that aspect that offends the deity, can mean "to act counter to one's duty, to be unfaithful, to deprive, take away something due to a person." It accurately describes the wrong done to Tamar and hence to Er or, more to the point, to equivalent Israelite players in the future land.[12]

Why is the verb *maʿal*, which has sacred overtones, employed in the rule? If we assume that the narrative has inspired the rule, we might note that the seed in a levirate situation is something deposited in trust with a surviving male family member by the deceased brother. It is precisely in matters of human trust that the notion of the sacred comes to prominence because, absent any legal instrument, trust is not enforceable and (as a second best) there can only be reliance on heaven. It is no surprise that in a biblical rule about deposit where one must rely on the good faith of the depositee not to act badly, the only quasi-legal remedy is resort to an oath (Exod 22:7–13), again but a second-best remedy.

A third peculiar feature of the narrative that is most suggestive for understanding the law is the role of Tamar. She is motivated to obtain seed from her father-in-law because she fears that otherwise her dead husband's name is going to die out. If no child is born to her husband, no heir inherits his estate. The Numbers rule takes into account the quite exceptional circumstances in which not only is the victim of the wrong dead, but a beneficiary to receive a promised property settlement is lacking; indeed, the main concern of the law is to address the consequences of the absence of an heir—precisely Er's situation had the levirate custom not been fulfilled.[13]

The story raises the distinct possibility that Tamar's husband might not (through a legal fiction) produce an heir. Onan, who should remedy the situation, dies when he offends against the levirate custom by spilling his seed during intercourse with Tamar. It looks as if greed was his motivation. He presumably reckoned that Er's part of the estate would become his. Onan's death leads Judah to hold back Shelah from taking Onan's place in fulfilling the custom. The rule has focused on the dilemma Judah creates: what is to be done with a man's share in a family estate when he has no heir? Should Er's share go to Shelah by default? This question is all the more understandable in that the lawgiver would undeniably have opposed Tamar's subsequent initiative. To produce an heir to reestablish her deceased husband's share of the patrimony, she has to resort to a deception. Thus she plays the part of a prostitute in order to seduce her father-in-law into impregnating her. Should she have failed to produce an heir, the part of the estate belonging to the dead Er and to the dead Onan might go to Shelah as Judah's one surviving son. Such a development, however, would constitute a trespass against the levirate custom.

The situation does not in the end result in failure to produce a firstborn, although it very much looked as if it would. The lawgiver, moreover, as just noted, would have opposed Tamar's deceptive act of prostitution to acquire an heir. He therefore has good reason to take up the question of what should happen to a benefit in a comparable, albeit hypothetical situation, in the absence of a beneficiary. If compensation cannot be given to an heir because of the failure to fulfill a sacred duty, it is to be consigned to the sanctuary. The law's levied donations—they are equivalent to the share of the patrimony that would have gone to Er's firstborn—go to a priest. Priests are, after all, Yahweh's firstborn (Num 3:11–13), Yahweh took Er's and Onan's lives directly (the extreme position is attributable to an anti-Canaanite bias in the narrative: Judah's sons are the product of a Canaanite mother, Gen 38:2), and the priest at the sanctuary becomes the stand-in to receive the goods. Levine comments on how the text has it that (in his translation and punctuation) "the liability that is to be repaid belongs to YHWH, [credited] to the priest."[14] The language, with Yahweh cited first, is a response to a situation that occurred in the pre-Israelite times of Genesis 38. Yahweh, not a priestly class, is active in the saga, and the lawgiver works out the equivalent situation in later Israelite life after the cult, representing Yahweh, has been established.

Looking at the unique and complicated aspects of a problem in the history of an important Israelite ancestor (Judah), the lawgiver has pursued the topic of the disposition of a significant kind of promised benefit. The complexity of the Judah–Tamar story is what inspires the lawgiver to tease out the issues in it. He references, for example, both a "man or a woman" breaking faith in some matter. Although Judah is clearly a culprit, it is also true from Judah's initial perspective that Tamar gives the appearance of being unfaithful to her dead husband when she becomes pregnant by pretending to be a prostitute. If Judah's accusation that she was pregnant by harlotry had proved correct, she would have been acting against her husband's claim from beyond the grave. Milgrom views the reference to "the man or a woman" in the rule as an example of how the language betrays a different source (H) from the supposed updated rule in Lev 6:2–7 [5:20–26], which he attributes to P. He also introduces the role of a false oath into the Numbers rule on the ground that "the Numbers version is patently a digest of its Levitic counterpart," which does involve a false swearing (Lev 6:5). What Milgrom assumes as a given becomes proof of his assertion.[15]

The two rules, Lev 6:2–7 [5:20–26] and Num 5:6–10, have much in common (although not as much as critics think), but that is because the cases in the narratives share elements. As I have consistently contended, the issues in every biblical law come from a narrative and not, as is the common view, from the reality of problems in the lawgiver's time.

5

JOSEPH AND MOSES AS SOURCES OF DISCORD (NUMBERS 7–14)

The focus on the establishment of the Israelite sanctuary in Numbers 7 is an example of the biblical narrator's consistent interest in beginnings. Significantly, in light of the previous focus on Judah in the rules in Numbers 5 and 6, he is cited first in the list of the twelve Genesis patriarchs in Numbers 7: "And Yahweh said unto Moses, They shall offer their offering, each prince on his day, for the dedicating of the altar. And he that offered his offering the first day was Nahshon the son of Amminadab, of the tribe of Judah" (Num 7:11, 12).

The sons of Levi, in turn, stand separate from the other sons of Israel, necessarily so in that they are the recipients of the offerings to the sanctuary from the "heads of the house of their fathers" (Num 7:2). In this list of chieftains, Joseph is represented by his two sons, Ephraim and Manasseh, a development that goes back to the episode in Genesis 48 when Jacob adopted them after reuniting with Joseph following his long separation from the family. Jacob singled Joseph out as his foremost son in anticipation of his formal rejection of Reuben as his firstborn (Gen 49:3, 4; 1 Chron 5:1).

Genesis 37–50	Numbers 7–14
Serving the God-King Pharaoh requests Joseph to have some of his brothers, expert in cattle, supervise the royal herds and serve in Pharaoh's household (Genesis 47).	*Serving the God-King* The later sons of Israel contribute to the sanctuary from their herds, and the descendants of Levi serve God, the sanctuary's sovereign (Numbers 7–8).
Disunity and accommodation Infighting in Jacob's family causes two members	*Disunity and accommodation* Those Israelites who cannot, on account of a

(continued)

to leave it: Joseph, allegedly dead, and Judah, separated at a distance. In the end all its members are united (Genesis 37, 38, 50).

Provision of food Joseph's divinely inspired plan enables Jacob's starving family to go to Egypt to be fed (Genesis 41–45).

Discord generated by leadership Viewing himself as godlike, an arrogant Joseph arouses the antagonism of the immediate members of his family (Genesis 37). In Egypt, he wields sole authority on behalf of Pharaoh (Genesis 41–47).

Spying The disguised Joseph causes his brothers despair when he tells them that they are spies in Egypt (Genesis 37, 42).

death or a long journey, be together at the Passover celebration are given the opportunity to participate in a second Passover (Numbers 9).

Provision of food The Israelites are wrong to wish to return to Egypt to obtain food because they fail to trust divine provision of it (Numbers 10–11).

Discord generated by leadership Moses is not to enjoy exclusive authority over the nation but to share it with seventy elders (Numbers 11). Despite his humble stance, Moses' immediate family members oppose his special standing with Yahweh (Numbers 12).

Spying The Israelite spies alarm their brethren with their account of the daunting task of conquering Canaan (Numbers 13–14).

Pharaoh and the Israelite deity are God-Kings, Pharaoh's role and the Israelite Yahweh's role being similar in many respects. The comparison shows up in many ways. Greifenhagen draws attention to the formula of self-introduction ("I am Pharaoh") that Pharaoh uses when elevating Joseph to his supreme leadership role over all the land of Egypt (Gen 41:44). The formula is found elsewhere in Genesis but only in the mouth of the deity (with an important exception, as we shall see in the next chapter, in regard to the exalted Joseph). It is especially used in God's promise to a patriarch about acquiring the land of Canaan, the primary focus of Numbers: "I am thy shield," "I am the Almighty God," "I am Yahweh" (Gen 15:1, 17:1, 8; note also 28:13, 35:11, 12).[1]

Genesis

Serving the God-King Pharaoh requests of Joseph that he have some of his brothers, expert in cattle, supervise the royal herds and serve in Pharaoh's household (Genesis 47).

Numbers

Serving the God-King The later sons of Israel contribute to the sanctuary from their herds, and the descendants of Levi serve God, the sanctuary's sovereign (Numbers 7–8).

SANCTUARY SERVICE

In Numbers 7 the twelve tribal groups contribute gifts to the altar for dedicatory purposes. (From the role assigned to them in Genesis 48 Ephraim and Manasseh in Num 7:48–59 make up the twelve tribes because the tribe of Levi is separate from the other tribes on account of its duties at the sanctuary.) The magnificent gifts of silver and gold are in keeping with the fact that God is like Pharaoh, a God-King, as well as a richly endowed father with an estate to which his sons have a claim. The altar is Yahweh's, and it is no surprise that the Levites, as his firstborn, find themselves attached to a magnificent edifice.

The Joseph story recounts how Jacob and his sons have herds (from Canaan) available to them (Gen 45:10, 46:32). Pharaoh honored these first sons of Israel by removing the stigma attached to foreign herdsmen, who were "an abomination unto the Egyptians" (Gen 46:34).[2] Thus Pharaoh had some of Jacob's sons serve in the royal Egyptian household as his special herdsmen: "And Pharaoh spake unto Joseph, saying, Thy father and thy brethren are come unto thee: The land of Egypt is before thee; in the best of the land make thy father and brethren to dwell; in the land of Goshen let them dwell: and if thou knowest any capable men among them, then make them rulers over my cattle" (Gen 47:6). In Numbers 7 the later sons of Israel give of their herds (from Egypt) to the service of the newly established sanctuary. The example of Joseph's brothers who brought some of their animals into the service of the God-King Pharaoh—for interbreeding purposes, for instance—has its counterpart when their descendants contribute animals to the service of Yahweh, the sanctuary's sovereign.[3] This is another instance of Numbers imitating in order to oppose the development in Genesis. Israelites in the service of the Egyptian pharaoh could not but signify their assimilation into Egyptian society, whereas their later counterparts' attachment to Yahweh declared a commitment to the Israelite community and its worship.

Other links between Pharaoh's treatment of Jacob's family when it came to Egypt and Yahweh's plan to take Israel to Canaan are also noteworthy. Pharaoh gives choice land, Goshen, to Jacob's family, and Canaan, in turn, will prove to be choice land (Num 13:19, 27). Joseph is to choose an especially skilled subgroup from among his brothers for Pharaoh's service, and God chooses a special subgroup among the tribes, the Levites, for his service. God goes a step further and chooses a smaller group, the Aaronites, from among the Levites.

Numbers 8 turns to the dedication of the Levites and the start of their form of elevated service. Although all of the Israelites became God's servants after he redeemed them as his firstborn son from slavery in Egypt (Exod 4:22), the father–son relationship particularly plays out in the Levites' role because in serving Yahweh they substitute for the larger collective that is Israel. God is the ruler, not the Egyptian pharaoh who was ruler first with Joseph and then later when his successor enslaved all the Israelites. Num 8:17, 18 explicitly recalls the enslavement in Egypt by way of explaining the role of the Levites at the sanctuary: "For all the firstborn of the children of Israel are mine, both man and beast: on the day that I smote every firstborn in the land of Egypt I sanctified them for myself. And I have taken the Levites for all the firstborn of the children of Israel." God was reenacting the slaughter of the firstborn in a milder form by taking the Levites "for all the firstborn."

Also in focus in Numbers 7 and 8 is, I submit, the preceding time of Joseph in Egypt. We might have anticipated this backward glance because Numbers 5 and 6 presented rules that took up from the Judah episode in Genesis 38—a story that is told as part of the history of Joseph's rise in Genesis 37–50. Just as Joseph's elevated service on behalf of Pharaoh followed his initial enslavement in Egypt, so the Israelites' special attachment to Yahweh followed their liberation from being slaves to the pharaoh, "who knew not Joseph" (Exod 1:8). Along similar lines, just as Joseph served under Pharaoh, the Levites (especially in Numbers 8) serve under God. Through Joseph's graces, after he had embraced Israelite identity again, God forgave the first sons of Israel for their wretched treatment of the young Joseph (Gen 50:15–21). In turn, through the mediation of the Levites' office, God extends forgiveness "to make an atonement" for the later sons of Israel (Num 8:19).

Genesis	Numbers
Disunity and accommodation Infighting in Jacob's family causes two members to leave it: Joseph, allegedly dead, and Judah, separated at a distance. In the end all its members are united (Genesis 37, 50).	*Disunity and accommodation* Those Israelites who cannot, on account of a death or a long journey, be together at the Passover to celebrate it are given the opportunity to participate in a second Passover (Numbers 9).

PASSOVER

The Sabbatical Year and the Year of Jubilee in Leviticus 25 set up Israelite policies in opposition to Joseph's in Egypt.[4] It is, therefore, not surprising that the institution of the Passover, because it recalls the enslavement of the Israelites after Joseph's death, is cited as the example of the first institution to be observed by the Israelites after leaving Egypt (Exodus 12). Numbers 9 introduces us to two Passovers, the regular one and another for those who miss the first one, and again there may be a link to the era of Joseph. Why is there a second Passover? There is, after all, no second Day of Atonement for those who cannot observe it. Numbers cites the Passover in a narrative context for the first time after it was established in the Book of Exodus (Exodus 12), but the focus is on introducing this second Passover.

The first Passover is set up to memorialize a past event, the liberation from enslavement in Egypt. Numbers 9 does not spell out the explanation for its observance. Numbers then institutes the second Passover for those Israelites and non-Israelites who were absent from the first one. Care is thus taken to ensure that everyone has the opportunity to celebrate the festival. No one—as in the two cases cited in Num 9:10, a nonattendee at the first Passover because he has been in contact with a corpse and a nonattendee because of a long journey—is to be denied participation in the celebration of the coming out of Egypt. Why, however, is there no explicit reference to the experience of the liberation from the enslavement in Egypt as the reason for observing the Passover? and why is there a stress on including everyone, Israelite and non-Israelite, in its celebration (Num 9:14)?

To answer these two difficult questions, I might repeat that the rules always come out of a narrative context, a current one in Moses' time but also, more often than not, one from the past too. Thus Numbers 9 harks back, I suggest, to the preslavery period, specifically, to the time when separations marred the family unity of Jacob's original family. First, Joseph was wrongly taken to Egypt, the initial act that led to the reason for the Passover: "Now Joseph was taken down to Egypt" (Gen 39:1). Then Judah "went down, away from his brothers"—the verb *yarad*, "to descend," is found in each instance—and lived a separate life away from his family in another part of Canaan (Gen 38:1). Esther Menn points out just how closely linked these two descents are in the narration of Genesis 37 and 38.[5] Neither Joseph nor Judah was in a position to rejoin the larger family for a celebratory purpose, let us say, some annual event when they might recall the family's deliverance from Laban. Or, probably more to the point because of the focus of the Numbers' narrator, if their situations were projected into the future settlement in Canaan, comparable if less dramatic experiences arise that would prevent those affected from celebrating the Passover.

Aside from the similar experiences of travels undertaken that led to separation from family, both of these brothers, for the first time in the nation's history, are associated with corpses, which, as noted, is the second cause cited for non-attendance at the Passover. Jacob identifies Joseph's blood-stained garment, which signified his dead body, and there is the actual corpse of Onan when he died in withdrawing from intercourse with Tamar. The passage in Numbers 9 is about making provision for times when separations prevent everyone from coming together for the appointed celebrations by enacting a second occasion for togetherness. The narrator of Numbers may then have taken stock of the original lack of unity in Jacob's family when they sojourned in Canaan. The narrator, that is, seeks to ensure that once the current period of sojourning in the wilderness is over, the settled nation is alert to comparable problems that might arise—an enforced absence from home or a state of temporary defilement because of contact with a corpse.

The return to the pre-Exodus history might also explain why there is no explicit recall of the liberation from slavery in Egypt. The history of Israel at this point is taking in more than just that period of time. There is also reflection back on the preceding time in Canaan that led up to the migration of Jacob and his family to Egypt. Joseph's journey to Egypt began, after all, the sequence of events that led to the eventual enslavement of the entire family. In the rule, sojourners observe the Passover. Their inclusion becomes intelligible too when we remember that Jacob's family had been sojourners in Canaan before moving to Egypt (Gen 37:1; Num 9:14). An acceptance of aliens characterizes Canaanites at that time, and Israelites, in anticipating their future in Canaan, are to extend to aliens inclusion in their commemorative ritual.

Numbers 10 concerns current events and journeying in a major way: the camp is on the move in the wilderness. In keeping with their respective roles, Moses and Aaron have trumpets made to assist them in assembling the people for political, military, and religious purposes. At the start of their journey the ensigns of the various tribal camps determine their formation. The names of the Genesis ancestors, Judah, Reuben, Ephraim, and Manasseh, etc., are listed and hence, as I have noted, their identity is known from the traditions we find in Genesis.

Genesis	Numbers
Provision of food Joseph's divinely inspired plan enables Jacob's starving family to go to Egypt to be fed (Genesis 41–45).	*Provision of food* The Israelites are wrong to wish to return to Egypt to obtain food because they fail to trust divine provision of it (Numbers 10–11).

COMPLAINTS

Numbers 11–14 signal a major, negative change of direction in the narration of Numbers. The people complain about food and about Moses' leadership. Burdened by the situation, Moses protests to God that his role is not like that of a mother of this firstborn son, Israel, who wants to return to Egypt: "Have I conceived all this people? have I begotten them, that thou shouldest say unto me, Carry them in thy bosom, as a nursing father [nurse?] beareth the sucking child, unto the land which thou swearest unto their fathers?" (Num 11:12). The wish to go back to Egypt is extraordinary because it means a life of renewed enslavement, "forgetting the oppression and slavery while remembering Egyptian delicacies."[6] God had redeemed them from slavery precisely because, in keeping with ideas derived from the social laws of the time, he was duty bound to do so, especially for a relative as close as a firstborn son.

The wrongfulness of the request to return to Egypt comes to expression in a rule in Lev 25:42. The Israelites are Yahweh's servants, "which I brought forth out of the land of Egypt: they shall not sell themselves by a slave-sale." The rule requires that the Israelites not pursue in their own land "after the doings of the land of Egypt wherein ye dwelt ... [nor] ... walk in their ordinances" (Lev 18:3). More to the point, the rule encapsulates a negative reaction to Joseph's policy in Egypt. In their own land the Israelites are to be slaves, not like the Egyptians to an earthly ruler such as the pharaoh but only to their own ruler, God. The model of the Egyptians as slaves to Pharaoh inspires the analogous model of the Israelites as slaves to God. The Israelites must "not sell themselves by a slave-sale" to any human master (Lev 25:42). The Egyptians sold themselves by just such a sale when, under Joseph, they gave themselves over to the pharaoh in return for grain. Whatever claims might be made about him, Pharaoh is a human, not a divine master. The correct translation of Lev 25:42 is not "They shall not be sold as bondmen" (AV, similarly RSV and NRSV), but, as in the JPS, "They may not give themselves over into servitude." That is, as in the case of those Israelites in Num 11:4–6, 18 and 14:3, 4, the slave, not the master, is blamed should an Israelite come under the authority of a human master. The Israelites are slaves to God on the ground that God stands in the role of a relative who redeems a kinsman enslaved at home or abroad. The redeemed relative then became the slave of the redeemer, though in a more benign subjugation, to be sure.[7]

The issues of food and leadership in Moses' situation in Numbers stand out in sharper relief when we view them in contrast to the position in Genesis 37–50. In Num 11:18–32 there is a miraculous abundance of food (the manna that had rained down from the heavens), but the question of its storage does not arise because of the unsettled nature of the people's existence in the wilderness. In Joseph's Egypt, on the other hand, not only was the food "beyond measure" (Gen 41:47–49), but it was stored for the future. In Egypt, Pharaoh could be relied on to make food available through Joseph's divinely inspired plan. In Numbers 11 its miraculous provision in the desert serves as an indictment of the Israelites' lack of trust in the deity's capacity similarly to provide abundance, at any time and in any conditions, without any plan being in place.

In Genesis 37–50 we find no judgment on the stance of Jacob's family readily going forth to Egypt to purchase supplies of food because of famine conditions. There is no negative reflection on their journeying from Canaan to Egypt to obtain it. Doubtless, the direction of the story regarding the wrong done to Joseph pushes aside any focus on the topic. In Numbers 11–14, however, there is no question that journeying to Egypt to obtain food is seen as a terrible wrong, a failure to trust in divine providence.

Genesis	Numbers
Discord generated by leadership Viewing himself as godlike, an arrogant Joseph arouses the antagonism of the immediate members of his family (Genesis 37). In Egypt, he wields sole authority on behalf of Pharaoh (Genesis 41–47).	*Discord generated by leadership* Moses is not to enjoy exclusive authority over the nation but to share it with seventy elders (Numbers 11). Despite his humble stance, Moses' immediate family members oppose his special standing with Yahweh (Numbers 12).

LEADERSHIP

We should look at the quality of Moses' leadership not only in his own time and place but also in light of the original problem of leadership in Jacob's family. In Num 11:16–30 seventy elders are to share authority with Moses. This distribution of power stands in sharp contrast to the single authority wielded by Joseph, whose sense of godlike capacity, as his dreams in Genesis 37 first reveal, provoked so much dissension within his family. The dissatisfaction with Joseph's lofty stance emerged with his own family members, and this is the case also with Moses' siblings regarding his preeminent position: "With him [Moses] will I [Yahweh] speak mouth to mouth, even apparently, and not in dark speeches; and the similitude of Yahweh shall he behold: wherefore then were ye [Aaron and Miriam] not afraid to speak against my servant Moses?" (Num

12:8). Like Joseph's brothers' objection in regard to his claim to divinity, the complaint of Moses' siblings, as the context in Numbers makes clear, centers on their displeasure at the uniqueness of Moses' position and the intimacy of his relationship with Yahweh: "Hath Yahweh indeed spoken only by Moses? hath he not spoken also by us?" (Num 12:2). Aaron and Miriam also speak against their brother Moses because of his marriage to a Cushite woman (Numbers 12). There is no indication why there is objection to the marriage to the foreign woman—she is probably North African (Nubian or Ethiopian)—just as we find no hint of negative reflection in the Genesis narrative on Joseph's marriage to a North African, Egyptian woman. The problem of Moses' standing in his family mirrors the original problem with Joseph's in his. In both instances, it is older siblings, Joseph's older brothers and Moses' older brother and older sister, who vent their feelings.

Although both Joseph's and Moses' leadership role undergoes challenge, they handle their elevated role and the challenges quite differently. Moses' example is in stark contrast to Joseph's. This distinction is played out in Numbers when Joshua, a descendant of Joseph (through Ephraim), stands out in opposing the addition to the seventy elders of two men, Eldad and Medad, despite their exhibiting charismatic qualities, the hallmark of leadership (Num 11:28). The Josephite Joshua is jealous because he does not wish to see Moses lose his preeminent position (Num 11:29). But Moses is quick to deny Joshua's request. In Gray's words, "Moses has more at heart the good of the community as a whole than his own personal honour or continued pre-eminence."[8] The intent of the new arrangement, we might infer, is to avoid the repetition of the situation where one son of Israel, Joseph, not only has so much power over the others but also exhibits arrogance that places him above all other humans on earth. He even imagines the sun, moon, and stars bowing down to him (Gen 37:9, 41:40–44, 57). In contrast, we read that "the man Moses was very meek, above all the men which were upon the face of the earth" (Num 12:3).

Of the members of that generation of Israelites who came out of Egypt, only two, Joshua and Caleb, are guaranteed to survive the wilderness wanderings and enter the Promised Land (Num 14:30). All the others are to die in the desert because of their lack of trust in the deity's capacity to provide for them. Two points might be relevant. One, the exclusion from future residence in Canaan of the generation that came out of Egypt is reminiscent of the generation of Jacob's sons, who had to remain in Egypt and not return to Canaan, where they had come from in order to obtain food in Egypt. Two, the stories of Joseph (Genesis 37–50) and Judah (Genesis 38) are about the precarious survival of the family line of each. In Numbers, their two tribal descendants, Joshua from

Joseph's line and Caleb from Judah's, emerge as the true survivors from the experience in Egypt, just as these two groups, the Ephraimites and the Judeans, continue to be dominant in the nation's affairs after settlement in the land of Canaan. Ephraim represented for Isaiah and Hosea, for example, the whole of the Northern Kingdom over against Judea in the south with its powerful center in Jerusalem (Isa 7:1–17; Hos 5:3–14). The continuing, highlighted interest in both Judeans and Ephraimites shows up in various parts of Genesis–2 Kings and is indicative of the integrated nature of the extended narrative.

Genesis	Numbers
Spying The disguised Joseph causes his brothers despair when he tells them that they are spies in Egypt (Genesis 37, 42).	*Spying* The Israelite spies alarm their brethren with their account of the daunting task of conquering Canaan (Numbers 13–14).

SPIES

The spying incidents in Genesis 42–45 and Numbers 13 bring out comparable issues. The context each time is the provision of food. Twice Joseph's brothers, ten of the sons of Jacob-Israel, go down to Egypt to buy food, and each time they experience hardship. Although food for purchase is available to them, they encounter a harsh Egyptian ruler, Joseph in disguise (Genesis 42), and a second time they come to Egypt the machinations of this Egyptian entrap them in seeming criminal activity (Genesis 44). Twice in Numbers 13 the Israelite spies go into Canaan to assess its agricultural potential, and they too fare badly. As is true for Joseph's brothers, a plenitude of food is on offer, but they encounter the daunting character of the inhabitants, and a second time when they make a sortie into Canaan to overcome the enemy, the native Canaanites defeat them. Moses unsuccessfully opposes making the sortie, just as Jacob-Israel unsuccessfully opposed the proposed second visit to Egypt by ten of his sons (Gen 43:1–14).

The Joseph story recounts another incident involving a negative and provocative report. The word *dibbah* used of the spies' report of Num 13:32 is the one found in Gen 37:2 when Joseph reports about his brothers to their father. At the time, Jacob and his family were sojourning in Canaan. Leveen sees an allusion to the Genesis narrative in Num 13:32: "This rather unusual term [*dibbah*] suggests that just as that report led to a disaster for Joseph, as he is kidnapped by his brothers and sold into Egyptian service, so too the negative reports of the spies lead to the punishment of these people, with the startling difference that they want to be returned to that very same Egypt that they now remember so favorably."⁹

Joseph's report leads to his future enslavement in Egypt, and the spies' report to the Israelites seeking to return to what would be renewed enslavement there. In Genesis, Jacob's family went of necessity and did not anticipate enslavement in Egypt. This Numbers generation, on the other hand, knows all about the slavery that would await them in Egypt but still contemplates willingly going back to it. Even more to the point, just as Joseph experienced sale of his person to Egypt, so the Israelites in the wilderness, as I have noted, intend in effect to sell themselves back into slavery in Egypt. Perhaps one reason for the perverse development is the perception that an appropriate penalty for the wilderness generation's wish to go back to Egypt should take the form of selling themselves to the Egyptians. Their ancestors' terrible treatment of Joseph that led to his sale has to be neither forgotten nor forgiven. Any association with Egypt will lead to negative consequences. The wrongful desire of the wilderness generation to return to Egypt, if acted on, would constitute unwitting, continued retribution for the offense of their ancestors. The Numbers generation, which is openly thought of as Yahweh's firstborn son and which is liberated from Egypt on account of that relationship, does not in fact return to Egypt. Instead, their fate is to die in the wilderness for accepting the description of the horrors in the spies' report (Numbers 14). Their end evokes the picture conveyed by yet another fateful, earlier report: Jacob's sons communicated to their father that Joseph ended up as a horrifically mutilated corpse in the wilderness (Gen 37:31–33). Num 14:33 refers to how forty years of desert wanderings will have to pass until the carcasses of those Israelites who came out of Egypt "be wasted in the wilderness." The sight of their carcasses is to remind the generation that will enter Canaan of their parents' offense in reacting so fearfully to the spies' report.

THE NEPHILIM

A major aspect of the report in Numbers 13 with which the spies dismay their fellow Israelites is their doom-laden communication that in encountering the Anakim-Nephilim they were confronting gods. The spies "were like grasshoppers" before them (Num 13:33). In Gen 6:1–4 the Nephilim were identified as the offspring of the daughters of men and the sons of the gods. Eryl Davies speaks of them as "a race of quasi-divine beings." Ashley points out that when Num 13:33 reports about "the sons of Anak, which come of the giants [Nephilim]," the clause citing the Nephilim "makes explicit the connection between the current statement and Gen 6:4."[10] That is, the Anakim are not known and are being encountered for the first time, but the Nephilim are known from Gen 6:4—evidence of just how pervasive the influence of Genesis on Numbers is.

The spies' report and the terrifying effect it has on the people cause Moses and Aaron to fall prostrate before the assembled Israelite community after they hear what Gray calls "the blasphemous murmurings of the people" (Num 14:5).[11] Gray presumably means the people's fear and hence their taking seriously the Anakim-Nephilim as godlike beings. Moses and Aaron experience anguish because their charges exhibit dread of alleged divine beings, the Anakim-Nephilim, instead of fearing and trusting their own god, Yahweh. 2 Kgs 17:35 expresses the matter well: Yahweh had made a covenant with the Israelites and "charged them saying, Ye shall not fear other gods."

We might look more closely at the scouting trip to the land of Canaan in Numbers 13 and 14 and recall how Joseph's brothers were supposedly spies in Egypt and how they bowed down before Joseph when purchasing grain (Gen 42:6). Their act of submission is intended to recall Joseph's dream about his brothers as sheaves of grain bowing down to him (Gen 37:6–8). In Egypt, his brothers, not recognizing him, bow down in awed reverence not as grasshoppers like the spies before the Anakim-Nephilim (Num 13:33), but in a movement recalling the "sheaves of grain" prostrate on the ground. Joseph's dream, which anticipates his future life in Egypt, will prove most significant for understanding why certain seemingly unrelated prohibitions follow in Numbers 15 (see chapter 6).

Joseph's accusation that his brothers are spies in Egypt is false. They are but visiting in order to bring back food for their starving family. In Numbers 13 the Israelites, who are again explicitly linked by name to their tribal ancestors in Genesis, are actual spies and thus do commit an offense against the country of Canaan. That infraction, however, is of no concern to the narrator. The primary focus is again on fraternal discord. These Israelite spies, by bringing troubling reports of frightening beings, upset their own brothers, whose hope had been set on entering Canaan. Although the spies report to their brethren back in the wilderness on the plentiful supply of food in Canaan, they frighten their fellow Israelites with accounts of the enemy's preternatural might. That might is not unlike the God-King Pharaoh's, which the brothers encountered in the person of "the Lord of the land," Joseph (Gen 42:30). That is, the terror of the Israelites in the wilderness when they hear about the Anakim-Nephilim is reminiscent of the fear that was engendered among the brothers after they encountered the disguised Joseph in Egypt, an encounter which they relayed to their father: "The man, who is the Lord of the Land, spake roughly to us, and took us for spies of the country" (Gen 42:30).

When the Israelites in Num 14:40–45 try to overcome the enemy by proceeding to attack the Canaanites, they suffer defeat. Divine aid is denied them, the deficit playing out when Moses chooses not to accompany them with the sacred Ark of the Covenant, the potent symbol of Yahweh's presence among them and a terror to any enemy of Israel (Num 14:44). Moreover, as a punishment for their preceding lack of trust the deity has decided to disallow any possession in Canaan for the generation to which the spies belong. Death in the wilderness will be their lot.

By any measure, the decision to deny the wilderness generation a settled existence in Canaan is exceedingly harsh: they have experienced enslavement in Egypt, to be followed by precarious, prolonged wandering in inhospitable terrain, all climaxing in death in the desert. There is, to be sure, recognition of the grimness that the people face and awareness of its source when they ask, "And wherefore hath Yahweh brought us unto this land, to fall by the sword, that our wives and our children should be a prey? were it not better for us to return into Egypt?" (Num 14:3). What accounts for such harshness? At stake, basically, are doubts about the deity's omnipotence, omniscience, and morality. Recognition of this aspect of the situation actually comes to expression in Moses' complaint to God: "Now if thou [Yahweh] shalt kill all this people as one man, then the nations which have heard the fame of thee will speak, saying, Because Yahweh was not able to bring this people into the land which he sware unto them, therefore he hath slain them in the wilderness" (Num 14:15, 16).

In order to quell doubts about God's justice, power, and governance, the ancient writer(s) introduces the idea that God has to test man. The Israelites have to spend forty years in the wilderness not because, in reality, God lacked the power to lessen the long length of time in such grim conditions, but because—in his defense—he needed to test and educate the people (Deut 8:2, 16). In regard to what transpires in Numbers 14, God punishes the Israelites because the people let themselves be misled by the spies' unfavorable report about the land of Canaan (Num 14:34).[12] Critics are readily caught up in the narrative's perspective and thus lack a dispassionate assessment. Ashley is typical when he writes, "The sins of the people are multiple. First, they have implicitly denied Yahweh's salvation and providential care by wishing to have died in Egypt or in their journey thus far. The reason for Israel's death wish is their fear of death at the hands of the Canaanites. This lack of faith is foisted on to Yahweh himself and is made to be his purpose in bringing the people into Canaan, where he will allow the Canaanites to slaughter the men and take the women and children as booty."[13] The matter is more complicated than these comments suggest. For one thing, the Canaanites on this occasion do slaughter Israelites. Underlying the write-up of Numbers 14 is, in fact, an apologetic intent. Human failings are seized upon in order to deflect attention from the fundamental unfairness that afflicts humankind and to maintain Yahweh's reputation: "Consider the work of God: for who can make that straight, which he hath made crooked?" (Eccles 7:13). The notion that a just God is in control of everything that occurs is upheld despite indications to the contrary: "The race is not to the swift, nor the battle to the strong, neither yet bread to the wise, nor yet riches to men of understanding, nor yet favour to men of skill; but time and chance happeneth to them all" (Eccles 9:11). The recorders of the traditions, and later commentators who are drawn into their perspective, are constantly constrained to justify the ways of God to humankind. He is their master and they are his disciples, whose responsibility it is to defend his conduct at every turn regardless of any perceived deficiency.

6

Joseph's Dreams and the Laws of Numbers 15

Just before the five rules in Numbers 15, we have the narrative about the Israelite spies. These spies, we saw, dismay their fellow Israelites with a report about the daunting nature of the people Israel has to displace in order to take over Canaan. The people are godlike, semidivine. They are called the Anakim-Nephilim. The name evokes the semidivine Nephilim of Gen 6:4. The Israelites attempt to defeat them but fail because their deity, Yahweh, withdraws his leadership. Why, then, do we move from those events to a rule in Numbers 15 about the grain offerings to be presented at the sanctuary, followed by rules about an inadvertent offense and a deliberately highhanded one, a person who gathers sticks on the Sabbath, and finally a requirement that an Israelite wear a blue cord on tassels attached to his garment?

The question about the arrangement of the material has been asked many times. The answer is invariably that no substantial connection of any kind is to be discerned between the rules and the narrative that immediately precedes them (and the one that follows them). Critics remark on what they perceive to be a bewilderingly unconnected list of rules. They think each displays subject matter that, aside from being quite unrelated to what comes before and what comes after, is also disconnected from anything that has come up elsewhere in the Book of Numbers. Expressing their perplexity at the seemingly disjointed sequence and disparate subject matter, critics offer comments such as, "But why an editor should have grouped together the laws contained in vv. 1–16, 17–21, 22–31, and why he should have included the legislation contained in the present chapter at this particular point in Numbers, must remain as much a mystery here as in the case of the similar collection of laws contained in chs. 5f. [breach of promise, suspected adulteress, and the nazirite]" (Davies); "Those laws [in Numbers 15], like those in c. 5 and 6, have little or no connection with one another . . . , and none with the narrative of the spies (c. 13 and 14) which precedes, or with the revolt of Korah which follows them" (Gray); "The abrupt transition from the spy story to the strange collection of cultic laws contained in this chapter [15] baffles commentators" (Wenham); "Like several other sections of Numbers, chapter 15 represents, in large part, an addition or appendix to other cultic codes, especially those in Leviticus. Numbers thus emerges as a repository of late ritual law" (Levine).[1] The last of these statements shows how major conclusions are drawn from the apparently haphazard way in which legal and narrative material is presented. In contrast to these views, I shall argue that the rules do indeed have the closest of links with both the narrative that precedes (the spies) and the one that follows (Korah's rebellion) and also with one another. The key to understanding the rules lies in the connections with the story of Joseph in Genesis 37.

Just as the Numbers account of the spies evokes the Nephilim of Genesis 6, so the ensuing Numbers rules recall Joseph's dreams in Genesis 37. It is a typical procedure. The narrator-lawgiver goes back to the first time within the budding nation (after the Nephilim of the primeval world in Genesis 6) that divine beings other than Yahweh came to prominence, namely, in the dreams of the supremely important Joseph in Genesis 37. In them, Joseph perceived himself as divine. His dream about the sheaves of grain pointed to a relationship between a godlike being and the first sons of Israel who bowed down in awe of him—a development that came to pass when Joseph provided food for the hungry in Egypt (Gen 42:6, 43:26). The Israelite spies in Numbers 14, in their quest for relief from hunger and thirst in the desert, viewed the Anakim-Nephilim as godlike and stood in awe of them. In each instance, the response of the brothers to Joseph and of their descendants to the Anakim-Nephilim has dramatic consequences.

If we assume that the Numbers narrator-lawgiver focuses on Joseph as well as on the Anakim-Nephilim, there is a second link between the Joseph story and the narrative about the spies that precedes the rules in Numbers 15. Numbers 13 and 14 portray, we saw, the division and disunity among the Israelites caused by the spies' report about the fearsome enemy Israel is about to face (Num 13:32, 14:36, 37). Each of the spies is a ruler of one of the twelve tribes who descended from the sons of Jacob. Numbers 15, in turn, while it primarily responds to Joseph's reporting of his dreams to his family, also takes up the immediately preceding and related evil report that Joseph brought to his father after spying on his brothers. That report, plus the reporting of his dreams, caused the first division ever among the sons of Israel. The rare word *dibbah* used of Joseph's report is the same word used of the spies' account in Numbers. At the same time as Joseph reported on his brothers, his father gave him a special coat. Joseph then relayed his dreams. Together, the nasty report, the special coat, and the description of his dreams aroused the brothers' hatred. I shall also be pointing out that the narrative that follows the rules in Numbers 15 continues the interest in the division among the sons of Israel. Thus Numbers 16 recounts how Korah and company rebel against their brother Levites, Moses and Aaron, precisely on the same grounds as Joseph's brothers, in disputing his divine standing, rebelled against him.

Joseph's dreams are highly ambiguous. They are unquestionably idolatrous, yet in their unfolding is the tale about how Yahweh brought good out of evil (Gen 50:20). Little wonder that the dreams receive so much detailed scrutiny in Numbers 15, as they do also in the Book of Daniel (see below). The contents of all five rules (quoted below) reflect back on the negative issues raised by Joseph's two dreams in Genesis 37 (also quoted below) and anticipate comparable problems after the land of Canaan has been conquered. Joseph's brothers and his father rebuked Joseph after he told them his dreams: "And his father rebuked him, and said unto him, What is this dream that thou hast dreamed? Shall I and thy mother and thy brethren indeed come to bow down ourselves to thee to the earth?" (Gen 37:10). Joseph cannot help having dreams, but his choosing to report them is another matter, a serious cause of concern and antagonism. The rules in Numbers 15 constitute a detailed critique of the dreams' offensive aspects, in particular Joseph's godlike stance and the awed response he imagined it elicited among the first sons of Israel. The topic, as indicated, very much ties in with the concern central to the preceding account of the spies in Numbers 14 when the Israelites are in awe of the godlike beings, the Anakim-Nephilim.

Joseph's eventual power in Egypt, which the first dream of the sheaves anticipated, allowed him to lay down rules about agricultural policy of far-reaching effect; for example, in return for food he enslaved the Egyptian population. Consistent with the position expressed in Lev 18:3, "After the doings of the land of Egypt, wherein ye dwelt, shall ye [the later sons of Israel] not do," it is no surprise that so many biblical rules constitute reactions to negative features of Joseph's role both before and after he became ruler in Egypt. Actions and attitudes viewed as unacceptable were not to be repeated in Israel's later settled life in Canaan.

As I indicated in chapter 1, the biblical law of the Sabbatical Year and the Year of Jubilee in Leviticus 25 illustrates the position well. That law serves to recall the Egyptian famine in Joseph's time by imposing a man-made interruption in the production of grain every seventh year throughout the entire land. The law goes on to single out a Jubilee Year that takes place after seven Sabbatical Years have come and gone, that is, after the equivalent of the seven years of famine in Egypt. The Jubilee Year memorializes the climax of the famine when the Egyptians had to sell their ancestral land and then themselves to the pharaoh. The intent of the law in Leviticus 25 is that the Israelites in their land should experience the opposite of what the Egyptians experienced in theirs. In a climactic fiftieth year, those Israelites who had sold their ancestral land are to return to it, and those enslaved are to be released from bondage. Like the law of the Passover, the Sabbatical-Jubilee law evokes the beginnings of the nation.[2]

Genesis 37	Numbers 15
Joseph's arrogance and idolatrous dream, which he proudly reported Sheaves of grain reverentially bow down to Joseph, an action signaling unwitting offenses by Joseph and his brothers. The stalks for the sheaves had been gathered for an idolatrous purpose, and just before his dream Joseph's special garment conveyed arrogance.	*Rules against arrogant and idolatrous conduct* Proper use of grain in paying homage to Yahweh (Num 15:1–16, 17–21); an inadvertent offense and a highhanded one (Num 15:22–31); prohibition against stick gathering on the Sabbath for an idolatrous purpose (Num 15:32–36); and colored fringes on a garment to remind any son of Israel to obey every rule (Num 15:37–41).

THE ROLE OF A GRAIN OFFERING IN WORSHIP

The first two of the five rules in Numbers 15 read as follows:

1 And Yahweh spake unto Moses, saying, 2 Speak unto the children of Israel . . . , When ye be come into the land of your habitations, which I give unto you, 3 And will make an offering by fire unto Yahweh, a burnt offering, or a sacrifice in performing a vow, or in a freewill offering, or in your solemn feasts, to make a sweet savour unto Yahweh, of the herd, or of the flock: 4 Then shall he that offereth his offering unto Yahweh bring a grain offering of a tenth deal of flour mingled with the fourth part of an hin of oil. 5 And the fourth part of an hin of wine for a drink offering shalt thou prepare with the burnt offering or sacrifice, for one lamb. 6 Or for a ram, thou shalt prepare for a grain offering two tenth deals. . . . 7 And for a drink offering thou shalt offer the third part of an hin of wine, for a sweet savour unto Yahweh. 8 And when thou preparest a bullock for a burnt offering, or for a sacrifice in performing a

vow, or peace offerings unto Yahweh: 9 Then shall he bring with a bullock a grain offering of three tenth deals. . . . 10 And thou shalt bring for a drink offering half an hin of wine . . . a sweet savour unto Yahweh. 11 Thus shall it be done for one bullock, or for one ram, or for a lamb, or a kid. 12 According to the number that ye shall prepare, so shall ye do to every one according to their number. 13 All that are born of the country [native-born] shall do these things after this manner, in offering an offering made by fire, of a sweet savour unto Yahweh. 14 And if a stranger sojourn with you . . . will offer . . . a sweet savour unto Yahweh; as ye do, so he shall do. 15 One ordinance shall be both for you of the congregation, and also for the stranger that sojourneth with you, an ordinance for ever in your generations. . . . 16 One law and one manner shall be for you, and for the stranger that sojourneth with you. (Num 15:1–16)

17 And Yahweh spake unto Moses, saying, 18 Speak unto the children of Israel, and say unto them, When ye come into the land whither I bring you, 19 Then it shall be, that, when ye eat of the bread of the land, ye shall offer up an heave offering unto Yahweh. 20 Ye shall offer up a cake of the first of your dough for an heave offering: as ye do the heave offering of the threshing-floor, so shall ye heave it. 21 Of the first of your dough ye shall give unto Yahweh an heave offering in your generations. (Num 15:17–21)

Genesis	Numbers
Joseph's idolatrous dream Sheaves of grain reverentially bow down to Joseph (Gen 37:5–8).	*Two rules about use of grain in worship* Proper use of grain in paying homage to Yahweh (Num 15:1–16, 17–21).

The bias of the two rules about grain is to direct attention to the amount to be offered with different sacrifices. Every commentator focuses on the concentration of interest in the grain offerings. They form the apodosis of the first rule (vs. 4), and they accompany all of the various sacrifices with details about differing amounts for a sheep or a goat, for large cattle, and for a ram. A grain offering is solely in focus in the second of the two sequential rules about offerings.

When an Israelite worshiper offers sacrifices he proclaims and praises the power of his god. With a primary focus on the accompanying grain offerings, the examples cited in the Numbers rule are "a burnt offering or a sacred feast for the purpose of setting aside a votive, or as a voluntary offering, or on the occasion of your festivals—producing a pleasing aroma for Yahweh, from the herd or from the flock." This is Levine's translation, and his heading for discussing this law is "Accompanying Grain Offerings."[3]

The term for the grain offering is *minḥah*. It means a gift or a tribute and conveys, in Levine's words, "the subsequent relationship of the worshipper to God so exactly." The person pays tribute to a higher being. Critics explain the remarkable attention to the grain as a reform that elevates the grain offering to the same status as an animal offering, or at the very least regularizes a practice to present it together with an animal sacrifice.[4] (The claim about a reform is another example of critics postulating a historical development with no substantiation for doing so.) The following, related rule in Num 15:17–21 is solely focused on grain and is special to Numbers. It requires the person paying homage to separate out some dough that is made from the grain and present it at the sanctuary: "Ye shall offer up a cake of the first of your dough for an heave offering [a gift]: as ye do the heave offering of the threshing-floor, so shall ye heave [make a gift of] it."

Instead of explaining the major attention given to the grain offering as reflecting changes to the Israelite sacrificial system at some unknown point in time, we might turn to a crucial incident in the life of Joseph, namely, to his dream in Gen 37:7 about a grain offering in worship: "Behold, we were binding sheaves in the field, and, lo, my sheaf arose, and also stood upright; and, behold, your sheaves stood round about, and made obeisance to my sheaf." Ron Pirson underlines that in the dream the verb *ḥawah* or *šaḥah*, "to bow down, to do obeisance," signifies, not "submission to someone" but "to prostrate oneself (in worship)."[5] The word occurs mainly in cultic contexts. Tribute is paid to Joseph as to a powerful, higher being.

In the overall story the dream anticipates key developments in Joseph's life; indeed, it encapsulates the entire story, from the recounting of the dream that so infuriates his brothers to his feeding them when they come to Egypt to purchase food. The narrator-lawgiver in Numbers reacts to the idolatrous implication of the dream about the sheaves and of the other dream about the sun, moon, and stars bowing down to Joseph. Unlike the prior dreams in Gen 20:3–7 (Abimelech), 28:12–15, 31:10–13 (Jacob), and 31:24 (Laban), God neither appears to nor talks to Joseph. Nor is there any later recognition at the end of the Joseph saga that God communicated the dreams to him. Within the context of the narrative, Joseph's dreams do not have God's legitimation.

Sheaves of grain, Joseph's brothers, bow down to him in one dream as if in homage to a god, as do the sun, moon, and stars, that is, his father, mother, and brothers, in the second dream. With his priestly concerns, the compiler of Numbers shows interest in sacred matters in the Book of Genesis. He counters the disturbing religious aspect of the sheaves dream, when the first sons of Israel paid homage to Joseph, by setting out the proper role of grain when the later sons of Israel are to pay homage to the true god, Yahweh. In the Num 15:2–21 rules, an exclusive interest in honoring a divine being might be seen in the fact that the rule does not cite a sin offering in its list of sacrifices. The focus is entirely on offerings whereby the worshiper honors his deity, and the aim is to parallel and oppose the homage paid to Joseph by his worshiping brothers.

Recent scholarship has shown interest in the idolatrous aspects of the Joseph story. Pirson expresses a restrained view of the matter: "Quite a few elements in the story of Jacob's sons add up and contribute to a portrayal of Joseph in which the divine not only plays an important role, but in which Joseph—now and then—presents himself as having divine knowledge, or in which he seems to absorb characteristics that are reserved and restricted to God or gods." That dreams are to be taken with the utmost seriousness is clear from Num 12:6–7: God speaks to Moses as a prophet and communicates with him by dreams. Joseph's dreams are prophetic but do not come from God. They are also idolatrous. Pirson points out that the first words spoken by Joseph urge his brothers to, "listen to this dream which I have dreamed" (Gen 37:6). That these are Joseph's first words in the story heightens the significance to be given to their contents. Gerhard von Rad is at pains to stress that Joseph's dreams in no way signify a religious dimension. They are, he implies, just the vivid imaginings of a young boy. One wonders why he feels the need to downplay troubling religious overtones. The issue that von Rad attempts to deny is precisely the one that lies behind the lawgiver's concern. Robert Alter's characterization of Joseph's dreams is also off the mark: they intimate "adolescent narcissism, even if the grandiosity eventually is justified by events." Both von Rad and Alter introduce psychological considerations as if the narrator in Genesis is intent on portraying irritating teenagers.[6]

Joseph says to his brothers at the end of the story that he is not in the place of God (Gen 50:19, 20), but the dreams present a more complex picture. At two places (Gen 45:3, 4), Joseph uses a formula of self-introduction ("I am Joseph") that is used only by the God-King Pharaoh ("I am Pharaoh") and the Hebrew God ("I am thy shield, almighty god," etc.).[7] Aaron Wildavsky comments on the brothers' later terrified response at coming upon the money they had given over for grain, "What is this that God has done to us?" (Gen 42:28): "We as the readers know it is Joseph who has done this to them, not the God of their fathers. Joseph is acting like a god. Joseph has done more than just become an Egyptian. As a high-ranking Egyptian official, he has assumed, on his own, the position of God, which the brothers acknowledge verbally, if unknowingly."[8]

In his first dream Joseph sees himself as in effect a nature god with his brothers as sheaves of grain bowing down to him. The information conveyed may echo non-Israelite, pagan practice associated with harvesting crops, when there is festive drinking and homage to a fertility god in the shape of a standing sheaf of grain. The welfare rule in Deut 24:19–22 about the forgotten sheaf at harvest time has led many commentators to speculate, as A. D. H. Mayes has, about "an ancient custom of leaving behind a portion of the produce of the field as an offering for the gods or spirits of fertility."[9] However that may be, Joseph's dream about the sheaves anticipates the role grain will play when he becomes governor of Egypt, how his brothers will obtain food from him, and how they will indeed bow down to him on the occasion (Gen 42:6, 43:26).

Insight into how a later biblical author viewed Joseph's dreams in a way similar to Numbers comes from the Book of Daniel. It is well recognized that the book owes much to the Joseph story.[10] Joseph and Daniel are the only two Israelites who, in the service of a foreign king, engage in the interpretation of dreams. Interesting links exist between Joseph's two dreams and Nebuchadnezzar's two dreams in Daniel 2 and 4:

> 31 Thou, O king, sawest, and behold a great image. This great image, whose brightness was excellent, stood before thee; and the form thereof was terrible. 32 This image's head was of fine gold, his breast and his arms of silver, his belly and his thighs of brass, 33 His legs of iron, his feet part of iron and part of clay. 34 Thou sawest till that a stone was cut out without hands, which smote the image upon his feet that were of iron and clay, and brake them to pieces. 35 Then was the iron, the clay, the brass, the silver, and the gold, broken to pieces together, and became like the chaff of the summer threshingfloors; and the wind carried them away, that no place was found for them: and the stone that smote the image became a great mountain, and filled the whole earth. (Dan 2:31–35)
>
> 10 Behold a tree in the midst of the earth, and the height thereof was great. 11 The tree grew, and was strong, and the height thereof reached unto heaven, and the sight thereof to the end of all the earth: 12 The leaves thereof were fair, and the fruit thereof much, and in it was meat for all: the beasts of the field had shadow under it, and the fowls of the heaven dwelt in the boughs thereof, and all flesh was fed of it. 13 I saw in the visions of my head upon my bed, and, behold, a watcher and an holy one came down from heaven; 14 He cried aloud, and said thus, Hew down the tree, and cut off his branches, shake off his leaves, and scatter his fruit: let the beasts get away from under it, and the fowls from his branches: 15 Nevertheless leave the stump of his roots in the earth, even with a band of iron and brass, in the tender grass of the field; and let it be wet with the dew of heaven, and let his portion be with the beasts in the grass of the earth: 16 Let his heart be changed from man's, and let a beast's heart be given unto him; and let seven times pass over him. 17

This matter is by the decree of the watchers, and the demand by the word of the holy ones: to the intent that the living may know that the most High ruleth in the kingdom of men, and giveth it to whomsoever he will, and setteth up over it the basest of men. (Dan 4:10–17)

In this dream in Daniel 4 the king sees himself as a tree towering over all the earth and all creatures receiving nourishment from it. Similarly, Joseph's dream about the sheaves anticipated his role of providing sustenance for all: "And all countries came into Egypt to Joseph for to buy corn; because that the famine was so sore in all lands" (Gen 41:57).

The important feature of the dream in Dan 2:31–35 is that it leads to an idolatrous act. The king's counselors inform Nebuchadnezzar that no man on earth can convey to him what he demands, namely, that the interpreter tell him not just the dream's elucidation but its actual contents. The counselors protest: "It is a rare thing that the king requireth, and there is none other that can shew it before the king, except the gods, whose dwelling is not with flesh" (Dan 2:11). When Daniel proceeds to do the impossible and convey as well as explain the dream's substance, the startling response is one of awe: "Then the king Nebuchadnezzar fell upon his face, and worshipped Daniel, and commanded that they should offer a grain offering [minḥah] and sweet odours unto him" (Dan 2:46). Joseph receives this kind of worship in his dream and later on in real life in Egypt: "And when Joseph came home, they [the brothers] brought him the present [minḥah] which was in their hand into the house, and bowed themselves to him to the earth" (Gen 43:26). If there is a link between Daniel 2 and the Genesis dream narrative, then the author of Daniel, through his depiction of Nebuchadnezzar, understands Joseph's dream as lending Joseph godlike character. The Daniel author does not introduce a psychological dimension but grasps the religious import of the dream.

A remarkable detail is, as just noted, the mention in Dan 2:46 of the grain offering to Daniel, the Jewish exile at the foreign court. Pamela Milne points out that much more than civic honor is implied in the king's command, that the honor is religious in character, which is underlined by the "strictly religious terms *grain offering* and *incense*."[11] For the purpose of my analysis of Num 15:1–21, the main point is that Nebuchadnezzar reacts to Daniel in real life in the same way the brothers of Joseph reacted to Joseph in the dream, by an act of worship involving grain. That is, the king's response to Daniel is in line with how the author of Numbers reads Joseph's dream. Evaluating the role of grain offerings in Israel's worship, the Numbers lawgiver has been troubled by the idolatry in Joseph's dream and wishes to establish the proper role of a grain offering in that worship. Matthew Rindge detects in the portrayal of Daniel similar opposition to Joseph's stance in Genesis 37–50. He is correct, but Numbers already reveals this stance.[12] Also noteworthy is that the outcome of Nebuchadnezzar's tree dream—the tree is cut down but is permitted to exist in a more modest form—contains the same judgment that the stance in Numbers implies. There can be a ruler, but he should not arrogate to himself God's power. God is the one who permits some people to have power over others, and he is the one who provides sustenance. Nebuchadnezzar's dream contains a negative judgment on arrogation of divine power. It is similar to Jacob's negative reaction to Joseph's dream—"Shall I and thy mother and thy brethren indeed come to bow down ourselves to thee to the earth?" (Gen 37:10)—and to the position of the lawgiver in Numbers.

By any reckoning Joseph's dreams are not minor. When Joseph initially relays the dream about the sheaves to his brothers, its effect, together with that of the second, even more blatantly idolatrous dream about the sun, moon, and stars doing him obeisance, is to arouse in them murderous intent. Pirson stresses how Joseph comes under a death sentence on account of the dreams' impact on them.[13]

In the first dream, sheaves of grain represent human beings. In commenting on the Numbers grain rule, Wenham points out that a cereal offering can sometimes replace the offering of an animal, and just as the offering of an animal represents the worshiper, so too can a grain offering. Wenham notes that the twelve wheaten loaves of showbread symbolize the twelve tribes of Israel (Lev 24:5–9).[14] Products associated with agriculture stand, then, not just metaphorically for humans but even represent them in cultic practice as in the dream. As for the metaphorical use, in Num 14:9 the Canaanites are said to be bread for the Israelites to consume in battle. The author of Numbers is well used to switching back and forth between literal and metaphorical meaning, for example, when he describes in the immediately following narrative about the death of Korah and his family: "And the earth opened her mouth" (Num 16:32, 26:10).

With its particular personification of grain, Joseph's dream about the harvest occurs at the point when Jacob and his sons originally settled as sojourners in the land of Canaan (Gen 37:1). Introducing the various rules in Numbers, verse 2 refers to "the land of your settlement." The phrase focuses on the post-Exodus settlement in Canaan, and Levine compares it to Gen 37:1, "the land of your sojourning," that is, Canaan in Jacob's time there. Num 15:19, in turn, speaks of eating "the bread of the land," in anticipation of the first harvest in Canaan after it is conquered. Wenham points out that the people are to enter Canaan and find large amounts of flour, oil, and wine readily available to them. Joseph's dream about the grain had anticipated an abundance of grain in Egypt.[15]

The Numbers rule takes into account persons who will be sojourners among the future settled Israelites (Num 15:14–16). Should they choose to participate in Israel's worship, they too have to observe the requirement about the grain offering. A factor may be to discourage them from their own peculiar religious rites. By participating in the Israelite cult, they are less likely to influence the Israelites with their own rites, fertility ones, for instance. Joseph's dreams occurred in Canaan, the land of his and his family's sojourning, and the judgment of the author of Numbers may have been that the Canaanite milieu influenced their idolatrous contents. We might infer that while Numbers thinks that it would not have been in order for Joseph and family to adopt idolatrous ways (for instance, as illustrated in the dreams), Numbers is not inimical to and may even want sojourners among the Israelites to adopt Israelite ways—an example, perhaps, of imitating in order to oppose.

AN UNWITTING OFFENSE AND AN INTENDED ONE

The next rule reads as follows:

22 And if ye have erred, and not observed all these commandments, which Yahweh hath spoken unto Moses, 23 Even all that Yahweh hath commanded you by the hand of Moses, from the day that Yahweh commanded Moses, and henceforward among your generations; 24 Then it shall be, if ought be committed by ignorance without the knowledge of the congregation, that all the congregation shall offer. . . . 25 And the priest shall make an atonement for all the congregation of the children of Israel, and it shall be forgiven them; for it is ignorance. . . . 27 And if any soul sin through ignorance, then he shall bring a she goat of the first year for a sin offering. 28 And the priest shall make an atonement for the soul that sinneth ignorantly . . . ; and it shall be forgiven him. 29 Ye shall have one law for him that sinneth through ignorance, both for him that is born among the children of Israel, and for the stranger that sojourneth among them. 30 But the soul that doeth ought with a high hand, whether he be born in the land, or a stranger, the same reproacheth Yahweh; and that soul shall be cut off from among his people. 31 Because he hath despised the word of Yahweh, and hath broken his commandment, that soul shall utterly be cut off; his iniquity shall be upon him. (Num 15:22–31)

Genesis	Numbers
Joseph's dreams Offenses by Joseph and his brothers (Genesis 37).	*Two rules* An inadvertent offense and a highhanded one (Num 15:22–31).

UNWITTING OFFENSE

A rule about any offense not consciously intended comes in a context that has just focused (in the previous rule about grain offerings) on proper worship. It is why some critics think that the type of offense under scrutiny must concern a previous infraction in the area of worship.[16] This notion proves to be accurate, but the law's language indicates that all commandments come under review ("all these commandments, which Yahweh hath spoken unto Moses, Even all that Yahweh hath commanded you by the hand of Moses, from the day that Yahweh commanded Moses"). To be sure, a switch from a focus on a grain offering to a concern with an unintentional offense of any kind does seem an odd transition but very much less so, we shall see, in light of the rule's more immediate, narrative inspiration, Joseph's dreams.

If we take into account the broader canvas on which the author of Numbers works, we can follow exactly how he proceeds, and Joseph's dreams continue to be very relevant. Joseph could not control having dreams, the contents of which have him think of himself as being godlike. Not only do sheaves of grain but also the sun, moon, and stars bow down to him. His overweening arrogance may not be consciously intended, but the offenses of idolatry implicit in the dreams are grave ones. Moreover, the imagined worshipful actions taking place in his dreams tie into the preceding rule's interest about the actual worship of Yahweh.

In the Num 15:22–31 rule, the congregation, a collective, commits a sin in ignorance. This focus on the worshiping community of the future sons of Israel—the interest in the generations is explicit ("among your generations," vs. 23)—corresponds to the situation of the first sons depicted in the dreams: in waking life they certainly did not wish to bow down to Joseph. In doing so in the dream, they unwittingly engaged in false worship. The rule also details an individual who offends unintentionally (Num 15:27). The example will correspond to Joseph himself, for he does not consciously intend idolatry. The first rule, then, is about the sin of a group (equivalent to Joseph's family), and the second rule is about the sin of an individual (Joseph). We do not learn what particular examples of unwitting offenses the lawgiver has in mind among later sons of Israel. In fact, he includes every infraction of Moses' rules: "Even all that Yahweh hath commanded you by the hand of Moses, from the day that Yahweh commanded Moses, and henceforward among your generations" (Num 15:23). The rule generalizes on the basis of the highly idiosyncratic example furnished by Joseph's dream.

There is a mental element in a dream, but it is out of the dreamer's control, just as in the rule the verb used to express the idea of inadvertence, *šagah*, "to err, go astray, meander, or reel," also points to a mental element that is difficult to control. Joseph's dream is deeply offensive, but he had no control over it. The idea it articulated constituted an inadvertent offense. The dream, nonetheless, does express Joseph's desires and self-perception. The actions in them do not take place in real life nor are they consciously intended, but that is not the end of the matter. When the brothers eventually go to Egypt to buy grain, they do indeed bow down to the Egyptian Joseph, who, unknown to them, has become "a father to Pharaoh, and lord of all his house, and a ruler throughout all the land of Egypt" (Gen 45:8). Pharaoh's status is that of a god. Surprisingly, in light of Joseph's rank, he deals directly with these foreigners who come to buy grain and not through one of his servants (Gen 42:6, 43:26, 45:8). We read: "And when Joseph came home, they brought him the present [minḥah] which was in their hand into the house, and bowed themselves to him to the earth" (Gen 43:26). The term for the present to Joseph is minḥah, exactly the term the preceding rule uses for the grain offering to be given to God. The language about bowing to the earth is the same language as in the dream in Gen 37:7, 10. At this point in the story the brothers cause Joseph's presumptuous dream to come true, but they are not aware of doing so. Their act of homage extends even to giving him a minḥah that is associated with worshiping God. Theirs is inadvertent wrongdoing.

DELIBERATE OFFENSE

The rule—it is found only here in Numbers—goes on to consider highhanded, intended action (Num 15:30, 31). Critics note that the language of the rule betokens someone who acts against God—exactly how the author of Numbers sees the Israelite Joseph doing in his dreams. Milgrom points out that the image of the "upraised hand" or "high hand" is one that, because of its background in religious language about the actions of deities, including Yahweh (Exod 14:8; Num 33:3), "is most apposite for the brazen sinner who commits his acts in open defiance of the Lord."[17] In focus, I suggest, is the fact that Joseph arrogantly communicated his dreams to his family. The first words he ever spoke were, "Hear, I pray you, this dream which I have dreamed." When his brothers and his father rebuked him he expressed no regrets and revealed no misgivings about the notion of a worshipful attitude to him on the part of his brothers and his parents. Nor is there any mention that God communicated the dream to him, as happens, we saw, with other dreams described in Genesis.

The dream about the sheaves proves to be accurate, for Joseph takes on divine status in Egypt. Pharaoh had presumably the status of a god, and Joseph became "even as Pharaoh," indeed, "as a father to Pharaoh." The brothers bow down to a disguised Joseph and receive grain from him in return. From a later Israelite perspective, Joseph's self-perception as the object of worship by members of his family certainly constitutes brazen sinfulness, or, at the very least, this type of person depicted in the Numbers rule is suggested. The rule states that the highhanded lawbreaker "shall be utterly cut off; his iniquity shall be upon him" (Num 15:31). This is exactly what happened to Joseph after he relayed his dreams—taken to Egypt, he was, indeed, utterly cut off from his people.

THE OFFENSE OF GATHERING STICKS ON THE SABBATH

The rule reads as follows:

32 And while the children of Israel were in the wilderness, they found a man that gathered sticks upon the Sabbath day. 33 And they that found him gathering sticks brought him unto Moses and Aaron, and unto all the congregation. 34 And they put him in ward, because it was not declared what should be done to him. 35 And Yahweh said unto Moses, The man shall be surely put to death: all the congregation shall stone him with stones without the camp. 36 And all the congregation brought him without the camp, and stoned him with stones, and he died; as Yahweh commanded Moses. (Num 15:32–36)

Genesis	Numbers
Joseph's dream about sheaves of grain The stalks for the sheaves had been gathered for an idolatrous purpose (Genesis 37).	*Rule about use of sticks* No gathering of sticks of wood on the Sabbath for an idolatrous purpose (Num 15:32–36).

We move from a rule about inadvertent and deliberate offenses to a rule about a stick-gatherer, which is communicated in the form of an actual incident. The shift in subject matter seems so abrupt, with little or no interest shared in common between one rule and the next. As for the story *cum* rule, we can at least note that it expresses a law in the context of a story—the very process that characterizes, if less directly, the relationship between biblical laws and narratives.

The rule has puzzling aspects, which has rendered it a most difficult one to interpret. Why is it so specific in condemning someone who gathers sticks on the Sabbath? It is clearly seen as a very serious offense, yet no one knows what the penalty is until God communicates it to Moses, and even then no explanation is forthcoming as to why the offense is so grave. If the focus is on a person breaking the prohibition against work on the Sabbath, why is the penalty, a death sentence, given for only this one action of picking up sticks of wood? The rule, moreover, does not say that the offense is working on the Sabbath. With negative intent, it states only that there was "found a man that gathered sticks upon the Sabbath day." Another indication of the gravity of the offense is that the matter has to be taken to God for adjudication. The preceding rule ends with a judgment against someone who acts against God in the most presumptuous of ways. Wenham correctly points out that from a formal point of view the rule about a deliberately highhanded offense and the rule about the offender on the Sabbath are one unit (Num 15:17–36), despite the striking difference in subject matter.[18] The stick-gathering offender has to be stoned outside the camp. The highhanded offender in the previous law "shall be utterly cut off" (Num 15:31). In other instances in which we find the location for the carrying out of a capital sentence to be outside of the camp it means that the person, a blasphemer, for example (Lev 24:14), has offended God directly. The severe penalty for the offense in Num 15:32–36 suggests that the wrong must be deliberately aimed against the prevailing sacred order. Meir Malul states of such an offender, "The violator is viewed as attacking the very embodiment of order and social structure and accepted laws of the group."[19] The seriousness of the stick-gatherer's offense has probably to be viewed in this light.

The rule is recounted in the form of an actual occurrence in contrast, I suggest, to the imagined event involving the sheaves in Joseph's dream. The Numbers lawgiver has raised the question: what offense among the later sons of Israel might compare to the one occurring in the dream about the sheaves? Joseph's dreaming, as Pirson emphasizes, brings him under a sentence of death, albeit a nonjudicial one—he provokes the brothers' rage.[20] The lawgiver takes the matter further. He views the dream as pointing to an action that would provoke divine jealousy. Just as the preceding rule focuses on the man who acts presumptuously in defying God, so the rule about the stick-gatherer focuses on the substance of the dream about the sheaves and hence on an offender deliberately setting himself up in competition with God.

Paul in 1 Cor 10:14–23 provides a later instance of someone who provokes divine jealousy. A Christian who arrogates the right to participate in pagan temple feasts acts contrary to God's warning not to provoke his jealousy. It is of the kind cited in Deut 32:21: "They have moved me to jealousy with a non-god, they have provoked me to anger with their vanities." The person hubristically claims to be stronger than God (1 Cor 10:22).

The man in the rule gathers sticks, possibly for making a fire, but his purpose is not cited. Fire is certainly present elsewhere in Numbers. In Num 15:3 we have "the offering by fire unto Yahweh," and in Num 11:1 God destroys the edge of the camp with fire, while in Numbers 16 God removes Korah and the other rebels by fire. Indeed, a rule in Exod 35:3 reads, "Ye shall kindle no fire throughout your dwellings on the Sabbath day." Fire is God's sacred element, a symbol of his holiness, and a person handling fire inappropriately competes with God and doubtless invites a capital sentence. He is, indeed, like the presumptuous person in the preceding rule in Num 15:30, 31. Why, however, does the Numbers rule not go further and spell out the gatherer's intention or the precise nature of the offense?

In the rule, all we learn is that the person gathers sticks on the Sabbath. The verb is *mqošeš*, a denominative of *qaš*, "straw," and it means "to gather into a bunch or bale."[21] In Genesis 37 the sheaves in Joseph's dream have already undergone the prior step when the individual stalks of grain were collected—*mqošeš*—and bound into sheaves, which then "stood all around" the sheaf Joseph and bowed down in reverence. In Zeph 2:1 the verb is used of assembling people. The gathering of the stalks in the dream is a preliminary step in the offense committed by the sheaves, the idolatrous reverence shown to Joseph. So too in the rule the gathering of the sticks appears to be a preliminary step for a pending idolatrous act. The interest in the initial stage of the offense is in line with the consistent interest in beginnings on the part of the narrator-lawgiver, whether it be in historical origins or in how an offense begins; for example, Abraham letting his wife, Sarah, be taken by a foreign king is the starting point for the law prohibiting the renovation of a marriage in Deut 24:1–4.[22]

In the Numbers rule, the person is placed under guard (*mišmar*) after gathering the sticks of wood. (Joseph's offensive dreams led to his exile in Egypt, and once there he was put under guard, *mišmar*, for offending against Potiphar's wife, who falsely claimed he left his garment with her after he tried to seduce her.) The key point is that the man who gathers sticks in the rule begins a course of action that very much looks intent on committing a serious offense against the sacred order. He is put under guard until God declares judgment on the nature of his activity.

If Joseph's dream is the context for the lawgiver's concern, we can infer that an idolatrous action is intended with the sticks of wood in the rule. The matter has to be taken before God. The reason for this step is the nature of the offense. The man is not breaking the Sabbath solely because he works on that day but because he moves to claim godlike powers on it. These powers he will presumably demonstrate with the gathered sticks, possibly involving the use of fire. He is setting himself up to receive acclaim for his divine standing on the very day, the Sabbath, when God is to be acknowledged as the unique creator of the universe and everything in it.

The man's hubris is like Joseph's when he saw himself as a bundle of stalks gathered together to be bowed down to by other bundles and, in the ensuing second dream, even by the sun, moon, and stars. The protest of Joseph's brothers centered on his claim to superior status: "Do you mean to be king over us?" (Gen 37:8). In Numbers, Moses' fellow Israelites bring the stick-gatherer to Moses, Aaron, and the whole congregation because they perceive the gravity of his offense: the man is challenging the divinely sanctioned leadership of Moses and Aaron and hence God's authority too. Their action is not taken because they do not know how to deal with the question, "What Shall We Do with the Sabbath-Gatherer?" which is neither a quote nor a question in the text, as Jonathan Burnside assumes.[23] The people all know to have God declare judgment because only God enjoys a status higher than that claimed by Israel's leaders and the stick-gatherer. As the man was challenging the recognized leadership, it was essential for the answer to come from one standing above both parties. When in Numbers 16 Korah and others who seek leadership rebel against Moses and Aaron and are found to be in the wrong, it is God who executes the sentence. As the culprits had challenged the leadership, it was essential for the answer to come from one standing above both parties. We might recall, in contrast, that in the Sabbath rule in Exod 31:13–17 there is a sentence of death for working on that day but no requirement that the matter be brought before God for judgment. In the Exodus context there is no comparable leadership struggle between one Israelite and another. The procedural step in the Numbers rule is further indication that the stick-gatherer's offense is not simply his breaking of the prohibition against laboring on the Sabbath, but his behaving in a presumptuous way in an attempt to arrogate undeserved high status.

The rule can be understood, I suggest, only by viewing it as exploring the issues involved in Joseph's dream about the sheaves of grain. We need to presume a scrutiny of the dream by the Numbers narrator-lawgiver in order to understand why his rule is formulated as it is, why it does not tell us more than that the person gathers sticks on the Sabbath. Law and narrative are bound together, presumably because in the scribal setting in which the texts are produced both are fitted together at the same time. The dream itself, in keeping with the nature of dreams, only hints at its meaning and cannot be interpreted without a context. Cryptic communication, characterizing both rule and dream, is always in need of a framework to be understood.

What exactly is the offense that the rule has in focus? The reference to the Sabbath is obviously important. Its concern is not with working on that day as such but with offending against the Sabbath because it is the day on which an Israelite should recognize God as Creator of the heaven and the earth and all that is found in them, the trees of the field, for instance, which produce sticks. The clearer clue to the rule's particular meaning comes from noting that in Joseph's second dream objects belonging to the created order, the sun, moon, and stars, bow down to him: "And he dreamed yet another dream, and told it his brethren, and said, Behold, I have dreamed a dream more; and, behold, the sun and the moon and the eleven stars made obeisance to me" (Gen 37:9). Because God created the heavenly bodies, it is idolatrous to think that they would bow down to a mortal like Joseph. Deut 4:15–19 prohibits the worship of the sun, moon, and stars—as well as of the Golden Calf, which was made by fire—yet here in the second dream these three astronomical bodies do homage to Joseph.

The offense in both of Joseph's dreams involves the worship of a being other than the God of Genesis 1, the Creator of the universe. In the Numbers rule the person, probably engaging in a magical endeavor with fire, is seen as setting himself up in competition not only with the recognized standing of Moses and Aaron, but also with this God of Genesis 1.[24] The corresponding activity in Genesis 37 is when in Joseph's first dream the stalks of grain have been gathered with a view to using them to acknowledge Joseph as mightier than nature. The one other rule laying down a death penalty for violating the Sabbath, in Exod 31:12–17, brings up issues similar to those underlying the rule in Num 15:32–36. The emphasis is very much on preserving the holiness of the day ("for it is holy unto you"). Most revealing is that the Exodus prohibition follows immediately after the approved appointment of two persons, Bezaleel and Aholiab, to work creatively—with fire in order to craft metals—on constructing sacred objects for the sanctuary (Exod 31:1–11). Permission is here legitimately granted to two persons to engage in creative work within a sacred precinct. The following prohibition, however, about the Sabbath is a dire warning that no such work can be done on that day for "it is a sign between me [Yahweh] and the children of Israel for ever: for in six days Yahweh made heaven and earth, and on the seventh day he rested, and was refreshed" (Exod 31:17). In this context the Sabbath is a reminder of the gulf between craftsmen who, even if engaged in sacred tasks that require great skill, come nowhere near God's capacity to create.

Another telling indication that the stick-gatherer is not just working on the Sabbath but is intent on demonstrating special creative powers at his disposal comes from noting that a miraculously sprouting product of a tree, a rod, is the means by which Aaron is legitimately able to show that God has conferred divine powers on him and not on the stick-gatherer (Num 17:8–10). The stick-gatherer is handling the kind of object that God used to denote Aaron's divine standing. I shall turn to Aaron's rod in the next chapter.

REMEMBERING THE COMMANDMENTS BY THE FRINGES ON ONE'S GARMENT

The rule reads as follows:

37 And Yahweh spake unto Moses, saying, 38 Speak unto the children of Israel, and bid them that they make them fringes in the borders of their garments throughout their generations, and that they put upon the fringe of the borders a ribband of blue: 39 And it shall be unto you for a fringe, that ye may look upon it, and remember all the commandments of Yahweh, and do them; and that ye seek not after your own heart and your own eyes, after which ye use to go a whoring: 40 That ye may remember, and do all my commandments, and be holy unto your God. 41 I am Yahweh your God, which brought you out of the land of Egypt, to be your God: I am Yahweh your God. (Num 15:37–41)

Genesis	Numbers
Joseph's dress His garment provoked his brothers to commit offenses against him and their father (Genesis 37).	*An Israelite's special garment* Colored fringes on an Israelite's garment are to remind him to obey every rule (Num 15:37–41).

A comparable, differently formulated rule turns up in Deut 22:12: "Thou shalt make thee fringes upon the four quarters of thy vesture, wherewith thou coverest thyself." I have argued that the Deuteronomic rule is inspired by the incident with Joseph's garment in Genesis 39: how the innocent Joseph resisted the sexual advances of Potiphar's wife. She falsely accused him of lusting after her and allegedly proved it by having in her possession his garment as evidence of his wickedness. The aim of the Deuteronomic rule for an Israelite audience is to make the tassels declare that an Israelite—Joseph is the model—is not given to licentious behavior. A Talmudic story captures the rule's meaning well. A disciple about to have intercourse with a prostitute holds back when the tassels on his garment strike him on the face. She is so impressed that she becomes a convert to Judaism and they marry (*b. Men.* 44a). An item of clothing plays a crucial role in the rule that follows the tassels one in Deut 22:13–21: if the cloth on which the wedding couple has lain to consummate their union is stained with blood, the Israelite woman is free of any accusation of harlotry her husband may have directed at her. If, however, there is no blood on the cloth she is guilty of licentious conduct and put to death.[25]

The Num 15:37–41 rule is more explicit about its purpose: it calls for obedience to all the commandments. The impetus, I submit, is again Joseph—only with a different garment of his in focus. The word for the tassels in the Deuteronomic rule is *gedilim*, while in Num 15:38 it is *tsitsit*. The problem with Joseph that the Numbers lawgiver has in focus is the special garment that his adoring father gave him. The coat, like the dreams, provoked not just his own misconduct; it also provoked his brothers into committing serious wrongs: an unintended one, slavery in Egypt, but not without their contributing a number of wrongs that led to it, assaulting and kidnapping Joseph, killing an animal from their father's herd and using in an unclean way its blood for a deceitful purpose, and causing their father to believe that his son was dead. The many wrongs explain why the Numbers rule about the garment is to be associated with obedience to all the commandments. The Israelite is to remember this particular garment of Joseph, note its negative impact on him and on his brothers, the first Israelites, and resolve to avoid any wrongdoing against a brother Israelite and their God, Yahweh.

The command to insert a blue cord into the garment is peculiar to the Numbers rule. The Hebrew word *tekelet* apparently indicates a blue cloth that, because the pigment was so expensive to manufacture, was reserved for royalty and for cultic vestments.[26] Joseph's garment enjoyed this dual role. In Gen 37:8 his brothers say to him, "Do you mean to be king over us," and, similarly angry, they react against his self-image as a godlike figure to be worshiped by them. (The link between the law and the narrative might support the traditional understanding of "the famous, and unfortunately untranslatable" coat as a colored one, "the coat of many colors.")[27]

In the rule, the wrongdoing referred to in the phrase about following one's heart and eyes "After which ye go wantonly" is usually, as Gray and Milgrom point out, some illegitimate cult or superstition of those who practice it.[28] This meaning is particularly pertinent to Joseph's situation. His eye-catching coat leads to false religious ideas about himself as indicated by his dreams. His dream about the grain follows immediately after he dons the unique garment (Gen 37:3, 5–8). A rule to look at one's blue-tasseled garment and commit to following the law (for example, no killing, kidnapping, or deceiving a father)—unlike the brothers who looked at Joseph's special garment and perpetrated all sorts of offenses against Joseph and Jacob—is forged in response to and as a remedy for the opening incident in the Joseph story. The special thing about his special coat was not just that it marked him as a favorite son, but that it stirred up a slew of offenses.

David Cotter writes, "Judah used a garment [Joseph's] to deceive his father, just as Tamar uses a garment [dressed as a prostitute] to deceive him."[29] More accurately, perhaps, Judah and his brothers used Joseph's garment to deceive their father about the fate of his beloved son, and Potiphar's wife used his garment to deceive her husband about Joseph's sexual wrongdoing. Much significance certainly attaches to Joseph's two garments, and we can readily see they might inspire different thoughts about garments in Deut 22:12 (sexual misconduct) and in Num 15:37–41 (a proliferation of offenses). So many rules come from reflection on the Joseph saga, and it is little wonder that a rule to remember all the commandments is forged in response to his story, especially the opening part of it, where his coat plays a major role in provoking wrongful behavior.[30]

The function of the fringes on the garment in the Numbers rule recalls comparable signs in other rules. Unleavened bread and animal and human firstborn serve to recall events at the time of the Exodus. The bread and the firstborn are to be thought of (in a way not entirely clear) as signs upon an Israelite's hand and as memorials between his eyes: "And it shall be for a sign unto thee upon thine hand, and for a memorial between thine eyes, that Yahweh's law may be in thy mouth: for with a strong hand hath Yahweh brought thee out of Egypt. And it shall be for a token upon thine hand, and for frontlets between thine eyes: for by strength of hand Yahweh brought us forth out of Egypt" (Exod 13:9, 16). For the Numbers lawgiver the fringes on an Israelite's garment serve, in turn, to recall the danger of Joseph's envy-producing coat that led to his exile to Egypt and to the Israelites' future oppression there. The rule explicitly mentions Israel's time in Egypt: "I am Yahweh, which brought you out of the land of Egypt, to be your God: I am Yahweh" (Num 15:41). The repetition of the divine name Yahweh appears especially apt given Joseph's unacceptable godlike stance.

The point of thinking of one's hand and eyes, according to Exod 13:9, is that by appealing to them one recalls the events in Egypt so that "Yahweh's law may be in thy mouth." There is interplay between law and story. In a mutually influencing way, some rules require certain actions to evoke historical events, and these events attract rules to ensure memory of them. One's bodily parts, in turn, reinforce memory of both story and rule. The fringes on the garment are to the end that the Israelite wearing them not follow his heart and eyes but instead look upon the accessory with a view to keeping the commandments. The fringes also allude to a story: how Joseph's splendid coat invited attention, even compelled it, and how the brothers reacted negatively and angrily to hearing his dream in which he saw himself as having divine status. As formulated in the Numbers rule, the fringes are to be looked upon with a view to alerting a later son of Israel to observe all the commandments, which certainly include those needed to counter the offenses triggered by Joseph's special coat. Bodily parts, heart and eyes, serve to respond to the sight of the fringes and reinforce memory of both history and law.

Contrary to common opinion, there is no problem in perceiving why there is a switch from the rules in Numbers 15 to Korah's rebellion in Numbers 16, which I shall turn to in the next chapter. The context for the five rules in Numbers 15 is the discord among the first sons of Israel. It is this same internal strife, only among the later sons of Israel, which prevails in the following narrative about Korah's rebellion in Numbers 16. Korah, moreover, like Joseph, claims a special sanctity and, as in the case of the stick-gatherer, God executes the death sentence because he stands above the two parties who claim holiness, Moses legitimately so and Korah not. Equally interesting is that the noun *beri'a*, "creation," which is derived from the verb *bara'*, appears only here in the Hebrew Bible, where it refers to a fearful punishment. Moses says to Korah and his followers, "If these men die the death of all men . . . Yahweh hath not sent me; but if Yahweh create a creation, and the earth open her mouth and swallow them up . . . then ye shall understand that these men have provoked Yahweh" (Num 16:29, 30). The stick-gatherer, setting up to compete on a par with Yahweh the supreme creator, also claimed the kind of special sanctity Korah claimed. In turning to the incidents with the stick-gatherer and Korah, the Numbers narrator updates trends that emerged in Genesis among the first sons of Israel so as to counter their disturbing character.

7

THE STATUS OF FIRSTBORN
(NUMBERS 16–18)

The rules in Numbers 15 took up issues arising from problems among Jacob and his sons, the first generation of Israelites. Under special scrutiny was the idolatrous aspect of Joseph's role as a superior being in his family and later as second only to Pharaoh in Egypt. His brothers expressed hostility to Joseph because of the divine status he communicated about himself in his dreams. Numbers 16, in turn, recounts the hostility of Korah and others to Moses because Moses is seen to enjoy divine status in his time. The Numbers 16 narrative hangs together well because of the concentrated focus on leadership, just as the seemingly haphazard collection of rules in Numbers 15 all come from reflection on the problem of Joseph's elevated status. The going back and forth between the generations, Joseph's and then Moses' in this instance, characterizes biblical historiography in general, and we have a particular example of it when we move from Numbers 15 to Numbers 16.

Critics find a complex combination of sources in Numbers 16 and think that issues having to do with control of the sanctuary have been brought into contact with a quite separate focus on the supreme status that Moses enjoys.[1] While such a combining of sources may have occurred, there is a quite specific reason why Numbers 16 reflects on the controversy surrounding Moses as national leader and Aaron as cultic leader. The narrator, I submit, so presents his material as to have the opposition to Moses' and Aaron's leadership roles reflect similar opposition to Joseph's role both as enjoying divine status (imagining his brothers bowing down to him) and as a political leader (laying down rules for Egyptian society). The Numbers (and Leviticus) narrator-lawgiver finds these aspects of Joseph's story unacceptable for Israelite society. Discriminatory, favorable upgrading of Joseph on the part of the father, Jacob, and of Moses and Aaron on the part of

God is at the root of each development. A complicating factor is that in the Genesis narrative God also favors Joseph. In Numbers, God's favor is conferred upon Moses (and Aaron), another example of *imitation par opposition*.

A primary feature of biblical history writing is that, whenever he can, the narrator-lawgiver pays attention to national origins and relates, explicitly or implicitly, what happens in later times back to these beginnings. To view issues in a narrative about Moses as inspired, in part, by a previous narrative about Joseph is not an allegorical reading of the texts, as one critic of my work asserted. His is an interesting distortion of my claim because behind history writing of the kind we find in the biblical sources lie beliefs about deeper meaning in history and insofar as an allegorical reading of a text uncovers a deeper, more important layer of meaning there is overlap between history and allegory. In fact, the historical reporting we have in biblical material shows up at all times. John Ramsden argues that a harmful aspect of the legend about Winston Churchill's opposition to appeasement with Adolf Hitler was the readiness of a following generation "to discover Munich in Vietnam," Suez, and elsewhere and to resort to war in the wrong circumstances. Being too ready to perceive events in light of previous ones, people make wrong judgments, he claims. It is, nonetheless, inevitable that a link between one generation and another is fashioned when one period of history is viewed as being tied to a previous one.[2]

The problems that showed up in Joseph's generation centered on the status of the firstborn, and similar problems had already turned up in the preceding generation of Jacob and Esau. In Moses' generation the issue of primogeniture again proves central in struggles for leadership when the nation takes shape at the time of the wilderness wanderings. The pattern of correspondence in Genesis and Numbers is as follows:

Genesis 25, 28, 37	Numbers 16–18
Complaints about leadership The brothers of Joseph oppose his ambition to be leader in the family (Genesis 37).	*Complaints about leadership* Brother Levites led by Korah, the Reubenites, and Israel's chieftains oppose Moses and Aaron as leaders (Numbers 16–18).
Primary firstborn Living on blood dishes from hunting but unsuccessful one day, Esau sells his birthright to Jacob for a "red, red" dish that turned out to be	*Primary firstborn* Chosen from among all twelve sons of Jacob-Israel and their descendants, Levi's descendants attain the status of Yahweh's firstborn. Their

(continued)

Genesis 25, 28, 37	Numbers 16–18
lentils (Genesis 25, 28:22). Jacob promises a tithe of all that God gives him in return for protection from Esau's wrath at losing firstborn status to Jacob.	brother Levites, Aaron and his descendants, enjoy an even higher status that is marked by the special tithe of agricultural produce assigned to them (Numbers 18).

KORAH'S REBELLION

Numbers 16 reads as follows:

1 Now Korah . . . the son of Levi, and Dathan and Abiram . . . sons of Reuben, took men: 2 And they rose up before Moses, with certain of the children of Israel, two hundred and fifty princes of the assembly, famous in the congregation, men of renown: 3 And they gathered themselves together against Moses and against Aaron, and said unto them, Ye take too much upon you, seeing all the congregation are holy, every one of them, and Yahweh is among them: wherefore then lift ye up yourselves above the congregation of Yahweh? 4 And when Moses heard it, he fell upon his face: 5 And he spake unto Korah and unto all his company, saying, Even to morrow Yahweh will shew who are his, and who is holy; and will cause him to come near unto him: even him whom he hath chosen will he cause to come near unto him. 6 This do; Take you censers, Korah, and all his company; 7 And put fire therein, and put incense in them before Yahweh to morrow: and it shall be that the man whom Yahweh doth choose, he shall be holy: ye take too much upon you, ye sons of Levi. 8 And Moses said unto Korah, Hear, I pray you, ye sons of Levi: 9 Seemeth it but a small thing unto you, that the God of Israel hath separated you from the congregation of Israel, to bring you near to himself to do the service of the tabernacle of Yahweh, and to stand before the congregation to minister unto them? 10 And he hath brought thee near to him, and all thy brethren the sons of Levi with thee: and seek ye the priesthood also? 11 For which cause both thou and all thy company are gathered together against Yahweh: and what is Aaron, that ye murmur against him? 12 And Moses sent to call Dathan and Abiram, the sons of Eliab: which said, We will not come up: 13 Is it a small thing that thou hast brought us up out of a land that floweth with milk and honey, to kill us in the wilderness, except thou make thyself altogether a prince over us? 14 Moreover thou hast not brought us into a land that floweth with milk and honey, or given us inheritance of fields and vineyards: do you think you can hoodwink men like us [NEB]? we will not come up. 15 And Moses was very wroth, and said unto

Yahweh, Respect not thou their offering: I have not taken one ass from them, neither have I hurt one of them. 16 And Moses said unto Korah, Be thou and all thy company before Yahweh, thou, and they, and Aaron, to morrow. . . . 32 And the earth opened her mouth, and swallowed them up, and their houses, and all the men that appertained unto Korah, and all their goods. 33 They, and all that appertained to them, went down alive into the pit, and the earth closed upon them: and they perished from among the congregation. 34 And all Israel that were round about them fled at the cry of them: for they said, Lest the earth swallow us up also. 35 And there came out a fire from Yahweh, and consumed the two hundred and fifty men that offered incense. [Numbers 17:1–15 in Hebrew numbering = Numbers 16:36–50 in English] 36 And Yahweh spake unto Moses, saying, 37 Speak unto Eleazar the son of Aaron the priest, that he take up the censers out of the burning, and scatter thou the fire yonder; for they are hallowed. 38 The censers of these sinners against their own souls, let them make them broad plates for a covering of the altar: for they offered them before Yahweh, therefore they are hallowed: and they shall be a sign unto the children of Israel. 39 And Eleazar the priest took the brasen censers, wherewith they that were burnt had offered; and they were made broad plates for a covering of the altar: 40 To be a memorial unto the children of Israel, that no stranger, which is not of the seed of Aaron, come near to offer incense before Yahweh; that he be not as Korah, and as his company: as Yahweh said to him by the hand of Moses. 41 But on the morrow all the congregation of the children of Israel murmured against Moses and against Aaron, saying, Ye have killed the people of Yahweh. 42 And it came to pass, when the congregation was gathered against Moses and against Aaron, that they looked toward the tabernacle of the congregation: and, behold, the cloud covered it, and the glory of Yahweh appeared. 43 And Moses and Aaron came before the tabernacle of the congregation. 44 And Yahweh spake unto Moses, saying, 45 Get you up from among this congregation, that I may consume them as in a moment. And they fell upon their faces. 46 And Moses said unto Aaron, Take a censer, and put fire therein from off the altar, and put on incense, and go quickly unto the congregation, and make an atonement for them: for there is wrath gone out from Yahweh; the plague is begun. 47 And Aaron took as Moses commanded, and ran into the midst of the congregation; and, behold, the plague was begun among the people: and he put on incense, and made an atonement for the people. 48 And he stood between the dead and the living; and the plague was stayed. 49 Now they that died in the plague were fourteen thousand and seven hundred, beside them that died about the matter of Korah. 50 And Aaron returned unto Moses unto the door of the tabernacle of the congregation: and the plague was stayed.

I turn first to an incident that proves crucial for the establishment of the priesthood in ancient Israel. It is written up against the background of the problem of leadership among the first sons of Israel as described in Genesis.

Genesis	Numbers
Complaints about leadership The brothers of Joseph oppose his ambition to be leader in the family (Genesis 37).	*Complaints about leadership* Brother Levites led by Korah, the Reubenites, and Israel's chieftains oppose Moses and Aaron as leaders (Numbers 16–18).

In Genesis 37 the brothers of Joseph are antagonistic to his ambition to become Jacob's leading son and his claim to divine status in his dreams. They are on the point of killing him for his arrogance when Judah takes on a leadership role by suggesting that they not kill Joseph but instead sell him for money. It is a counsel to which the brothers assent—with one exception. As the eldest son in the family, presumably responsible to their father for the well-being of all his brothers, Reuben seeks to restore Joseph to his father. He is not successful. A series of overlapping events sets Joseph on his way to Egypt and to future power over his brothers. All of them, Joseph, Reuben, Judah, and those siblings who go along with him, are caught up in the tension resulting from rivalry among them.

In the situation that Moses confronts in Numbers 16, the power struggle repeats itself. The sons of Israel are again caught up in opposing a supreme leader, in this instance, Moses, along with his brother Aaron: "Ye [Moses and Aaron] take too much upon you, seeing all the congregation are holy, every one of them, and Yahweh is among them: wherefore then lift ye up yourselves above the congregation of Yahweh?" (Num 16:3). Korah is the leader of a group of Levites, which as a tribe enjoys the status of firstborn above that of the other Israelites who together with the Levites constitute Yahweh's firstborn. Korah protests the even higher position enjoyed by Moses and Aaron, their fellow firstborn Levites. There is an interesting ambiguity. The priests are more firstborn than the Levites, who in turn are more firstborn than the rest of the Israelites. Joining the protesters led by Korah are the Reubenites, whose eponymous ancestor Reuben was Jacob's original firstborn and who lost the status to Joseph. Critics suggest that the involvement of the sons of Reuben in the Korah rebellion is to be attributed to the fact that they "once possessed, but had lost, the primacy" and here in Numbers seek to assert their original firstborn standing among the twelve tribes of Jacob-Israel.[3] Indeed, two kinds of firstborn, a company of Levites and the Reubenites, gang up against the now primary firstborn, Moses and Aaron. In addition, 250 chieftains of the Israelite assembly join the revolt. Like the parties in conflict in Genesis 37—Jacob's firstborn, Reuben; Judah, who would like to have the role of leader; the brothers who support Judah; and Joseph, who views himself as leader—various identifiable factions show up among the sons of Israel in Numbers 16 and 17. The tension is again an outgrowth of competition for control of political and religious matters.

Other links between the two stories are observable. Moses requests that God not accept Korah's offering, a judgment that perhaps renews the critical attitude to the situation in Joseph's dream, which depicts an unacceptable act of devotion by his brothers to Joseph. Even absent foreign religious infusion, when internal Israelite affairs alone are involved certain acts of worship are illegitimate. The making of the Golden Calf in Exodus 32 is a dramatic precedent.

Moses defends himself against the accusation of two Reubenite chieftains that he has hoodwinked—I accept the NEB translation—the starving people by promising to feed them well after taking them out of Egypt. Moses protests to God, affirms his integrity, and asserts that he has not "taken one ass from them" (Num 16:14, 15). Two curious features stand out. It is difficult to see how Moses could be seen to have tricked his fellow Israelites. Nothing in the Numbers story suggests deception on his part, and he faced the same plight as they did. Moreover, it is curious of Moses to cite in his defense that he has not stolen a single ass: he had not been accused of theft. Illumination may be forthcoming if the Moses portrayed in Numbers is understood to be a contrasting type to Joseph in Genesis, whose conduct toward the brothers included both deception and the threat of theft. When Joseph, to the surprise of the brothers, invited them to dine with him, with some justification they viewed the invitation as a trick to "take us for bondmen, and our asses" (Gen 43:18).

Levine points to a similar use of language in both stories. In Num 16:5 courtly language about being an intimate is applied to certain priests in relation to God: "And he spake unto Korah and unto all his company, saying, Even to morrow Yahweh will shew who are his, and who is holy; and will cause him to come near unto him: even him whom he hath chosen will he cause to come near unto him." In Gen 45:10 the same language is used when the godlike, Egyptian Joseph invites Jacob, his sons, and his grandsons to be his intimates after they come to Egypt ("And thou shalt dwell in the land of Goshen, and thou shalt be near unto me, thou, and thy children, and thy children's children, and thy flocks, and thy herds, and all that thou hast"). Levine also notes that similar language—"By this shall ye know"—asserting the authentic nature of an action is common to Num 16:28 (the type of destruction to be visited upon Korah and his family as proof that they had offended the deity) and Gen 42:33 (the type of proof necessary to convince a hostile, disguised Joseph that the brothers are not spies).[4]

AARON'S ROD

Ashley points out that the complaint of Korah that the sanctity claimed by Aaron and his descendants conflicts with the holiness of all the Israelites is "a clear tie to the previous passage in which Israel was to use tassels on their garments as a reminder to do Yahweh's will and to be holy" (Num 15:40).[5] The tassels rule, we saw, focused on Joseph's unwarranted holiness when he perceived himself as possessing divine status. The Numbers narrator wrestles with the same problem but this time in order to uphold the legitimacy of Aaron's special sanctity. The resolution of the problem in favor of Aaron comes about by a miracle that recalls the central feature of Joseph's dream about the sheaves.

Numbers 17 contains the miracle story and reads as follows:

> 1 And Yahweh spake unto Moses, saying, 2 Speak unto the children of Israel, and take of every one of them a rod according to the house of their fathers.... 7 And Moses laid up the rods before Yahweh in the tabernacle of witness. 8 And it came to pass, that on the morrow Moses went into the tabernacle of witness; and, behold, the rod of Aaron for the house of Levi was budded, and brought forth buds, and bloomed blossoms, and yielded almonds. 9 And Moses brought out all the rods from before Yahweh unto all the children of Israel: and they looked, and took every man his rod. 10 And Yahweh said unto Moses, Bring Aaron's rod again before the testimony, to be kept for a token against the rebels; and thou shalt quite take away their murmurings from me, that they die not. 11 And Moses did so: as Yahweh commanded him, so did he. 12 And the children of Israel spake unto Moses, saying, Behold, we die, we perish, we all perish. 13 Whosoever cometh any thing near unto the tabernacle of Yahweh shall die: shall we be consumed with dying?

Levine claims that the sprouting of Aaron's rod in Num 17:8 is unique in biblical literature precisely because such growth occurs detached from the soil.[6] The rod signifies Aaron's distinction as God's supreme firstborn, and the miraculous sprouting singles his rod out from among the twelve rods of the other tribes, which do not blossom. I am not so sure, however, about the uniqueness in question. The incident may reflect the influence of Joseph's dream pointing to his supremacy. A comparable miraculous sign in his dream is when his standing sheaf of grain is bowed down to by the sheaves representing his eleven brothers. The sheaf is like the rod because in both instances something contrary to nature happens to each. In both instances as well something that had its origin in the earth indicates Joseph's and Aaron's superior status. We might recall that in the rule about the man who gathers sticks from the ground on the Sabbath, his aim was to display, via the gathered sticks, his superior standing (Num 15:32–36). In all three instances, sticks/stalks connote either wrongful arrogation (Joseph, stick-gatherer) or bestowal (Aaron) of divine authority.

There might also be detectable in the background another negative stance toward Joseph, this time as a diviner when he exercised supreme control over his brothers by means of his divining cup (Gen 44:1–17). The sign of Aaron's supremacy in conveying divine mysteries is a different object, a rod, to which potency is attributed and which is judged to constitute a proper sacred object. The topic we confront is about the factors at play that lend legitimacy to religious authority. So long as some source of authenticity is recognized, certain human beings are permitted to display divine powers. (Jacob Haberman reminded me of Thomas Hobbes's view: "Feare of power invisible, feigned by the mind or imagined from tales publicly allowed, RELIGION; not allowed, SUPERSTITION.")[7]

CULTIC LEADERSHIP

In Numbers 16–18 the question of who controls the official cult is the major concern, and the outcome is that among the twelve tribes primary leadership is conferred on the tribe of Levi. As I have indicated, a further distinction in rank is then introduced. The larger body of Levites has a lesser standing than those Levites who are directly descended from Aaron's family. Thus in the prime position are the priests, the Aaronites, who are responsible for the most sacred rites connected with the sanctuary—they enter the Tent of Meeting and officiate at it—and in a subsidiary role are the other Levites, who are guardians of the sacred precinct. In larger perspective: after the events recorded in Genesis and part of Exodus, leadership in the sacred sphere comes about no longer mainly by direct divine intervention, as when God struck down Er and Onan (Genesis 38) and when he is "a man of war" against the Egyptians (Exod 15:3, cp. 14:14). To be sure, we saw that even when earthly jurisdiction prevails after God visits violence upon the Egyptians there can still be divine intervention, for example, when judgment necessarily has to come from an authority ranking above two competing earthly rulers. Mainly, however, in place of direct divine involvement in sacred matters, leadership comes indirectly through the persons of Aaron's family and the Levites who carry out duties at the sanctuary in accordance with instructions laid out for them.

FOOD SPECIAL TO THE AARONITES

Numbers 18 concerns tithes for the Levites and a special tithe for the Aaronites. The text reads as follows:

> 1 And Yahweh said unto Aaron, Thou and thy sons and thy father's house with thee shall bear the iniquity of the sanctuary: and thou and thy sons with thee shall bear the iniquity of your priesthood. 2 And thy brethren also of the tribe of Levi, the tribe of thy father, bring thou with thee, that they may be joined unto thee, and minister unto thee: but thou and thy sons with thee shall minister before the tabernacle of witness. 3 And they shall keep thy charge, and the charge of all the tabernacle: only they shall not come nigh the vessels of the sanctuary and the altar, that neither they, nor ye also, die. 4 And they shall be joined unto thee, and keep the charge of the tabernacle of the congregation, for all the service of the tabernacle: and a stranger shall not come nigh unto you. . . . 8 And Yahweh spake unto Aaron, Behold, I also have given thee the charge of mine heave offerings of all the hallowed things of the children of Israel; unto thee have I given them by reason of the anointing, and to thy sons, by an ordinance for ever. 9 This shall be thine of the most holy things, reserved from the fire: every oblation of theirs, every meat offering of theirs, and every sin offering of theirs, and every trespass offering of theirs, which they shall render unto me, shall be most holy for thee and for thy sons. 10 In the most holy place shalt thou eat it; every male shall eat it: it shall be holy unto thee. 11 And this is thine; the heave offering of their gift, with all the wave offerings of the children of Israel: I have given them unto thee, and to thy sons and to thy daughters with thee, by a statute for ever: every one that is clean in thy house shall eat of it. 12 All the best of the oil, and all the best of the wine, and of the wheat, the firstfruits of them which they shall offer unto Yahweh, them have I given thee. 13 And whatsoever is first ripe in the land, which they shall bring unto Yahweh, shall be thine; every one that is clean in thine house shall eat of it. 14 Every thing devoted in Israel shall be thine. 15 Every thing that openeth the matrix in all flesh, which they bring unto Yahweh, whether it be of men or beasts, shall be thine: nevertheless the firstborn of man shalt thou surely redeem, and the firstling of unclean beasts shalt thou redeem. 16 And those that are to be redeemed from a month old shalt thou redeem, according to thine estimation, for the

money of five shekels, after the shekel of the sanctuary, which is twenty gerahs. 17 But the firstling of a cow, or the firstling of a sheep, or the firstling of a goat, thou shalt not redeem. . . . 25 And Yahweh spake unto Moses, saying, 26 Thus speak unto the Levites, and say unto them, When ye take of the children of Israel the tithes which I have given you from them for your inheritance, then ye shall offer up an heave offering of it for Yahweh, even a tenth part of the tithe. 27 And this your heave offering shall be reckoned unto you, as though it were the corn of the threshingfloor, and as the fullness of the winepress. 28 Thus ye also shall offer an heave offering unto Yahweh of all your tithes . . . and ye shall give thereof Yahweh's heave offering to Aaron the priest. 29 Out of all your gifts ye shall offer every heave offering of Yahweh, of all the best thereof, even the hallowed part thereof out of it. 30 Therefore thou shalt say unto them, When ye have heaved the best thereof from it, then it shall be counted unto the Levites as the increase of the threshingfloor, and as the increase of the winepress. 31 And ye shall eat it in every place, ye and your households: for it is your reward for your service in the tabernacle of the congregation. 32 And ye shall bear no sin by reason of it, when ye have heaved from it the best of it: neither shall ye pollute the holy things of the children of Israel, lest ye die.

Genesis	Numbers
Primary firstborn Living on blood dishes from hunting but unsuccessful one day, Esau sells his birthright to Jacob for a "red, red" dish that turned out to be lentils. Jacob promises a tithe of all that God gives him in return for protection from Esau's wrath at losing firstborn status to Jacob (Genesis 25, 28:22).	*Primary firstborn* Chosen from among all twelve sons of Jacob-Israel and their descendants, Levi's descendants attain the status of Yahweh's firstborn. Their brother Levites, Aaron and his descendants, enjoy an even higher status that is marked by the special tithe of agricultural produce assigned to them (Numbers 18).

A major issue that arises in Numbers 18 is, what dues should the Levites and the Aaronites receive? They turn out to be quite splendid, in keeping with the best part of an inheritance for the primary son: "I [Yahweh] am thy part and thine inheritance among the sons of Israel" (Num 18:20). Their food comes from offerings to the sanctuary from the other Israelites. As a collective, the status of the priests and the Levites is that of Yahweh's firstborn son, and even within this privileged position a distinction, as noted, is made between Aaron's family, the priests, and the other Levites. The distinction shows up in a particular distribution of food that the Levites collect from the agricultural tithes of the people. A tenth of this portion, the best part of it, the Levites must give over to the favored priests. A concluding statement warns the Levites to avoid any profanation of this food "lest you die" (Num 18:32). The final focus, then, is on one group of Levites serving their brother Levites, the sons of Aaron, by providing the latter with an especially sacrosanct tithe from threshing floor and winepress that is taboo even to consecrated persons, the Levites. Only the supreme group of firstborn, Aaron and his descendants, can consume the food in question.

JACOB'S ATTAINMENT OF FIRSTBORN STATUS FROM ESAU

The Aaronites attain paramount status in a struggle for power between one firstborn, a group of Levites, and another firstborn, the Aaronites. The Aaronites prove to be superior, and their position is highlighted by a certain kind of vegetable food, the special tithe, which is made available solely to them. Numbers 16 and 17 depict this struggle and, as we have observed, it mirrors the power struggle in Jacob's family in Genesis 37. But this infighting also mirrors an even earlier, similarly tension-laden interchange at the nation's origin, and it does so in a particular way that again highlights a special food, a blood dish, as a distinctive marker of Isaac's firstborn at the time, Esau. Only in this instance the special food causes Esau to lose the birthright to his cleverly exploitative younger brother Jacob. By a binding oath requested by Jacob, Esau had to give over the status of the firstborn to Jacob, who achieved it by substituting vegetable food, lentils, for Esau's desired blood dish (Gen 25:19–34). Esau's wrath at losing his birthright to his brother required God to protect Jacob, who in turn pledged a tithe to God of all that God would give him and his descendants (Gen 28:22). The time frame includes the period in the future when the sanctuary will come into operation and the tribe of Levi serves there and collects every Israelite's tithe. That tithe is the one under consideration in Numbers 18, and in each instance God's regard for the supreme firstborn, Jacob and the Aaronites, is a central feature. Whereas Jacob will give God the tithe in return for protection, the Levites acting on God's behalf give it to their brothers, the Aaronites, who act as God's intimates in the sanctuary.

In Numbers 18 the Aaronites are made responsible for offenses against the sacred order: "Thou [Aaron] and thy sons and thy father's house with thee shall bear the iniquity of the sanctuary: and thou and thy sons with thee shall bear the iniquity of your priesthood" (Num 18:1). The concern is a central one in Numbers 18 and continues the awareness of the wrongfulness of Joseph's cultic aspirations that so dominated the rules in Numbers 15. But even Joseph's iniquity had its precedent. In his father Jacob's generation, a sacred offense involving the ingestion of blood lay at the heart of how Israel became a nation—the incident when Jacob acquired the birthright from Esau. That the Numbers narrator should turn to this momentous event occasions no surprise. A primary feature of biblical lawmaking is that the laws take up issues arising in the nation's history, especially at its start, with the laws incorporated into a coherent, chronological narrative that begins in Genesis and concludes in 2 Kings.

INTRODUCING THE RITUAL OF THE RED HEIFER

Although my next chapter will go into the subject in detail, I begin a discussion of the long-standing mystery of the Red Heifer at this point by way of puzzling out the difficult question of why the topic might turn up in Numbers 19 after the topic of the special tithe for the Aaronites in Numbers 18.

Jacob, not Esau, became the firstborn in the favored line of Abraham and Isaac on the vivid occasion when Esau sought to devour a "red, red" dish that Jacob was cooking and that Esau took to be a death-defying blood dish. Esau received instead a dish of red lentils. His misperception, which involved a ruse by Jacob, prevented Esau from eating blood, which would have been an offense against the sacred order (Gen 25:19–34). On the occasion, the benign vegetable dish served both to save Esau from dying and to avoid the wrongful use of blood. The positive outcome for Jacob was transference of the right of the firstborn to him, as a result of which he became the father of the nation Israel. The incident is, I will argue, the key to understanding the ritual of the Red Heifer that follows in Numbers 19: the colored animal's flesh and blood are reduced to ashes and, when mixed with water, serve to repel death.

Aside from a continuous interest in exploring aspects of how the notion of God's firstborn plays out and how the nation's history progresses, why should the Numbers narrator turn to this particular episode about Esau's birthright? The explanation appears to be that, in keeping with his focus on sacred matters that turn up in the life of Jacob and his family, the narrator responds to the potential offense involving blood at the heart of the Jacob–Esau story. In doing so, as we shall see, he dramatizes and transforms the offense into a ritual for use by Jacob-Israel's descendants (and Esau's too). In brief outline: Esau was famished and desperately needed to consume a blood dish in order to stave off the threat of death. Numbers 19 lays out a ritual that, imitating the situation in the story of a slaughtered animal with its blood intact, opposes consumption of blood to fend off death. Even in a dire situation like Esau's, blood is to be avoided. Connected with the sanctuary, however, blood can be used by the Aaronites to signify life. Outside the sanctuary, as in Esau's situation, blood is linked to death that causes contamination. The institution of the Red Heifer ritual is inaugurated for the purpose of removing pollution associated with death. Because the ritual has been shrouded in mystery, I will (in the next chapter) examine in detail the way in which the Jacob–Esau narrative—the core firstborn struggle at the creation of the nation—inspired its construction.

8

THE RITUAL OF THE RED HEIFER
(NUMBERS 19)

David Daube began his book *Studies in Biblical Law* by quoting a line from John Bunyan's *Pilgrim's Progress:* "Would'st thou read Riddles, and their Explanation?" In what follows I attempt an explanation for a riddle, the ritual of the Red Heifer, which has baffled interpreters down the ages. Crucial to the solution, I will contend, is Daube's explanation of one of the key events he addressed in his book: how Jacob acquired the birthright from Esau. The incident is recounted in Gen 25:20–34 and is so written as to anticipate later developments concerning Jacob and Esau and their descendants, Israel and Edom:

20 And Isaac was forty years old when he took Rebekah to wife, the daughter of Bethuel the Syrian of Padan-aram, the sister to Laban the Syrian. 21 And Isaac intreated Yahweh for his wife, because she was barren: and Yahweh was intreated of him, and Rebekah his wife conceived. 22 And the children struggled together within her; and she said, If it be so, why am I thus? And she went to inquire of Yahweh. 23 And Yahweh said unto her, Two nations are in thy womb, and two manner of people shall be separated from thy bowels; and the one people shall be stronger than the other people; and the elder shall serve the younger. 24 And when her days to be delivered were fulfilled, behold, there were twins in her womb. 25 And the first came out red, all over like an hairy garment; and they called his name Esau. 26 And after that came his brother out, and his hand took hold on Esau's heel; and his name was called Jacob: and Isaac was threescore years old when she bare them. 27 And the boys grew: and Esau was a cunning hunter, a man of the field; and Jacob was a *tam* [whole, civilized?] man, dwelling in tents. 28 And Isaac loved Esau, because venison was in his mouth: but Rebekah loved Jacob. 29 And Jacob cooked a stew: and Esau came from the field, and he was faint: 30 And Esau said to Jacob, Feed me, I pray thee,

with that red, red stuff; for I am faint: therefore was his name called Edom. 31 And Jacob said, Sell me this day thy birthright. 32 And Esau said, Behold, I am at the point to die: and what profit shall this birthright do to me? 33 And Jacob said, Swear to me this day; and he sware unto him: and he sold his birthright unto Jacob. 34 Then Jacob gave Esau bread and pottage of lentils; and he did eat and drink, and rose up, and went his way: thus Esau despised his birthright.

Esau, red in color at birth and hairy to depict his later wild nature, becomes "a man of the field," a hunter. Jacob, gripping his brother's heel at birth to indicate that he will later supplant Esau's role in the family, becomes "a tent-dweller." One day Esau comes back from an unsuccessful hunting trip and is in a fearful state of hunger. As Daube demonstrates, Esau is depicted as being desperately dependent for food on his game dishes with blood the vital ingredient. To Esau, blood has special, life-giving properties capable of reviving an exhausted hunter.[1] The problem he confronts, I emphasize, is not lack of food. He could easily obtain something to eat, let us say, roots or berries picked along the way. What he craves is the life force that supposedly comes from blood dishes.

Coincidentally with Esau's return from his hunt, or, much more likely, opportunistically, Jacob is cooking a dish, the substance of which is not specified but is red in color. Esau begs, literally in Hebrew, "to gulp" some of "that red, red [dish]." The redness of the dish is what is so important to him. Daube is correct to retain the double reference to the word "red" in the Hebrew text. When Esau asks permission not to eat but to gulp (*laʿat*) Jacob's food, the allusion appears to be to a mode of eating comparable to that of a wild beast when it consumes its prey's flesh with the blood. In postbiblical Hebrew, as Robert Alter points out, the verb *laʿat* is reserved to describe how animals eat. As Alter further points out in his translation, "Isaac loved Esau for the game in his [Esau's] mouth" (Gen 25:28), the idiom appears to allude to "Esau as a kind of lion bringing home game in its mouth."[2] Gen 25:27 further describes Esau as "a knowing hunter." In Job 28:7 the same verb is used of a bird of prey.

In any event, Esau thinks that a meat dish is cooking on the fire, presumably from one of Jacob's domestic animals. The dish's red color signifies to Esau the blood that is supposedly present in the pot, the very substance he believes he needs to recover from his dire condition.[3] I repeat: it is the red contents of the dish on the stove, not just the food as such, that will save him from death. Esau is quite specific when he asks to eat the red stew (with its blood) in order to live. It is at this point that Jacob suggests to Esau that he sell him his birthright.

The birthright is sold to Jacob. Esau believes that it is of no use to him because he thinks he is about to die. Jacob has him swear to the transaction.

Esau then finds that instead of receiving the revivifying blood dish he receives a paltry plate of red lentils. He lives on, and on account of the role the color red plays in the transaction Esau's name is changed to Edom (*'edom*), the "red one." The name, in this context, evokes the Hebrew word for blood, *dam*. The same play upon words, *dam* and *'edom*, involving errors similar to Esau's, occurs in other contexts concerning, directly or indirectly, his descendants, the Edomites: water made red by the sun shining on it is mistaken for blood because of the red stone characteristic of the terrain of the Edomites, and blood on God's garments is initially mistaken by Edom for red grape juice (2 Kgs 3:20–22; Isa 34:5–7, 63:1–6).[4] Esau's change of name underlines just how much significance attaches to the redness of Jacob's dish and the consequence of Esau's confusion about its contents. Esau had become the firstborn son in a state of red (Gen 25:25). He loses the status by ingesting food of the same color.

We learn from Gen 27:36 that Esau has no doubt that Jacob cheated him out of his birthright. A "tripping up" is how Esau describes both the purchase of the birthright in Genesis 25 as well as the theft of the blessing later in Genesis 27 when Jacob took advantage of his father's blindness. In Genesis 25 Jacob exploits Esau's misperception about the contents of the "red, red" dish by having him swear to a transaction that has Jacob give the dish to Esau in return for the status of the firstborn in the family. More precisely, the sleight of hand consists in Jacob's responding to Esau's request for his habitual blood dish by taking advantage of Esau's careless request for "red, red [food]." Adhering to the letter of their agreement, Jacob cynically makes use of the sacred nature of an oath. The swearing renders the deal beyond recall, for by it the agreement enters the sphere of the absolute. Esau has no option but to accept as inviolable the transaction of a birthright for a red dish that turns out to be lentils.[5]

For Jacob to make Esau swear an oath is not a strange step in the ordinary way of doing business. Behind an oath's sacrosanct nature is the serious matter that in a society lacking legal instruments a person's word is of enormous significance. What might appear odd from our perspective is quite rational within such a society. Jacob cleverly uses the oath because it ensures that the transaction cannot be undone even though it involves underhandedness.

Esau's sale of his birthright to Jacob is the foundational event in the history of the nation. All later developments about Israel's rescue from Egypt as God's firstborn son, and Israel's religious and sacrificial life as centered on the Levites representing that firstborn son (Num 3:40–51), begin with the episode in Genesis 25. From the point of view of the Book of Numbers, so concerned with primogeniture (Num 3:11–13, 40–51; 7; 8; 16–18; 26), the transaction between

Esau and Jacob at the creation of the nation is of enormous interest and lies at the heart of the mysterious Red Heifer ritual in Numbers 19.

THE RITUAL OF THE RED HEIFER

The institution of the Red Heifer or Red Cow as a rite to rid of contamination those who have been in contact with corpses and the like is proverbial for its obscurity. Typical is *Numbers Rabba* on 19:3 (a medieval compilation) that has King Solomon say that while he understands the Torah's commandments, the one about the Red Heifer is quite beyond his comprehension. R. Johanan ben Zaccai (middle of the first century CE) expresses an earlier view when to outsiders he admits that magic seems to be involved. But he tells his disciples in private that neither is uncleanness caused by a corpse nor cleanness by the ritual's "water of separation." The statute was one of those that had to be accepted as the will of God, although no rational basis could be discerned even by the rabbinic authorities (*Pesiqta de Rab Kahana* 4:7).

Numbers 18, we saw, has to do with sanctuary matters in a major way, but Numbers 19 introduces the sanctuary in a curiously peripheral way. As I outlined at the end of the previous chapter, Numbers 19 introduces the Red Heifer ritual as commemorating the moment in Genesis 25 when Israel commenced on the path of firstbornhood, which occurred long before the official cult was set up at Sinai.

The ritual is laid out in Num 19:1–22 and reads as follows:

> 1 And Yahweh spake unto Moses and unto Aaron, saying, 2 This is the ordinance of the law which Yahweh hath commanded, saying, Speak unto the children of Israel, that they bring thee a red heifer without spot, wherein is no blemish, and upon which never came yoke: 3 And ye shall give her unto Eleazar the priest, that he may bring her forth without the camp, and one shall slay her before his face: 4 And Eleazar the priest shall take of her blood with his finger, and sprinkle of her blood directly before the tabernacle of the congregation seven times: 5 And one shall burn the heifer in his sight; her skin, and her flesh, and her blood, with her dung, shall he burn: 6 And the priest shall take cedar wood, and hyssop, and scarlet, and cast it into the midst of the burning of the heifer. 7 Then the priest shall wash his clothes, and he shall bathe his flesh in water, and afterward he shall come into the camp, and the priest shall be unclean until the even. 8 And he that burneth her shall wash his clothes in water, and bathe his flesh in water, and shall be unclean until the even. 9 And a man that is clean shall gather up the ashes of the heifer, and lay them up without the camp in a clean place, and it shall be kept for the congregation of the children of Israel for a water of separation: it

is a purification for sin. 10 And he that gathereth the ashes of the heifer shall wash his clothes, and be unclean until the even: and it shall be unto the children of Israel, and unto the stranger that sojourneth among them, for a statute for ever. 11 He that toucheth the dead body of any man shall be unclean seven days. 12 He shall purify himself with it on the third day, and on the seventh day he shall be clean: but if he purify not himself the third day, then the seventh day he shall not be clean. 13 Whosoever toucheth the dead body of any man that is dead, and purifieth not himself, defileth the tabernacle of Yahweh; and that soul shall be cut off from Israel: because the water of separation was not sprinkled upon him, he shall be unclean; his uncleanness is yet upon him. 14 This is the law, when a man dieth in a tent: all that come into the tent, and all that is in the tent, shall be unclean seven days. 15 And every open vessel, which hath no covering bound upon it, is unclean. 16 And whosoever toucheth one that is slain with a sword in the open fields, or a dead body, or a bone of a man, or a grave, shall be unclean seven days. 17 And for an unclean person they shall take of the ashes of the burnt heifer of purification for sin, and running water shall be put thereto in a vessel: 18 And a clean person shall take hyssop, and dip it in the water, and sprinkle it upon the tent, and upon all the vessels, and upon the persons that were there, and upon him that touched a bone, or one slain, or one dead, or a grave: 19 And the clean person shall sprinkle upon the unclean on the third day, and on the seventh day: and on the seventh day he shall purify himself, and wash his clothes, and bathe himself in water, and shall be clean at even. 20 But the man that shall be unclean, and shall not purify himself, that soul shall be cut off from among the congregation, because he hath defiled the sanctuary of Yahweh: the water of separation hath not been sprinkled upon him; he is unclean. 21 And it shall be a perpetual statute unto them, that he that sprinkleth the water of separation shall wash his clothes; and he that toucheth the water of separation shall be unclean until even. 22 And whatsoever the unclean person toucheth shall be unclean; and the soul that toucheth it shall be unclean until even.

Genesis

Encountering death Jacob exploits Esau's need for a blood dish to fend off his fear of death by giving him a red dish that, despite lacking blood, keeps Esau alive. Esau, in fact, avoids the polluting presence of death which blood represents.

Numbers

Encountering death Ashes from a red heifer, which has been incinerated with its blood and other red items added to the conflagration, serve to ward off the polluting presence of death.

The ritual's puzzling features are manifest. Levine states, "Numbers 19 provides a unique instance in priestly legislation of riddance rites separate from the Sanctuary and its sacrificial altar." George Buchanan Gray writes, "The fact that the sacred victim is slaughtered outside the camp is quite exceptional, and is inconsistent with the view that it is a sacrifice, an offering to Yahweh." Gray, like all other critics, views the institution's placement in the Book of Numbers as decidedly problematical, for no link is seen with what comes before or what comes after.[6] But there is a link. In the sequence, Numbers 18 and 19, we move from the threat of death for wrongful eating of tabooed food, the special tithe for the priests, to the law about applying the ashes of a red heifer to a person, Israelite or non-Israelite, who comes upon death in, for example, the form of a corpse. How do we account for what seems a baffling change of subject matter?

To understand the ritual, we have, as I have indicated, to go back to the occasion at the starting point in the nation's history when Esau sought meat with blood that he usually obtained from his hunting expeditions. But such a dish from an Israelite perspective is taboo because it is an offense against the sacred order. Eating meat with blood is contrary to the rule laid down for all humankind after the flood: one can eat meat but only after removing its lifeblood and returning the blood to the deity (Gen 9:3, 4). As I will argue below, the rule in Numbers 19 is about blood that only priests can be involved with for sacred purposes, and it opposes, via the drama of the ritual, the eating of meat with blood, as Esau had wanted to do.

Esau's dilemma was not just a need to avoid starving to death by consuming food of any variety but a need—denied to him in the event—for a special kind of food, namely, animal meat with its blood intact. He saw such meat as a means of sustaining life to ward off death. Being a sacred substance, however, blood should not be put to the use Esau sought. Because life peculiarly comes from God in the form of blood and life returns to God, it is not for humans who are not priests to use blood in fending off death (or for any other purpose). Indeed, from a priestly perspective the blood in animal meat that Esau thinks is necessary for life signifies the opposite, the contaminating presence of death. The Numbers law transforms what priests would have regarded as potential wrongdoing in the Esau narrative into a ritual way to confront death. The ritual restores life by countering the polluting presence of death, as when, in circumstances more likely than Esau's, an Israelite or a non-Israelite encounters a corpse or the like. With blood playing a unique role, a priestly rite of separation is required to undo the contaminating encroachment of death on life.

The capacity of blood to transform the threat of death into the preservation of life shows up in the ritual of the Passover. That ritual commemorates how blood on the doorposts of the Israelite houses in Egypt preserved Israelite lives but brought death to the Egyptian firstborn (Exodus 12 and 13). Critics are alert to the role of life and death in the Passover ritual and in the story of the Exodus because it is spelled out. They are not alert to the similar links between the institution of the ashes of the Red Heifer in the Book of Numbers and the Esau saga about the right of the firstborn because the links are not spelled out in the text. The occasion in Genesis 25 took place before Moses was born, and the connections to later developments are not made manifest, unlike the Exodus epic that Moses and his audience experienced in their lifetime. As in many other instances, via a literary strategy that contributes to the fiction that Moses delivers the laws, only some events in his lifetime, not those that occur before or after it, are ever cited in the laws. (There is, for example, the lack of the obvious reference to King Solomon in the prohibition in Deut 17:14–20 that the king not multiply horses, wives, silver and gold, and the similar lack of reference to Rachel and Leah in the rule in Deut 21:15–17 about upholding the right of a hated wife's firstborn son.) Once the ties between Genesis 25 and Numbers 19 are observed, the proper context for the institution of the ritual of the Red Heifer can be understood. Not only is the issue of the firstborn a dominant theme in Numbers as in Genesis, but the quite particular topic of food and assistance to a firstborn through the provision of food is the concern in Numbers 18, the subject matter that immediately precedes the ritual of the Red Heifer in Numbers 19. I consequently cannot agree with the critics. There is a close relationship between Numbers 18 about sacred food for firstborn (as the Levites and Aaronites are considered to be) and Numbers 19 about the ritual of the Red Heifer.

The lawgiver in Numbers 19 is alert to previous developments in the nation, and he considers the food that Jacob gave Esau in place of a meat dish. At the time in question Esau was Isaac's firstborn. Esau was denied, after an unsuccessful hunt, his usual source of sustenance. Just as the Passover enacts and recalls the rescue of Israel as God's firstborn, so the Red Heifer ritual enacts a recapitulation of and silent comment upon how Jacob became the firstborn. In the episode that occurs almost immediately after the institution of the Red Heifer, Jacob's relationship to Esau is brought up among their descendants. Moses has messengers request the king of Edom to permit Israel to pass through Edomite territory. The appeal is based on their original fraternal tie: "Thus says your brother Israel" (Num 20:14). The implicit reference is to the brothers Jacob and Esau, precisely the two figures at the heart of the Red Heifer ritual.[7]

When critics ask about the site of the animal's slaughter and debate whether or not its slaughter is a real sacrifice, they are, I think, pursuing the wrong question. The proper question to ask is, why must the animal be red in color? Why is a color mentioned at all? In attempting to make sense of the matter I want to recall Gray's statement—although not made in regard to the Red Heifer ritual—that it is entirely in the manner of priestly procedure "to connect the origin of an institution with an event."[8] This is true for the institution of the Red Heifer.

RESPONSE IN NUMBERS 19 TO JACOB'S ACQUIRING THE STATUS OF FIRSTBORN IN GENESIS 25

Because of its supposed blood content, the stage before its true contents (the lentils) emerge, the dish made by Jacob that Esau craved would have been anathema from a priestly point of view. Outside of the priests' use of it in the sanctuary, blood contaminates and signifies death. Only in association with the sanctuary does blood have the opposite effect, life-giving because it absorbs and removes impurity, a state equated with death ("Impurity [*tum'a*] is the realm of death").[9]

In reacting negatively to the Genesis saga, the ritual-maker opposes the "red, red" (blood) dish by producing a mixture that, after any contact with death in the form of a corpse, a human bone, or a grave, will restore purity and hence life. By highlighting an animal that has been reduced to ashes without removing all of its blood, the ritual imitates the event in which Esau thinks Jacob has slaughtered a domestic animal and roasted the meat without first removing the blood. Hebrew *parah*, "heifer" or, more accurately, "cow," is a term used loosely in biblical Hebrew for a domestic animal and covers the beast Jacob had supposedly used to cook the "red, red" dish.[10] The ritual, we shall see, even enhances the red color of the animal.

(There may be a wordplay in Num 19:2 that points to the story, or perhaps the vocabulary of the story is carried over into the law. The animal, *parah*, is to be *'adumah*—red, *temina*—whole, in which there is no defect. The Rabbis understood the reference to *temina*, whole, as pointing to the heifer's total redness, whereas modern critics have typically applied *temina* to the next part of the sentence, which concerns the healthy condition of the animal. These critics recognize the redundancy, but they claim that it must be for emphasis.[11] In Gen 25:25, 27 Esau is *'admoni*, ruddy, and Jacob is *tam*, the same two words that describe the heifer or cow, *'adumah temimah*. Esau, moreover, is "red all over [*kulo*] like an hairy mantle," conjuring up the image of a fully red creature. The description of the animal in the law might then point to the significant features of each brother, even if it has never been clear what quality *tam* suggests about Jacob. Esau's error about the animal meat comes to define his person: the hunter Edom is "the red one," and the tent-dwelling Jacob is *tam*, possibly the civilized one, who, in contrast to his animal-like brother, knows human ways and how to exploit Esau's bestial need for blood. Perhaps the description of the animal in Numbers as *'adumah temimah*, with its linguistic echo of a major characteristic of each brother, is an appropriate way to draw attention to an animal that never existed. Esau reckoned that it did, and Jacob pretended that it did, so it can be thought of as recalling the nonexistent *'adumah*—the wild Esau, the red one—*temimah*—the domesticated Jacob, the civilized one—animal.)[12]

From Esau's perspective there is blood in Jacob's dish from a slaughtered domestic animal. It is not true, but Jacob is happy to have Esau think that it is. Indeed, Jacob seems fully prepared to be making a blood dish for eating, and in the eyes of the Numbers lawgiver doing so would render him culpable along with Esau. As a result, the confusion (some think of it as deception) wins Jacob Esau's birthright. When we turn to the Red Heifer, as commentators well note, the designation of its color is decidedly puzzling. It is a clue that something out of the ordinary lies behind the ritual, which in my view is Jacob's ruse with "the red, red" dish.

The ritual incorporates a negative reaction to the supposed kind of meat dish Jacob cooks. The Numbers lawgiver's disapproval of Esau's desire and Jacob's apparent willingness to have him consume blood is the reason the animal in the ritual is burnt to ashes along with its blood. The ritual imitates in order to oppose. The requirement to burn the blood of a slaughtered animal is unique to this law, "something without parallel elsewhere in the Old Testament."[13] The ritual highlights redness, the quality associated with blood in Jacob's preparation. In the first place, in the ritual what exactly is a *red* heifer? Did such a fully red-colored animal actually exist? Most likely not (then as now), and hence it is common to rationalize the problem away in order to enhance the plausibility that the ritual was actually practiced.[14] Thus Milgrom has the color as reddish-brown because, he states, brown cows are plentiful, but a fully red one would not have existed or if it did would have been extremely rare. But then why bother to designate a color for the animal at all if it was commonly found? Noth, while similarly rationalizing about the heifer's color, is more alert to the problem when he writes about the animal "whose red (reddish-brown) color is obviously considered to be important for the intended effect" (to which he appends the statement "There is nothing in the Old Testament with which to compare this last point").[15]

The heifer's red color is all the more puzzling because in the end the animal is totally incinerated and reduced to ashes. Yet, remarkably, the color red is emphasized by the explicit references to how its blood and its dung are burned and how a scarlet cloth is thrown into the fire. Critics commonly insist that the Hebrew *piršah*, usually translated "its dung," refers to its (bloody) entrails. Milgrom argues that cedar wood is used because its red color symbolically adds to the quantity of blood in the ashes.[16] Yet the red ingredients eventually disappear in the fire, so we have to wonder all the more why redness comes into the ritual at all. The highlighting of the color seems an unnecessary, gratuitous facet of the ritual. The ashes, once cold, will not be red, so the role of redness has no obvious relevance.

The color is highlighted because it harks back to the role of the color red in the episode in Genesis 25. In Jacob's cooking activity no animal is, in fact, involved, but in an illusory way the redness of the dish indicates to Esau that one is. If Esau had not mistaken what the redness in Jacob's dish signified, the transaction of the sale of the birthright would not have taken place. In the final outcome of the Genesis story, as in the ritual, the essential significance denoted by the color—life, blood—disappears. Esau finds out that the redness comes from lentils and not from the blood of an animal for which he has a craving. The blood inside the heifer is burnt to ash.

We can also explain another major puzzle: while the function of the burnt heifer is to purify those defiled by death in one form or another, the burning process defiles those conducting the ritual. The animal confers uncleanness on the person burning the animal, on the priest who casts into the fire the cedar wood, the hyssop, and the scarlet material, and on the layperson gathering its ashes. These participants in the ritual become unclean on account of their duties and remain so until, by undergoing cleansing with water, they achieve purification in the evening. Why do they become unclean? In effect, they mirror the original potential offense in Genesis because they do not remove the animal's blood in accordance with priestly law. That is, in mimicking the scene with Esau and Jacob, they become unclean by association with the failure on the part of Esau, certainly, and Jacob, possibly, to recognize that blood must always be totally drained from a dead animal. Actually, Isaac too loved to eat meat with blood. It is what he loved Esau for. Indeed, all three, Jacob, Esau, and Isaac (Rebekah, too, who prepared Isaac's meat dish), seem to have been accustomed to preparing meat with blood. The literal translation of Gen 25:28, "Isaac loved Esau for the game in his [Esau's] mouth," portrays Esau with meat dripping with blood in his mouth. Isaac loved him for this. The later lawgiver, who has in mind the prohibition of consuming blood, was put off by this image of Esau and Isaac eating blood.

Why is the ritual "a purification for sin" (Num 19:9)? Milgrom and Wright argue, despite many indications to the contrary, that we are in fact dealing with a sacrifice. For them, the ashes act as a prospective purification or purgation offering for a person after he or she has been in contact with a dead body. Somehow the blood retains its power to purify even though it has been burnt. One problem with this view, which I do not entirely discount, is that it is difficult to understand how blood subjected to fire retains its power. Another problem is that elements of the procedure do not bear the usual hallmarks of a ritual that requires a sacrifice. As Milgrom and Wright recognize, the animal is slaughtered outside the camp by a nonpriest, its blood is not splashed over the altar, and the use of cedar, hyssop, and scarlet material, as here, is never found in sacrifices. The term used for its ashes is *'eper* (vs. 9) and *'apar* (vs. 17), not *dešen* as in the ashes left after a cultic offering. Noth says of the statement about the removal of sin by the cow's ashes that "it is left hanging in the air and is all the more surprising since a sacrificial action has precisely not taken place." Noth sees the statement as an addition but gives no reason why a scribe bothered to add it.[17] The slaughtered animal is not a sacrificial offering, even along the lines that Milgrom and Wright argue. Rather, in my view, the ritual is meant to recall a historical moment associated with the original ancestor Jacob. The ritual contains, from a later priestly perspective, a critique of the willingness to prepare a meat dish, especially one having blood in it, as portrayed in the Jacob–Esau narrative. As "purification for sin," the ritual retrospectively counteracts the offense in the story in Genesis 25.

In sum, for the Numbers lawgiver the incident in which Jacob acquires the right of the firstborn presents an objectionable belief about blood. The redness of the heifer in the ritual is crucial for understanding it because the institution's focus is on the supposed magical effect of Esau's "red, red" dish. The magic here is Esau's wrongful idea that he can control his world by attributing a power to blood that it does not have outside of its approved use by a priest at the sanctuary. By reducing the animal and its blood to ashes under the supervision of a priest (Eleazar), the lawgiver has the redness attaching to the cow totally obliterated in order to oppose the consumption of blood and death-defying power attributed to the blood that Esau thought was in Jacob's dish.

POSITIVE SIGNIFICANCE OF THE RITUAL

Ritualized actions with two goats on the Day of Atonement in Leviticus 16 turn to good the evil of Joseph's brothers' deed with the blood of a slaughtered goat (as Jub 34:18, 19, rightly interpreted). The creator of the Red Heifer ritual in Numbers, responding negatively to how Jacob attained the birthright from Esau, likewise exploits the incident for a constructive use. The Numbers lawgiver derives the beneficial aspect of the Red Heifer ritual from the idea that is central to the story: Esau's need to keep death at bay. Because no animal is actually used in Genesis 25, Jacob's deception inspires the question, what kind of ritual might be constructed that does have a slaughtered animal serve to repel death (other than by eating it without its blood)? The move is comparable to the one that lies behind the construction of the Day of Atonement in Leviticus 16. The live goat that is sent to the demonic being Azazel ("Mighty Goat") in the wilderness represents the fictional wild beast that killed Joseph and that serves, in turn, the need to undo that offense and all later offenses of the sons of Israel.[18] Similarly inventing the ritual in Numbers 19, the lawgiver takes the fictitious animal killed in Genesis 25, transforms that illusion into an actual slaughtered animal, and has it first serve to recall the offense, approval of eating meat with blood. The ritual is then put into service to emphasize the primary feature of Jacob's make-believe: the red color associated with blood that Esau linked to life overcoming death.

The ritual applies to various instances in which an Israelite or a resident non-Israelite encounters death: when he is exposed to a corpse on entering a tent or is near an open vessel in a tent that has been exposed to a corpse; when he touches someone in open fields who has been slain by a sword or who has died naturally; or when he touches a human bone or a grave (Num 19:14–16). There is opposition to one use of animal blood, as a counter to death on Esau's part, with a view to exploiting its use in another, acceptable way, that is, as a counter to the miasma of death. The two cases of death cited in the ritual concern death in a tent and death in the open field. Noteworthy is the fact that in the story Jacob is a "tent-dweller" and Esau is a "man of the field": "And Esau was a knowing hunter, a man of the field; and Jacob was a *tam* [civilized?] man, dwelling in tents" (Gen 25:27). The prey-deprived, death-fearing Esau comes from the open field and receives the death-defying red dish from the tent-dwelling Jacob.

A human corpse is manifestly like animal meat that has not had the blood thoroughly and immediately removed from it. Both human corpse and animal carcass contaminate; in Howard Eilberg-Schwartz's terms, each represents not just something dead but additionally death as impurity.[19] For the lawgiver, blood does indeed repel death, but it can do so only if it is linked to the sanctuary. Blood under the control of the priests is associated with life and is thought to ward off death. Central to the positive role of the ritual is the action by the priest (Eleazar) at the beginning, when he takes some of the newly slain animal's blood on his finger and sprinkles it seven times in the direction of the sanctuary (Num 19:4). The action plainly signifies some removal, however little, of blood from a slaughtered animal. Its symbolic transfer from the animal in the direction of the sanctuary serves to indicate that "the blood is the life" (Deut 12:23; Gen 9:4) and should properly return to the deity who resides in the sanctuary.

The subsequent placement in a vessel of the ashes of the burnt, dead animal with the "water of separation" (*me niddah*) serves an efficacious function. Like

Esau thinking that the blood in animal meat will keep death from him, so the mixture of ashes and water achieves its end in a manner not open to rational scrutiny. The fact that the heifer, before its slaughter, is without blemish and never bore a yoke indicates that the animal is to be put to a positive use (Num 19:2). Wright thinks that because a firstling could not have a yoke put on it (Deut 15:19), the heifer may well have been a firstborn animal, a point of some interest given the issue of primogeniture that dominates both the story in Genesis 25 and the context in Numbers.[20]

On the one hand, then, there is recall of the fiction of Jacob killing an animal and opposition to what he supposedly made from it: a blood dish capable of giving life to an expiring Esau. On the other hand, there is the affirmative action of reducing an animal and its blood to ashes and preserving them with a view to achieving the very end that Esau sought and Jacob supported, namely, resisting the realm of death. Certainly not resistance to impending death by eating meat with blood but a different application: to counter the fear of a corpse and the like. More particularly, the focus is on countering the contamination caused by death, a focus that is determined by the consideration that Esau would have become contaminated if, in seeking to ward off death, he had proceeded to consume his usual meat dish.

The law's reference to more usual situations evoking death than Esau's plight is illuminating. Just as Esau's fear of dying from the failure to obtain his favorite blood stew is irrational (he could have eaten anything, not just meat, to ward off starvation), so too is the fear generated by a corpse or by a tent or an open vessel infected by a corpse, a human bone, or a grave. In each instance, moreover, the decisive element in addressing the problem is the red quality attaching to, respectively, Jacob's dish in the story and the heifer in the law. A notable gap between story and law also proves illuminating. In Gen 25:32, Esau urgently seeks by the immediate consumption of a blood stew recovery from his exhausted state ("Behold, I am at the point to die: and what profit shall this birthright do to me?"). His urgency sharply contrasts with the duration of time and delay built into the ritual for countering the contaminating power of death. Not until the third day is there to be a sprinkling of the water of separation on the affected person, and not until four days later is there to be a second and final sprinkling. A hurried response like Esau's to the presence of death is markedly absent. The feature of a third day sprinkling and another on the seventh day is, I might add, unique.

The seemingly magical element in the institution can be minimized once we realize that it is a dramatization of a foundational moment in the life of the nation. The law has no historical reality in the sense of reflecting ongoing cultic life in ancient Israel. The reference to the role of Eleazar in the ritual suggests that its institution is to be forever thought of as peculiar to the wilderness period. The elements in the law that echo a past event in Genesis introduce a historical dimension. We are dealing not with a legislative prescription for cultic practice but with a law that is more like a drama—"Ritual shapes identity through drama"—or a monument emblematically recalling and commemorating the past.[21] The statute, rather than its application, is to be remembered.

Numbers 16 and 17 provide a parallel to the commemorative, emblematical nature of the law of the Red Heifer. First, there is a narrative incident to be recalled: the occasion when Moses has the rebels led by the Levite Korah fill censers with fire and incense to test whether their claim to have equal status with the Aaronite priests is justified. Korah's proves to be a wrongful claim, and the rebels perish by fire. There follows the commemoration: flattened into a casing, the censers are kept in the sanctuary in the form of the altar's copper covering to recall the offense. The institution of the ritual of the Red Heifer serves the same commemorative function but because the incident occurs in Jacob's lifetime, and not during Moses', the original occasion is not explicitly cited.

The ritual of the Red Heifer is a product of reflection on Israelite tradition and I doubt has anything to do with a transformation of some remote, pre-Israelite rite of exorcism for dealing with contamination coming from corpses and the like. Such rites may well have existed in the lawgiver's time, but if they did they are probably not especially relevant to the ritual of the Red Heifer. My view stands in sharp contrast with those of other scholars. Milgrom, for example, assumes a biblical transformation of a preexisting ritual and postulates that "the demonic impurity of corpses of a bygone rite has been devitalized." Even if Milgrom is right about the adaptation of preexisting ritual, in no way has the Red Heifer devitalized anything. If one takes the ritual as being real and the ideas about the contaminating power of things associated with death as being truly held beliefs, the ritual is vital indeed—odd, mysterious, and magical. Noth also assumes that some primitive, magical rite has been transformed with the introduction of Israelite priestly supervision of it. The supposed primitive stage "has been brought into at least an outward connection with the legitimate (Yahweh) cult." S. Wefing argues that the ritual was originally a form of ordeal inveighing against pagan sacrifice. Roland de Vaux writes, "This rite certainly originated in pagan practices, and it must have been originally a magic rite"; here "certainly" is assertiveness making up for lack of substance. Paul Mpungu Muzinga provides a rare negative critique of the view that we are dealing with some primitive rite that has been surprisingly preserved. The Numbers ritual is not "une 'survivance,' lequel faisait partie des 'pratiques archaïques et magiques' que les Hébreux ont hérité et ont assimilé à un 'sacrifice d'expiation pour le péché'" [a "survival" going back to "archaic and magical practices" that the Hebrews had inherited and assimilated to an "expiatory sacrifice"].[22]

The ritual of the Red Heifer is, in my view, an invention inspired by and critical of the transaction between Jacob and Esau about the privilege of being firstborn. It is doubtful that the ritual was ever intended for institutional realization. For one thing, as Eryl Davies points out, in other texts washing in water alone was sufficient to remove contamination associated with an animal carcass (Lev 11:24–28) or, more to the point (for the sons of Aaron), with a human corpse (Lev 22:4–6): "It is not clear why this particular method of lustration should have been instigated at all, for provisions elsewhere in the OT indicate that washing in plain water was sufficient to remove any contamination incurred by contact with the dead."[23] De Vaux notes that biblical texts describing funerary rites "do not remotely suggest that contact with a corpse brings on defilement (cf. especially Gen 46:4, 50:1)." He puts forward the odd argument that the Red Heifer ritual is an archaic rite that was not part of the ordinary life of the people but somehow lived on side by side with the official religion.[24] In my view, the institution in Numbers 19 is a hypothetical construction specifically derived from the Genesis story and hence a product of an ancient scribal school's project of integrating narrative and law in Genesis–2 Kings.

The ritual reenactment of what takes place between Jacob and Esau, that is, Israel and Edom, applies to non-Israelites too (Num 19:10), and Levine is much struck by the inclusion of a resident alien in the rule.[25] But Edomites, the descendants of Esau, who might choose to reside in Israel, would fall into this category and therefore, in light of Esau's central position in Genesis 25, it is less of a surprise that the resident alien comes into consideration. In the ongoing narration of events in Numbers, the Edomites' encounter with the Israelites in the wilderness, as noted, next comes into reckoning (Num 20:14–29).

The one other biblical source outside of Numbers in which there appears to be a reference to the Red Heifer ritual is Ezek 36:25. Significantly, Edom again plays a prominent role.[26] There is particular mention of the ancient enmity between Edom and Israel, that is, of the struggle between Esau and Jacob (Ezek 35:5–6). There are references also to the judgment upon the nations, Edom being the only nation singled out by name (Ezek 36:5), and to the blood that defiled the land of Israel (Ezek 36:16–21). Ezekiel, who is quite familiar with priestly lore, speaks metaphorically of how the ritual washing will cleanse Israel after it has experienced its enemies' destructive power, that is, when Edom took possession of its land, which the Israelites themselves had previously defiled with blood. Like the original Jacob and Esau in dealing with the "red, red" dish, there is joint guilt.

Some more general points may be set down by way of summary. How Jacob achieved top status in his family surely demanded attention among those who surveyed Israelite beginnings. It is, therefore, not surprising that the disturbing incident comes to expression in seemingly mysterious elements of a ritual. It is a general truth, especially in law, that the more important the subject matter, the transfer of primogeniture for instance, the more it is likely to attract ritualistic forms. The conveyance of land is an example, as in the role of the shoe in Ruth 4:7.

As is common the world over, often the aim of a ritual is to reverse an unwelcome situation. The ritual of the Red Heifer, which imitates the offense in Genesis 25 in order to recall and oppose it, fits this pattern. Somewhat comparable is how the bow that appears in the cloud after the Flood originally represents the bow with which God wages his battles (Gen 9:13; Exod 15:3; Hab 3:9, 11). Its placement in the cloud is a sign that God has ceased his hostilities against man.[27]

The magic associated with the Red Heifer ritual is really not magic at all but is about dramatizing Esau's desire, with Jacob's collusion, for a bloody meat dish. After all, deceiving the senses is what magic is about, and once we are undeceived the magic vanishes. To speak of a magical component as characterizing the ritual, as has been the universal judgment, is a confession of bewilderment about strange practices. The bafflement disappears when we view the ritual of the Red Heifer, like those of the Passover and the Day of Atonement, as a dramatic, stylized retelling of a foundational story that by its very nature depicts a highly unusual happening.

There is, to be sure, a magical factor to be evaluated in Esau's situation. What supposedly saves him from dying is not just the partaking of food in the form of lentils, but his belief in the magical properties of the "red, red" dish. There is thus an odd element in Esau's situation: he needs food, but he needs, from his viewpoint, much more than food. He gets the lentils but not the magical ingredient, blood. The situation is derisory—in seeking to keep death away he was about to be in contact with death in the form of an animal's blood—and in this light he deserves to be despised for giving up his birthright (Gen 25:34). The narrative, like the ritual, condemns Esau.

Overall, Genesis 25 and Numbers 19 share a considerable number of correspondences. There is the fraternal relationship between Jacob and Esau, which shows up again in the episode in Numbers 20 that follows the establishment of the Red Heifer ritual. There is blood in the story that is suggested and emphasized by the red dish, and there is blood in the ritual. Potential contamination caused by blood in the story has its counterpoint in the law when it requires a purifying mixture of water and ashes from an animal burnt with its blood. Fire is a feature of both texts. Redness is highlighted in both. There is a sacred component in both: in the narrative, the oath that Jacob has Esau swear, and in the ritual, priestly supervision of the proceedings. The fear of death is central to both. Indeed, if we wanted to capture in essence the curious outcome of both the Genesis narrative and the rule in Numbers 19, we might borrow the words of Virginia Woolf: "I meant to write about death, only life came breaking in as usual."[28] Finally, story and ritual share an interest in a domestic animal, illusory in the story, apparently real in the ritual but for the following reason I think illusory also.

The ritual is invented tradition to record the narrator's judgment on a crucial but decidedly questionable event at the nation's beginning. When commentators recognize that red heifers or cows never existed they do not conclude that the ritual probably did not exist either. Instead, they rationalize the problem away by suggesting other colors. Their unquestioned assumption is that the biblical texts must reflect social and religious practice in ancient Israel. I think that is an unsafe assumption. Numbers 19 is not part of a historical archive but a literary invention.

9

SPEECH ACTS (NUMBERS 20–24)

From this point on, in Numbers 20–36, the narrator evokes the history of Jacob: from the point when, acquiring the birthright through trickery, Jacob aroused Esau's antagonism to his ending up in Joseph's Egypt. A succession of events in Genesis comes under scrutiny: Jacob's need of divine protection because of his fear of meeting a hostile Esau after he flees with his two wives from his father-in-law Laban (Genesis 28–31); his deliverance from Esau's enmity (Genesis 32 and 33); the problem of sexual seduction by a Canaanite that causes consternation in Jacob's family at the Hivite city Shechem (Genesis 34); the return to Bethel, where Jacob had earlier vowed to give his allegiance to Yahweh in response to the latter's protection (Gen 28:20), and the death of Rachel (Genesis 35); Esau's settlement at Mount Seir (Genesis 36); and Jacob and his family's sojourn in Canaan followed by their settlement in Egypt (Genesis 37–50). By and large, the author is systematic in evoking the episodes in Genesis 27–50. What we find overall is that Numbers 20–36 (Israel's migration from enslavement in Egypt to the imminent settlement in Canaan) link up with Genesis 25–32 (the migration of Jacob and his family from their form of enslavement under Laban in Aram to their taking up residence in Egypt).

Genesis 25–32	Numbers 20–24
Power of speech Jacob had the famished Esau swear an oath to sell his birthright for a "red, red" dish. Exploiting the power associated with the sacred, Jacob caused Esau to lose his birthright (Genesis 25).	*Power of speech* Moses fails to speak God's words to the rock to obtain water for those urgently needing it. He loses his personal inheritance in Canaan as a consequence (Numbers 20).

(continued)

A vow Jacob utters a vow seeking divine assistance for relief from troubles (Genesis 28).

A vow Israel utters a vow seeking divine assistance for relief from troubles (Numbers 21).

Life-threatening divine encounter An angel wrestles with Jacob, who survives the encounter and extracts a blessing that changes his name to Israel. The result is Jacob's survival of Esau's threat on his life (Genesis 32–33).

Life-threatening divine encounter Israel survives Moab's threat after a life-threatening angel confronts Balaam. By not opposing Yahweh's words on the occasion, Balaam's life is spared and, as a consequence, Israel's too (Numbers 22–24).

MOSES' OFFENSE AT THE ROCK AND THE POWER OF SPEECH

Numbers 20 recounts an incident about obtaining water from a rock for the thirsty Israelites. Although the water is forthcoming, the two sons of Levi, Moses and Aaron, are punished for failing to heed the deity's directions about how to go about obtaining it. The punishment consists in their being denied future entrance to the new land. The offense that brought the punishment has long engendered puzzlement as to what exactly the wrong is. The focus on Esau's loss of his birthright to his younger brother Jacob in Genesis 25, which was crucial for understanding the preceding institution of the ritual of the Red Heifer in Numbers 19, may aid in comprehending the offense at the rock. The key is the role of speech acts. At least three events—transfer of the right of the firstborn in Genesis, obtaining water from the rock in Numbers, and the immediately following story of Israel's denial of secure passage through Edomite territory—turn on the role of utterances.

In Numbers 20 the people in the wilderness complain because of their lack of water:

> 1 Then came the children of Israel, even the whole congregation, into the desert of Zin in the first month: and the people abode in Kadesh; and Miriam died there, and was buried there. 2 And there was no water for the congregation: and they gathered themselves together against Moses and against Aaron. 3 And the people chode with Moses, and spake, saying, Would God that we had died when our brethren died before Yahweh! 4 And why have ye brought up the congregation of Yahweh into this wilderness, that we and our cattle should die there? 5 And wherefore have ye made us to come up out of Egypt, to bring us in unto this evil place? it is no place of seed, or of figs, or of vines, or of pomegranates; neither is there any water to drink. 6 And Moses

and Aaron went from the presence of the assembly unto the door of the tabernacle of the congregation, and they fell upon their faces: and the glory of Yahweh appeared unto them. 7 And Yahweh spake unto Moses, saying, 8 Take the rod, and gather thou the assembly together, thou, and Aaron thy brother, and speak ye unto the rock before their eyes; and it shall give forth his water, and thou shalt bring forth to them water out of the rock: so thou shalt give the congregation and their beasts drink. 9 And Moses took the rod from before Yahweh, as he commanded him. 10 And Moses and Aaron gathered the congregation together before the rock, and he said unto them, Hear now, ye rebels; must we fetch you water out of this rock? 11 And Moses lifted up his hand, and with his rod he smote the rock twice: and the water came out abundantly, and the congregation drank, and their beasts also. 12 And Yahweh spake unto Moses and Aaron, Because ye believed me not, to sanctify me in the eyes of the children of Israel, therefore ye shall not bring this congregation into the land which I have given them. 13 This is the water of Meribah; because the children of Israel strove with Yahweh, and he was sanctified in them. (Num 20:1–13)

Genesis	Numbers
Power of speech Jacob had the famished Esau swear an oath to sell his birthright for a "red, red" dish. Exploiting the power associated with the sacred, Jacob caused Esau to lose his birthright (Genesis 25).	*Power of speech* Moses fails to speak God's words to the rock to obtain water for those urgently needing it. He loses his personal inheritance in Canaan as a consequence (Numbers 20).

What precisely is Moses' and Aaron's offense? The people fear they will die because of lack of food, but the lack of water is the only problem God is seen to solve when he tells Moses and Aaron that he will provide the people with water from a rock. We might recall that Esau in his time feared death because of lack of food and, more to the point, because he needed a blood dish. In the Numbers incident God instructs Moses to take the rod, which betokens Moses' special authority, and assemble all the people. He is then to speak to the rock before their eyes (Num 20:8). Instead of speaking to the rock, however, Moses addresses the people: "Hear now, ye rebels; must we fetch you water out of this rock?" (Num 20:10). We then learn that "Moses lifted up his hand, and with his rod he smote the rock twice: and the water came out abundantly, and the congregation drank, and their beasts also" (Num 20:11). There is no speaking to the rock in the name of God.

Moses' failure to address God's words to the rock appears to be where the problem lies. The fault is taken up in God's condemnatory statement to Moses: "Because ye believed me not, to sanctify me in the eyes of the sons of Israel, therefore ye shall not bring this congregation into the land which I have given them" (Num 20:12). The point of oaths, vows, divine words, and the like is precisely *belief* in their effectiveness. The failure to sanctify appears to refer to Moses' ignoring the capacity of words alone, the speaking to the rock, to bring about a divinely directed result. More to the point, Moses, by using the rod (*his* symbol of authority) only, by not using God's name, and by saying "must we fetch you water out of this rock?" emphasized not God's power but his and Aaron's power. Moses takes full credit for the miracle by word and by deed; God is upset that Moses did not believe and did not sanctify him in the eyes of the children of Israel. It is a dishonoring of God's name, that is, of his reputation among the people for accomplishing the miraculous. Sirach, of the early second century BCE, brings out well the proper stance. Referring to the miracle in Exod 15:25 in which Moses follows God's command to throw a piece of wood into contaminated water, Sirach states, "Was not the water made sweet by the wood, that he might make known to all men his [God's] power?" (Sir 38:5). The improper stance in later Jewish ethics is called *ḥillul haššem* (profanation of the name of God), the particular gravity of public sinning. When Moses uses the rod he fails to follow God's instruction solely to speak to the rock: "Speak ye unto the rock before their eyes; and it shall give forth its water" (Num 20:8). Whether he is aware of it or not, Moses' use of the rod instead of addressing the rock by divinely sanctioned oral communication showed lack of trust in the power of language to enhance God's reputation.

There is a link between the incident of Jacob's "red, red" dish—the inspiration for the preceding institution of the ashes ritual in Numbers 19—and the incident at the rock. Jacob opportunistically exploited the sacred by having Esau utter an oath whose effect could not be changed because the uttered promise took on a power of its own. Numbers 20, in turn, relays what should have been a proper example of the sacred use of words to bring about a good result, but one which was not acted on. In each incident life is at stake, Esau's and the life of the Israelite people, each of whom lacks vital nourishment (food of a certain kind, water). Esau continues to live on, but he loses the birthright and hence inclusion in the promise to Abraham and Isaac to inherit the land of Canaan. Esau's oath was also wrongful speech because he had despised his God-given birthright by conveying it to Jacob in the most careless and offensive of ways: the use of loose language in seeking to consume blood (Gen 25:34). In Numbers, at Kadesh, Moses and Aaron in turn also continue to live on, as do the people, but the two brothers are denied entrance to Canaan because of a failure to use divinely commanded speech. Each time, then, a firstborn, Esau and these two Levites, Yahweh's firstborn, suffers a loss of inheritance and a speech act or its omission plays a crucial role.[1]

We are dealing with the power of the numinous. Esau's swearing away his birthright for the "red, red" dish cannot be undone. Similarly, in Gen 27:27–29, 33, a blessing once uttered is beyond recall, as in Isaac's blessing of Jacob. Words spoken to the rock should alone have served to save the Israelites from dying of thirst.

Immediately following the incident at the rock there is a clear retrospective reference to the Genesis relationship between the two brothers Jacob and Esau. At the meeting between the messengers of Moses and the king of Edom in Num 20:14–21, the Israelites fail to obtain from the Edomite king a binding promise that they can pass through his territory on their way to the new land. Moses' request touches on the fraternal tie we first learn about in Genesis 25 and 27. The tie between the two brothers had broken down in Genesis 27 because of utterances by their father, Isaac, that could not be undone and that resulted in Esau's hostility to Jacob. The tension between the two eponymous ancestors of Israel and Edom surfaces again at this particular point in Numbers because the king of Edom still appears to be upset with his founding ancestor's loss of birthright: he threatens force should the Israelites try to traverse Edomite territory. Unlike the promise that Jacob pressured Esau into making, Moses' pressure to have the king of Edom promise to grant Jacob's descendants protected passage and sustenance in trying circumstances, even if the latter is paid for (Num 20:14–21), is not successful. The Edomite king refuses to give his word guaranteeing secure transit to the Israelites.

The power of speech is also the central point of the episode that follows after Israel's request of the king of Edom to promise safe passage through Edomite territory (Num 20:14–21). Thus in Numbers 22–24 Balak hires Balaam to curse Israel, but Balaam cannot do so because he can speak only that which Yahweh puts into his mouth: "I cannot go beyond the word of Yahweh to do less or more" (Num 22:18) with the further statement in Num 23:13 that Balaam cannot do "of mine own mind; but what Yahweh saith, that will I speak." The power of speaking features prominently at this point in Numbers. In sum, what emerges from these different episodes is that the potency attributed to the act of speech symbolizes its magical, numinous component. From an anthropological perspective, such speech resembles magic in that it "attempts to control the environment primarily by manipulative and mechanistic incantation of words."[2]

An episode in Exodus further highlights the significance given to the role of speaking in Numbers 20. Exod 17:1–7 describes another incident during the wilderness wanderings about obtaining water from a rock, this one at Horeb: the people, having journeyed to Rephidim, complain about the lack of water, and God commands Moses to smite the rock. In the Exodus narrative, contrary to the corresponding Numbers narrative, Moses is indeed commanded to strike the rock with his rod. No mention is made, as critics observe, of speaking to it.[3] Ashley points out significant differences between the story in Exodus 17 and the one in Numbers 20. His conclusion is that the differences, "although not disproving that the author of Numbers simply reshaped Exod. 17 for a different purpose, are sufficient to show that he wished his readers to consider this a separate incident." I would substitute for the author of Numbers the narrator-lawgiver or school of scribes responsible for the entire write-up of Genesis–2 Kings. In any event, we have a good example of how in the integration of materials into Genesis–2 Kings similar stories are set out in different ways to emphasize different ideas in focus in each narration. The occurrence of similar stories is worth further comment because the phenomenon is far from being an isolated one. It turns up in both narratives and laws.

DOUBLETS

We sometimes find in the narrative history double retribution for someone's offense. The two punishments represent much reflection on different aspects of a narrative, exactly as when two similar rules take up different facets of an offense. As illustration we might note the Sabbath command in Exod 20:8–11 and the similar one in Deut 5:12–15. Each responds to a different feature of the story in Exodus 32 about the making of the Golden Calf. Aaron sets aside a special day for the calf, which he refers to as Yahweh, so that the Israelites celebrate its role in bringing the Israelites out of Egypt. Of concern to the narrator—and to other biblical writers (Hos 8:6 and Ps 106:19)—is the celebration of a man-made god. In response to this offense Deut 5:12–15 takes up the first issue of who was responsible for bringing Israel out of Egypt. The Deuteronomic Sabbath commandment emphasizes that it was the God Yahweh, not the Golden Calf Yahweh, who performed the miracle: "Keep the Sabbath day to sanctify it, as Yahweh thy God hath commanded thee. Six days thou shalt labour, and do all thy work: But the seventh day is the Sabbath of Yahweh thy God. . . . And remember that thou wast a servant in the land of Egypt, and that Yahweh thy God brought thee out thence through a mighty hand and by a stretched out arm: therefore Yahweh thy God commanded thee to keep the Sabbath day." Exod 20:8–11, in turn, takes up the second issue of who is the true Maker of everything that exists in order to counter any notion that humankind can fashion divinity: "Remember the Sabbath day, to keep it holy. Six days shalt thou labour, and do all thy work: but the seventh day is the Sabbath of Yahweh thy God: in it thou shalt not do any work.... For in six days Yahweh made heaven and earth, the sea, and all that in them is, and rested the seventh day: wherefore Yahweh blessed the Sabbath day, and hallowed it." Unlike the rule in Deuteronomy, which affirms the God Yahweh over against the calf Yahweh in the role of rescuer from Egypt, this rule affirms the God Yahweh's power to create all things over against man's attempt to create a god. We should be careful before resorting to source analysis to explain the differences between one story or one law and another similar story or law. The differences need not be attributed to presumed preexisting sources.

The following examples are of double retribution in the narrative history; how pondering the nature of an offense in some incident, the biblical narrator often fashions scenarios in which the offender experiences different kinds of retribution in later incidents, depending on what aspect of the offense is under scrutiny. Judah's punishment for his role in the disposal of Joseph (Gen 37:26–35) takes two forms. From the father Jacob's point of view, his son Joseph is dead. Retribution befalls Judah when he loses sons himself in his dealings with Tamar (Genesis 38). Later, Joseph, in disguise, proves to be alive and causes Judah to pledge that he will become a bondman to him and remain in a foreign land, Egypt (Gen 44:33). Judah's fate mirrors what befell Joseph after Judah got his brothers to go along with his scheme to sell him into slavery (Gen 37:26–28).

A second example of double retribution is when Jacob experiences fallout for deceiving his father, Isaac. With his mother's help, Jacob tricks his father by taking advantage of his blindness. As a result, Isaac gives the blessing of the firstborn to the younger son Jacob and not to the elder son Esau (Genesis 27). Jacob in turn is tricked by Laban, his mother's brother. On Jacob's wedding night, when he cannot see properly because it is dark and he is probably drunk from feasting, Laban substitutes his elder daughter Leah for the younger daughter Rachel so that Leah, not Rachel, becomes his wife (Genesis 29). Jacob receives further retribution for another aspect of his offense against Isaac. Dressing up as his hairy brother, Jacob uses garments to deceive his blind father into thinking that he is Isaac's other son Esau, and as a consequence Jacob again receives the chief blessing. Isaac's anguish over the deception is visited upon Jacob as a father when his sons use Joseph's blood-soaked garment to deceive their father and convince him that Joseph is dead (Gen 27:33; 37). A third example of double retribution in the narrative record is how Saul dies twice, first by suicide, that is, directly seizing death himself (1 Samuel 31), and then by the hand of a lowly Amalekite camp follower (2 Samuel 1). We are probably not dealing with badly edited stories by some compiler of Genesis–2 Kings who does not see the contradiction. Instead, we have two different accounts of Saul's end because of two grave offenses he committed in his lifetime: he reached into the realm of death to raise Samuel from the dead (1 Samuel 28), and he let the highest member of the Amalekites, the king, live when he should have dispatched him (1 Samuel 15).[4]

Genesis	Numbers
A *vow* Jacob utters a vow seeking divine assistance for relief from troubles (Genesis 28).	A *vow* Israel utters a vow seeking divine assistance for relief from troubles (Numbers 21).

VOW AT ARAD

In Numbers 20, in presenting Moses' communication with the king of Edom, the narrator looks back to the past: to the more recent post-Exodus wilderness events, then further back in time to the enslavement in Egypt, and further back again to the original family tie between Jacob and Esau (Num 20:14: "Thus saith thy brother"). From this point on, in Numbers 21–36, the narrator continues a focus on the history of Jacob-Israel from the time when, acquiring the birthright through trickery, Jacob aroused Esau's antagonism to his ending up in Joseph's Egypt. The formation of the nation Israel in the wilderness takes off from and mirrors the experiences of its first family in Genesis.

In Numbers 21 we probably have the precedent of Jacob's vow at Bethel in focus when, in escaping Esau's enmity, Jacob sought protection from God (Gen 28:20–22):

> 20 Jacob vowed a vow, saying, If God will be with me, and will keep me in this way that I go, and will give me bread to eat, and raiment to put on, 21 So that I come again to my father's house in peace; then shall Yahweh be my God: 22 And this stone, which I have set for a pillar, shall be God's house: and of all that thou shalt give me I will surely give the tenth unto thee.

The words "So that I come again to my father's house in peace" refer to Jacob's safe return to Bethel in Gen 35:1: "And God said unto Jacob, Arise, go up to Bethel, and dwell there: and make there an altar unto God, that appeared unto thee when thou fleddest from the face of Esau thy brother." The context for Gen 28:20–22 is one in which Jacob anticipates future troubles such as encountering a murderous Esau (Edom) intent on revenge for losing his birthright to his younger brother. In the event, as we shall see, divine protection prevented the dire outcome.

In the post-Exodus situation in Numbers 20, potential Edomite enmity is, we saw, a factor with which Israel contends. Because the king of Edom is opposed to Israel's request for passage through Edomite territory and will not guarantee safe passage through it, Israel avoids confrontation by seeking a different entry into Canaan. Taking a different route and skirting Edom, Israel confronts the Canaanite king of Arad, whose troops capture some Israelites. Seeking divine assistance for deliverance from the enemy, Israel makes a vow similar to their ancestor's at Bethel. Both the Genesis and Numbers contexts—"Give me bread to eat" (Gen 28:20) and "There is no bread, neither is there any water" (Num 21:5)—concern the problem of sustenance. The vow at Arad proves efficacious, for Yahweh duly enables the Israelites to defeat their enemy: "And Yahweh hearkened to the voice of Israel, and delivered up the Canaanites; and they utterly destroyed them and their cities" (Num 21:3).

THE SERPENTS

Avoiding the land of Edom, the people are again in despair about their dire condition. We read in Numbers 21:5–9,

> 5 And the people spake against God, and against Moses, Wherefore have ye brought us up out of Egypt to die in the wilderness? for there is no bread, neither is there any water; and our soul loatheth this light bread. 6 And Yahweh sent fiery serpents among the people, and they bit the people; and much people of Israel died. 7 Therefore the people came to Moses, and said, We have sinned, for we have spoken against Yahweh, and against thee; pray unto Yahweh, that he take away the serpents from us. And Moses prayed for the people. 8 And Yahweh said unto Moses, Make thee a fiery serpent, and set it upon a pole: and it shall come to pass, that every one that is bitten, when he looketh upon it, shall live. 9 And Moses made a serpent of brass, and put it upon a pole, and it came to pass, that if a serpent had bitten any man, when he beheld the serpent of brass, he lived.

A key feature of the presentation of the material in Genesis–2 Kings is the thoroughness with which certain issues are explored. The incident about the serpents illustrates. In Numbers 20 (obtaining water from the rock) we had the same despair exhibited by the people when complaining about their lack of food and water. That incident, however, does not focus on what is perceived in Numbers 21 (the serpent incident) to be a serious fault of the people when they express despair and show lack of trust in the deity's capacity to provide for them. Yahweh punishes them with a plague of serpents. The focus in Numbers 20 (the rock incident) had fallen on their leaders, Moses and Aaron, who do not sanctify Yahweh before the people by acknowledging his miraculous capacity to deliver water from the rock by speaking to it. In the similar (serpent) incident in Numbers 21, a negative focus falls this time on the people's failure to appreciate the deity's capacity to provide sustenance for them even in harsh desert surroundings. The outcome is a clear, unambiguous demonstration of Yahweh's power, but not this time in a miraculous supply of sustenance (water), as in Numbers 20.

The sacred dimension lies in another direction: serpents bite the people, and some die from their wounds, but those who look at a molten serpent crafted by Moses are cured, thereby demonstrating their faith in Yahweh. Numbers includes two episodes, then, that appear on the surface to be very similar—the people complain each time that Moses has brought them into the desert to experience suffering. We can also add a third incident: in Exod 17:1–7 when the people, again expressing anger about their suffering in the wilderness, are accused by Moses of testing God, and Moses strikes the rock with his rod and it produces water. The traditional (JEDP) view when confronting similar stories and rules is to sort them into the various strands J, E, D, P (and H) and to assume that they have been put together awkwardly by a redactor. I would argue, however, that, whatever their origin, similar occasions are recorded in order to explore and thoroughly examine different issues: the first concerning Moses' acknowledgment of Yahweh's power (Numbers 20), the second concerning the belief of the people in their God (Numbers 21), and the third expressing the notion about the people testing God (Exod 17:1–7).

Genesis	Numbers
Life-threatening divine encounter An angel wrestles with Jacob, who survives the encounter and extracts a blessing that changes his name to Israel. The result is Jacob's survival of Esau's threat to his life (Genesis 32–33).	*Life-threatening divine encounter* Israel survives Moab's threat after a life-threatening angel confronts Balaam. By not opposing Yahweh's words on the occasion, Balaam's life is spared and, as a consequence, Israel's too (Numbers 22–24).

The history of Jacob's dealings with a hostile Esau in Genesis 32–33 dominates the write-up of the next episode about Balaam in Numbers 22–24, when Jacob-Israel's descendants face another enemy, the Moabites. As a preliminary step before launching an attack, King Balak of Moab seeks to have the diviner Balaam curse Israel. In the end, however, Balaam, after being confronted by an angel with a sword, acts counter to the king's request and instead blesses Israel. The Numbers episode provides a prime example of the replication and reworking of a Genesis event. That event is when Jacob confronts an angel before being well received by a previously hostile Esau (Genesis 32–33).

AN INTENDED CURSE THAT CHANGES TO A BLESSING

What mainly determines the outcome of the Balaam story is the blessing owing to the firstborn that back in Genesis Isaac was compelled to confer, not on Esau but on Jacob (Genesis 27). As part of that blessing, Isaac told Jacob, "Cursed be every one that curseth thee, and blessed be he that blesseth thee" (Gen 27:29). So blessed is Jacob from that Genesis episode that he cannot be cursed in the later Numbers one, despite the lengths to which the king of Moab goes to have Balaam do so. Yahweh compels Balaam to bless Israel in the same words that Isaac relayed to Jacob: "Blessed is he that blesseth thee, and cursed is he that curseth thee" (Num 24:9).

Balak, who hires Balaam to curse Israel, is like Esau in that each protests vigorously the conferral of the blessing on Jacob-Israel (Gen 27:34–41; Num 23:25), but neither plea is successful. Living by his sword, Esau can expect to continue losing out to Jacob: "By thy sword shalt thou live, and shalt serve thy brother" (Gen 27:40). Isaac's original blessing on Jacob in Gen 27:28–29 also means that, Israel's good fortune being irreversible, Balaam in his time has to predict disaster for both Moab and Edom in their future dealings with Israel. The two nations are cited together in a longer list of the enemies of Israel that Balaam pronounces negatively upon in Num 24:17–25. What happens throughout Numbers 22–24 plays out in line with Isaac's blessing in Gen 27:29 because the earlier blessing cannot be revoked.[5] Even the curious discrepancy, much remarked upon by commentators, between God telling Balaam to accompany Balak's men (Num 22:20), which is then followed by the contrary statement, "But God's anger was kindled because he went" (Num 22:22), parallels Jacob's similarly topsy-turvy situation in Genesis 31 and 32.[6] God told Jacob to leave Laban's Aram and go to the land of his birth (Gen 31:13), but after Jacob started on that very journey his divine messenger acted with hostile intent against Jacob (Genesis 32).

In Genesis, Esau's and Laban's hostility played a major role in the background as Jacob migrated, but an encounter with a divine being transformed the situation. In Numbers, Balak's hostility through Balaam's actions plays a similar role in the migration of Jacob's descendants, but again an encounter with a divine being transforms the scene. Esau's curse on Jacob in Gen 27:41 changed in Genesis 32 and 33 to favorable treatment of Jacob after the incident at Peniel with the divine wrestler. Balak's attempt, in turn, to curse Jacob's descendants in Num 22:6 turned into a blessing on them after the incident with the divine figure and Balaam's donkey (Num 22:22–24:25).

In each episode neither the hostile Esau nor the hostile Balak engages Israel directly. Jacob was on his way to meet with what he expected would be a menacing Esau when an angel in the form of the divine wrestler first encountered Jacob in an openly hostile way. The belligerent wrestler acted as a substitute for Esau, that is, like Esau he was initially menacing but, again like Esau, who receives Jacob well after the incident, ended up conferring a blessing (Gen 32:29). In Numbers, Balak's proxy, Balaam, is directed to curse Israel and menace them, but a divine being, confronting Balaam and threatening him, transforms the peril of a curse into a blessing upon Israel.

As noted, an angel plays an initial adversarial role in each story, the one who wrestled with Jacob in Gen 32:24 and the one in Num 22:22 who stands in the way "for an adversary against him [Balaam]." Jacob and Balaam are alone with God when the divine being confronts each of them (Gen 32:25; Num 22:8, 13, 23:3). Both occasions involve a physical struggle of a supernatural character: the wrestler who seemed to be antagonistic to Jacob but was actually on his side; and a donkey, controlled by an angel and given the power of speech, who seems to go against his master, Balaam, but actually opposes him for his good, which means for Jacob-Israel's benefit. (Both names, Jacob and Israel, are used in Num 23:23.) Stubbornness is a feature of each adversary, but both times it is in the best interests of Jacob-Israel. In Num 22:21–35, the angel, acting through the she-ass and causing Balaam to be jammed against a wall, does physical harm to the prophet just as the divine figure did harm to Jacob: "And when he [the divine being] saw that he [Jacob] prevailed not against him, he touched the hollow of his thigh; and the hollow of Jacob's thigh was out of joint, as he wrestled with him" (Gen 32:25). In each instance the injury is to a leg. If the concept of agency has it that "the messenger of a man is like the man" (*m. Ber.* 5:5; *b. Ber.* 34b; *b. Kidd.* 41b), then in both episodes "the messenger of God is like God."

The divine wrestler's initial action serves as a substitute for Esau's potentially murderous attack on Jacob. The hostility, however, changes into a positive disposition. When Jacob prepared for his fearful meeting with Esau, seven applications of the word "face" are used in Gen 32:16–21. The use of the word so many times relates to the place Peniel, "the face of God," where Jacob encountered the divine being before meeting Esau (Gen 32:30, 33:10). The connection between the mysterious figure and Esau comes out in Gen 33:10 when Jacob says to Esau, after he unexpectedly received Jacob well, "If now I [Jacob] have found grace in thy [Esau] sight, then receive my present at my hand: for therefore I have seen thy face, as though I had seen the face of God." A comparable miraculous transformation occurs in the Numbers episode. The donkey, being made to talk, is the agent of God whereby Balak is coerced to accept Israel. Balak's change of attitude corresponds to Esau's. Although gifts do play a role in each episode—Jacob to Esau through intermediaries in Gen 32:14–22, and Balak to Balaam through intermediaries in Num 22:17–18—in each instance it is favorable divine interference and not the presents that brings about the transformation.

What also may have contributed to the write-up of the incident with the donkey is the incident in Genesis 27 when Jacob, dressed in animal skins, deceives the blind Isaac into thinking that he is Esau and receives the chief blessing as a result. The donkey in Numbers 22 is made to behave like a human by uttering speech. Relying on their senses, both Isaac and Balaam come to a wrong conclusion. The blind Isaac thought that Esau stood before him because Jacob's goatskins conveyed that he was his hairy son who had brought him his favorite game dish. By trusting his sense of touch, Isaac persuaded himself that he was dealing with Esau and not with Jacob. He was wrong, the consequence being that the blessing he intended for Esau went to Jacob. The animal-like person before the blind Isaac was not the crude huntsman Esau but Jacob, the skillful exploiter of human ways. An animal-human overlap shows up in the incident with the talking donkey, in which both touch and blindness again play a role. Balaam feels sure that his donkey, jamming him against a wall, solely shows the unwanted stubbornness so characteristic of a donkey: "And when the ass saw the angel of Yahweh, she thrust herself unto the wall, and crushed Balaam's foot against the wall" (Num 22:25). Balaam is wrong, for he is blind to the presence of the angel acting on behalf of Jacob-Israel. Thus "Yahweh opened the eyes of Balaam, and he saw the angel of Yahweh standing in the way, and his sword drawn in his hand: and he bowed down his head, and fell flat on his face" (Num 22:31). As in Genesis, to the advantage of Jacob-Israel touch prevails over sight at a certain point in the narrative. The donkey causing Balaam to be jammed against a wall leads Balaam to see that he is bound to bless Israel. The donkey then tells Balaam in words where his duty lies. We are reminded of the constraint on Isaac to confer his blessing on Jacob.

IMPENDING ATTACK

The military setting is pronounced in each episode, and large numbers play an important role. Jacob feared Esau because four hundred of Esau's men were approaching. Balak fears the Israelites because, although his own Moabites are many, there are so many more Israelites. There is, indeed, in Gen 32:13 an anticipation of the great numbers of Israelites in Num 22:3. In Gen 32:13, Jacob prayed, "Deliver me, I pray thee, from the hand of my brother, from the hand of Esau: for I fear him, lest he will come and smite me, and the mother with the children. And thou [Yahweh] saidst, I will surely do thee good, and make thy seed as the sand of the sea, which cannot be numbered for multitude." In Num 22:3 we hear that "Moab was sore afraid of the people, because they were many." In God's blessing on Jacob at Bethel, there was reference to his future seed being "as the dust of the earth" (Gen 28:14). Balak, in despair, asks, "Who hath numbered the dust of Jacob?" (Num 23:10). The emphasis on great numbers points to Israel's expansion in keeping with the earlier blessing on the Genesis patriarchs.

Jacob and his entourage encountered angels at Machanaim (God's military camp) before one of them confronted him alone at night. He had just passed over the river Jordan (Gen 32:11). Israel in Num 22:1 is at the Jordan river at Jericho. The incidents occur during a time of difficult travel. Journeying from Laban with his wives and children, Jacob anticipated a fearful meeting with Esau, and, following the fortunate outcome, the incipient nation faced the harmful prospect of forging connubial relations with the Canaanite group, the Hivites (Genesis 34). The Israelites, in turn, in Num 25:1, are journeying from Egypt and, following the unexpectedly favorable encounter with the enemy Balak and Balaam, they wrongfully attach themselves to Moabite women.

Israel in Num 23:9 is "a people dwelling apart." We recall that in Gen 33:14 the emphasis is on Jacob remaining apart from Esau despite Esau's unexpectedly kind offer to accompany Jacob on his journey. When Jacob's family came into contact with the Hivites in Genesis 34, Simeon and Levi resolutely insisted that there be no relations, especially marital, with the Hivites. This hostile attitude to intermarriage is the entire point of Numbers 25, as we shall see in the next chapter, about Israelite men taking up with Moabite women.

INTERNATIONAL ASPECT

Fleeing from the Aramean Laban, Jacob journeyed from Aram to Edom (Genesis 33 and 34). Num 23:7, in turn, has Israel, in its flight from Egypt, arrive at the territory of Edom and Moab, and it is Balaam who declares "from Aram has Balak brought me." Balaam is the son of Be'or, and in the Edomite genealogy in Gen 36:31–43 there is a Bela', a son of Be'or, who is cited as the first king of Edom. Gray says of Gen 36:32 that "the ultimate identity of Bela' king of Edom and Balaam is highly probable," and he finds that sometimes Balaam is Edomite, other times even Ammonite or Midianite. Mainly, however, in Numbers 22–24 Balaam is Aramean. One source of the mixed identity, Aramean or Edomite, may be the influence of the Genesis narratives about Laban the Aramean and Esau the Edomite because each was similarly intent on doing harm to Jacob. God revealed himself to Laban in a dream by night (Gen 31:29) and to the outsider Balaam also at night (Num 22:9, 19, 20, stated directly for the second visitation in vs. 20).[7] That is, both Laban and Balaam are from Aram, and the message to each from the Israelite god is that no harm must be done to Jacob (Gen 31:24, 29; Numbers 22–24). Laban was basically ill-disposed to Jacob, but God had him provide for Jacob's welfare. A similar element of hostility shows up with Balaam, but God has him treat Israel well (Num 24:14, 25:1, 31:16; Deut 23:5; Josh 24:10; Neh 13:2). The climax to the Esau saga in Gen 33:16 and to the Moabite Balak saga in Num 24:25 is that each enemy ends up going home without committing to hostile action against Jacob-Israel.[8]

The story of Balaam in Numbers 22–24 is a particularly tantalizing example of how recall of the past influences communication about the present. Just as there is no human experience without some transfer from the past, so no account of Israel's history, or any history, is free of transfer from previous experiences. The point is commonplace but, so far as I am aware, the extensive transfer of elements from the stories in Genesis to the write-up in Numbers has gone unnoticed. The phenomenon is undoubtedly more complicated than I have presented, and one aspect I shall not pursue is the impact of the reverse phenomenon: the impact of the later history, for example, Israel's dealings with Edom and Moab, on the recording of the original phase of history to be found in Genesis.

10

SEXUAL AND RELIGIOUS SEDUCTION (NUMBERS 25-31)

Israel's dealings with foreign groups dominated the previous accounts of events in Numbers 20–24. The king of Edom refused Israel passage through Edomite territory, and the king of Moab employed the Mesopotamian diviner Balaam to curse the migrating Israelites. In Numbers 25–31 Arameans, Canaanites (Hivites, for example), Edomites, Moabites, and Midianites, explicitly or implicitly, all come into reckoning. The following outline suggests how certain Genesis narratives continue to exert their influence on Numbers 25–31. The Genesis narratives recount the history of the first Israelite family, Jacob's, when they were migrating and encountering foreign groups (or the ancestors of such groups), Edomite, Aramean, and Canaanite.

Genesis 28–35	Numbers 25–31
Fierce treatment of seduction Simeon and Levi slaughter all male Hivites because one of them seduces their sister Dinah. She had introduced herself to the Hivites. The two brothers totally oppose any mixing with the foreign group (Genesis 34).	*Fierce treatment of seduction* Moses, a Levite, has the judges slaughter those Israelite men involved with Moabite women. Phinehas, also a Levite, slaughters a Simeonite chieftain and the Midianite woman whom he had introduced into Israel's camp (Numbers 25).
Loss of fathers and sons Hivite sons and fathers die at the hands of Simeon and Levi. Jacob fears that the same fate of extinction will befall the House of Israel	*Loss of father and sons* Lists the generations of Jacob's descendants and counts the living members for the purpose of fighting the Canaanites. An Israelite fa-

(continued)

Genesis 28–35	Numbers 25–31
because the surrounding Canaanite enemies will avenge the deaths (Gen 34:25–30).	ther dies with no sons to succeed him, but a rule permits daughters to inherit (Numbers 26–27).
Leadership Simeon and Levi are model leaders because they exhibit a commitment to Israel's distinctive identity in the midst of the Canaanites (Genesis 34).	*Leadership* Joshua succeeds Moses and bows to the authority of Aaron's successor, Eleazar, a Levite, who will maintain proper standards in the acquired land of Canaan (Numbers 27).
Religious commitment Anticipating Israel's future worship, Jacob builds an altar at Bethel in fulfillment of an earlier vow there (Gen 28:20–22, 35:1–7).	*Religious commitment* Moses gives an exhaustive list of the altar offerings that the Israelites are to present at the sanctuary in the new land (Numbers 28 and 29).
Jacob's vow and oath Escaping the wrath of Laban and Esau, Jacob begins to fulfill his vow at Bethel. He receives a blessing of fertility, but Rachel, who earlier avoided death despite her husband's oath about her possession of her father's gods, dies in childbirth (Gen 31:32, 35:9–20).	*Vows and oaths* A man's vow or oath is comprehensively binding, as is the vow or oath of a woman. It makes a difference, however, if she is under the authority of her husband or her father (Numbers 30).
Sexual and religious seduction After the slaughter of the Hivite males on account of Shechem's seduction of Dinah, Jacob takes in the Hivite women and children. On his way to build the altar at Bethel, Jacob removes their gods (Gen 34:29, 35:2–4).	*Sexual and religious seduction* Moses exterminates the Midianite married women and their male children. Like the Moabite women in Numbers 25, the Midianite women had seduced the Israelites with their gods (Numbers 31).

In his magnificent oracle in Num 23:9, the foreign diviner Balaam refers, we noted, to Israel as "a people dwelling apart." A precedent for Israel's stance of independence in Genesis was when Jacob and his family declined Esau's invitation to accompany them inside Edomite territory, despite the welcome Esau gave them (Gen 33:14). The next stage in the history of the first family in Genesis was the incident involving Dinah, when two of Jacob's sons, Simeon and Levi, fiercely resisted any attempt to forge relations, especially marital, between their group and the Canaanite group, the Hivites (Genesis 34). The motivation was again a need to underscore the separate identity of the Israelites. A feature of Numbers in relation to Genesis is that Numbers is even more committed to stressing Israelite identity. Numbers reinforces apartness by combating any tendencies in the opposite direction that are suggested in the Genesis narrative.

Genesis	Numbers
Fierce treatment of seduction Simeon and Levi slaughter all the male Hivites because one of them seduces their sister. She had introduced herself to the Hivites. The two brothers totally oppose any mixing with the foreign group (Genesis 34).	*Fierce treatment of seduction* Moses, a Levite, has the judges slaughter those Israelite men involved with Moabite women. Phinehas, also a Levite, slaughters a Simeonite chieftain and the Midianite woman whom he introduces into Israel's camp (Numbers 25).

The fierce stance of Simeon and Levi in Genesis 34 to the prospect of Israel's loss of a distinctive identity very much comes to the surface again in Numbers 25 and particularly shows up in the person of Phinehas, a descendant of Levi. (The same stance also appears, as we shall see, in the resumption of Numbers 25 in Numbers 31, when there is a mass slaughter of the Midianites with Phinehas again the leading antagonist, vs. 6). The hostility in Numbers to non-Israelite groups is, indeed, taken much further than in Genesis 34. Phinehas, "the son of Eleazar, the son of Aaron," that is, a leading Levite, spears to death an Israelite head of household, Zimri, and a Midianite woman, Cozbi, whom Zimri had introduced into the Israelite camp (Num 25:6–8). Not only is the outsider slain, as with the Hivites in Genesis 34, but the insider, Zimri, who has been receptive to a marital relationship with a Midianite woman, is slain also. In Genesis 34, Dinah escapes unscathed but is not heard of again. The compiler of Genesis–2 Kings, in the spirit of Phinehas, perhaps deliberately extirpated her from the historical record.

Dinah in Gen 34:1 had introduced herself into the Hivite camp. In Numbers 25 it is the reverse and much more likely situation where the Israelite male takes the initiative and introduces a foreign woman into his camp. But in each instance it does not alter the fact that attention is given to a single, named, and initially unattached woman, Dinah and Cozbi. Like his ancestor Levi in Genesis 34, Phinehas acts to preserve the separation of the Israelites from other groups by resolutely opposing any mixing, in this instance, with Midianites or Moabites because they had led Israel into idolatry (Num 25:1–7, 16–18, cp. Gen 36:35 on Midianites living in Moab). Israel had "joined itself unto Baal-Peor, committed whoredom with Midianite women, and sacrificed to the Moabite gods" (Num 25:1–3).

THE ZEAL OF PHINEHAS

The development in Numbers 25 relives not just the unacceptable sexual involvement of the Hivite prince, Shechem, with Jacob's daughter, Dinah, but also unwanted religious influence on the house of Jacob-Israel. In Genesis 34 a concern with idolatry emerged both before and after Simeon and Levi slaughtered all the male Hivites. Jacob initially purchased a parcel of land from the Hivites, settled there, and proceeded to build an altar to Israel's god and call it El-elohe-Israel, "God, the God of Israel" (Gen 33:20). The altar served as a marker of Israelite identity. Immediately following the slaughter of the Hivites, God instructed Jacob to go to Bethel and build an altar at the place where God appeared to him after he fled from Esau. Jacob called it El-Bethel, "God of Bethel" (Gen 35:1), the aim no doubt being, again, to reinforce group solidarity.

At that time Jacob instructed his household to divest themselves of the foreign gods in their midst: "Then Jacob said unto his household, and to all that were with him, Put away the strange gods that are among you, and be clean, and change your garments: And let us arise, and go up to Bethel; and I will make there an altar unto God, who answered me in the day of my distress, and was with me in the way which I went" (Gen 35:2, 3). The strange gods are the ones that the Hivite (Canaanite) women will have brought with them after Jacob's sons took them captive (Gen 34:29). One implication is that if the Hivite women had been permitted to keep their gods they would have invited the Israelite men to sacrifice to them, as happens later, in Num 25:2, when the women of Moab do invite the Israelites to sacrifice to their gods. Focusing on Israel's anticipation of entry into Canaan, the Numbers narrator is alert to the unwelcome implications of the events, sexual and religious, in Genesis 34 and 35. In keeping with his desire to depict the more intense commitment to exclusiveness in Moses' generation, the Numbers narrator certainly has nothing corresponding to Jacob's accommodating attitude to the foreign group's request for marriage alliances (Gen 34:5, 30, 31). Instead, Simeon's and Levi's antagonistic stance is the model. Indeed, the Numbers narrator goes much further. In Israel's later dealings with the Moabites and the Midianites, especially in the resumption of the story in Numbers 31 when nonvirginal women and their male children are also killed, there is even less tolerance of foreign influence and the Israelite offenders are themselves extirpated. Leniency such as that shown to the Hivites, when the lives of the women and children were spared and no punishment befell Dinah for her initiative in visiting the foreign group, is not viewed as an option. Contrary to Dinah's boldness going unpunished, God orders the death of Israel's leaders (Num 25:4).

In Numbers 25 it is the Levite Phinehas who makes a name for himself by stamping out an unwanted sexual and idolatrous relationship. He shows the same zeal as Simeon and Levi in Genesis 34, of whom Jacob had angrily and, we may infer from the attitude of the Numbers narrator, wrongly condemned for wielding "instruments of violence" against the Hivites (Gen 49:5). Why, then, if the Genesis narrative exerts its influence on the write-up of the Numbers narrative, do we not find a descendant of Simeon also listed as continuing to exhibit zeal for Israelite identity in dealing with the Moabites and the Midianites? Simeon's conduct in Genesis 34 against the Hivites is as praiseworthy as Levi's. Why, for that matter, in a broader context, are the Simeonites not chosen along with the Levites as temple employees who qualify to represent Yahweh's sacred interests?

One reason for there being no priestly role for the Simeonites, certainly for the absence of a zealous role for any Simeonite in Numbers 25, is that the offender who brings a Midianite woman into the camp is himself a Simeonite. He is Zimri, the head of a Simeonite family (Num 25:14), and he clearly does not share the attitude of Phinehas, the Levite. Zimri's perceived wrongdoing may have contributed to the judgment that the entire tribe of Simeon did not deserve the status the Levites enjoy because of the original exemplary stand Simeon and Levi exhibited against the Hivites in Gen 34–35:4. It is noteworthy that in Gen 46:10 Simeon has sons by a Canaanite wife, which suggests that already in Genesis, before the establishment of the priesthood, there is reason to deny Simeon's tribe priestly status. The Simeonite tribe's loss of standing reflects less perhaps a historical development than one aimed at accounting etiologically for the downgrading of Simeon's position in later Israelite life.[1] After all, there is much inventiveness in the write-up of all the traditions, which are not archival records but legends imbued with certain ideological stances.

In later tradition Phinehas is the model zealot who provides the paradigm for the exercise of jealousy (*qin'a*, jealousy, zeal) in the religious-political arena. As an emotion, jealousy might often be momentary, as presumably with Phinehas's action against the Simeonite in Numbers 25. As a religious-political concept, however, it primarily depicts a person like him who breaks away from a routine, conventional loyalty, to exhibit a fervent, even violent and total commitment to a cause. In pursuit of that cause, a zealot's behavior transcends the legal process and is not subject to its strictures. Phinehas is viewed not as murdering Zimri but as executing him and his companion in accordance with a higher order. His act is excused not because the passion on display overcomes his self-control, a defense that sometimes mitigates conduct, but because the conduct on the occasion is worthy from a religious perspective. In this regard also Phinehas is reminiscent of Simeon and Levi. By wiping out all the Hivite males they appalled their father by not conforming to, as Jacob perceived it, the proper international order of the day. Over the issue of Shechem's wish to marry Dinah, Jacob appeared to have been open to negotiating a reasonable settlement with Hamor (Gen 34:30, 49:5–7).

We do not move immediately, as we might have expected, to the problem in Numbers 31 of the sexual and religious seductiveness of the Midianites at Baal-Peor (Num 25:18). The account in Numbers 31 is an obvious extension of the one in Numbers 25. The reason for the break in and later resumption of the narrative in Numbers 31 is not that legends and laws in Numbers 26–30 have been added at some later time to the Book of Numbers, which is the view of most critics, even conservative ones.[2] Instead, the process of taking up issues from the same Genesis narratives that underlay the account of the slaughter of Zimri and the Midianite woman in Numbers 25 continues. The replication of these Genesis issues in the wilderness period accounts for the topics that show up in the intervening texts of Numbers 26–30. In particular, before he again takes up his account of the slaughter of the Midianites in Numbers 31, the Numbers narrator focuses on important but related matters of the repercussions that followed the slaughter of the Hivites in Genesis 34 and 35. I turn, then, to the aftermath of the Hivites' fate, again to demonstrate just how powerful Genesis is as an introductory, foundational document.

Genesis	Numbers
Loss of fathers and sons Hivite sons and fathers die at the hands of Simeon and Levi. Jacob fears that the same fate of extinction will befall the House of Israel because the surrounding Canaanite enemies will avenge the deaths (Gen 34:25–30).	*Loss of father and sons* Lists the generations of Jacob's descendants and counts the living members for the purpose of fighting the Canaanites. An Israelite father dies with no sons to succeed him, but a rule permits daughters to inherit (Numbers 26–27).

First, however, a description of the narrative in Numbers 26 is in order. The topic of inheritance, the continuity of name and possessions through the oncoming generations, dominates much of the remainder of Numbers, from Numbers 26 through Numbers 36. In Numbers 26, because the old generation dies of the plague in the wilderness (Num 26:64, 65), a new census is necessary of those who survive. This census replaces the one in Numbers 1. The reason for each census is to count the people available for war and thus to prepare the way for conquering the land wherein the Israelites will take up their inheritance. On the subject of inheritance, Yahweh declares to Moses,

> 53 Unto these [the tribal clans of the sons of Jacob] the land shall be divided for an inheritance according to the number of names. 54 To many thou shalt give the more inheritance, and to few thou shalt give the less inheritance: to every one shall his inheritance be given according to those that were numbered of him. 55 Notwithstanding the land shall be divided by lot: according to the names of the tribes of their fathers they shall inherit. 56 According to the lot shall the possession thereof be divided between many and few. (Num 26:53–56)

The use of the lot, according to Wenham, is "to avoid any dissension"—of the kind, I suggest, so familiar from the struggles for dominance among Joseph and his brothers in Genesis 37, the very ancestors cited in Numbers 26.[3]

As for the connections to Genesis in Numbers 26, Milgrom points to a particularly telling example. The names of the clans of the House of Jacob in Numbers 26 "are closely related to those in Gen 46:8–24, with the difference that there [in Genesis] they are persons, whereas here [in Numbers] they are clans." He draws the link with Genesis even closer when he notes that "Israel—having entered Egypt numbering seventy individuals (Gen 46:27; Exod 1:5)—has become a nation of seventy clans" about to enter Canaan.[4] The Levites are not included among the twelve tribes for the purpose of inheritance but have a separate census. In that they enjoy a special (and especially rich) inheritance at the sanctuary, they also do not have shares in the land on the same basis as the other clans.

Numbers 1–25 has been an extended commentary on issues in Genesis 25–38 to convey counterpart developments at the time of the wilderness wanderings and to right the wrongs that occurred at the inception of the Israelite nation. The commentary continues until the end of Numbers (Numbers 26–36). For instance, the topic of loss of inheritance is an important issue and reflects a similar one in Genesis. I note the concern in Num 26:63–65 first: "These are they that were numbered by Moses and Eleazar the priest, who numbered the children of Israel in the plains of Moab by Jordan near Jericho. But among these there was not a man of them whom Moses and Aaron the priest numbered.... For Yahweh had said of them, They shall surely die in the wilderness. And there was not left a man of them, save Caleb the son of Jephunneh, and Joshua the son of Nun." Out of all the parents of families who were previously numbered in the census that was conducted after they left Sinai (Numbers 1), only Caleb and Joshua are to take up an inheritance in the new land. Their contemporaries die in the wilderness because of their unacceptable response to the fearful report of the spies about the Canaanite enemies and a corresponding failure to trust Yahweh in conquering them (Numbers 14). Theirs is seen as a justified loss of personal inheritance.

The situation in Numbers 26, about the loss of an inheritance in Canaan to the head of every Israelite family except Joshua and Caleb, mirrors a major concern in Genesis 34 and 35. In Numbers 26, aside from the decimation by plague to be visited upon the wilderness generation, the surviving generation faces a threat from the surrounding Canaanite enemies. We recall that, in Genesis 34, Jacob expected neighboring Canaanite groups to take up arms in retaliation for the action of Simeon and Levi in depriving the Hivites of sons and fathers. As Jacob in despair expressed the matter to his two zealous sons Simeon and Levi, "Ye have troubled me to make me to stink among the inhabitants of the land, among the Canaanites and the Perizzites: and I being few in number, they shall gather themselves together against me, and slay me; and I shall be destroyed, I and my house" (Gen 34:30). Like the later Numbers generation confronting Canaanite enemies in the wilderness, Jacob too showed no trust in the power of his God to overcome them. Fortunately, the threat did not materialize because divine protection was indeed provided. After Jacob had the residents of his camp give up the foreign gods in their midst—an acknowledgment of the correctness of Simeon's and Levi's stance—as they journeyed "the terror of God was upon the cities that were round about them and they did not pursue after the sons of Jacob" (Gen 35:5).

The "sons of Jacob"—it is they who would have been targeted for what they did to the son of Hamor and all the other sons of the Hivites. Jacob's feared outcome, the cutting off of lines of succession by removal of sons, did not occur. But the topic remains under consideration and plays out in two specific ways: first, in Num 26:64, 65, when God decides to exterminate all heads of Israelite households, except Joshua and Caleb, but allows their sons to survive; and, second and even more to the point, in Numbers 27, when a particular Israelite family, Zelophehad's, experiences the loss not just of a father but of his sons too. We might recall that we have to account for the apparently awkward move, in Numbers 25–27, from the subject of religious and sexual seduction to that of inheritance, specifically, Israel's acquiring the land of Canaan and the threat of loss of inheritance within Zelophehad's family on account of the absence of any son to succeed the father. The narrative background of Genesis 34 is the key: the Canaanite Shechem's seduction of Dinah, Simeon's and Levi's response to it, and the bleak consequence for Israel's future that Jacob worried about. The rule in Num 27:1–11 reads as follows:

> 1 Then came the daughters of Zelophehad, the son of Hepher . . . the son of Joseph: and these are the names of his daughters; Mahlah, Noah, and Hoglah, and Milcah, and Tirzah. 2 And they stood before Moses, and before Eleazar the priest, and before the princes and all the congregation, by the door of the tabernacle of the congregation, saying, 3 Our father died in the wilderness, and he was not in the company of them that gathered themselves together against Yahweh in the company of Korah; but died in his own sin, and had no sons. 4 Why should the name of our father be done away from among his family, because he hath no son? Give unto us therefore a possession among the brethren of our father. 5 And Moses brought their cause before Yahweh. 6 And Yahweh spake unto Moses, saying, 7 The daughters of Zelophehad speak right: thou shalt surely give them a possession of an inheritance among their father's brethren; and thou shalt cause the inheritance of their father to pass unto them. 8 And thou shalt speak unto the children of Israel, saying, If a man die, and have no son, then ye shall cause his inheritance to pass unto his daughter. 9 And if he have no daughter, then ye shall give his inheritance unto his brethren. 10 And if he have no brethren, then ye shall give his inheritance unto his father's brethren. 11 And if his father have no brethren, then ye shall give his inheritance unto his kinsman that is next to him of his family, and he shall possess it: and it shall be unto the children of Israel a statute of judgment, as Yahweh commanded Moses.

THE DAUGHTERS OF ZELOPHEHAD

A specific example of unjust loss of inheritance is laid out in Numbers 27. The five daughters of a man, Zelophehad, who died as a member of the wilderness generation that is denied entrance to Canaan, find that when their sonless father dies they are excluded from inheriting his estate. The prevailing rule was plainly that, in the absence of sons, a man's estate passed to the nearest male relative (agnation), with the consequence that the man's own name was extinguished. This is the outcome the daughters cite when pleading their case. They imply that the male relative acquires an unfair addition. In our terms it is the wrong of unjust enrichment and a remedy is given: daughters are to inherit in the absence of sons. Concentrating on the loss of their father's name should they not inherit his land, these daughters plead their case before Moses and the verdict is, "Right speak the daughters of Zelophehad." The Hebrew term for "right" is *ken*, meaning "straight," "honest," a term well suited to someone expressing a desired remedy for a benefit that inappropriately goes to another party.[5]

Why do we move to this particular topic of the inheritance rights of daughters in the absence of sons? Again, as I indicated, an issue arising from Genesis 34 and 35 determines the narrator's agenda. Specifically, he takes stock of the implications of the incident involving the action of Simeon and Levi that caused the Hivites to lose sons and fathers. From Jacob's angle, the slaughter of all the male Hivites was grossly unfair. The opening statement of a rule in Deut 24:16 judges the slaughter from a viewpoint that might be Jacob's: fathers are not to be put to death on account of the offenses of their sons. The initial spotlight on fathers suffering for their sons' wrongdoing—it is not the usual situation in biblical sources, which is that sons typically suffer because of their fathers' offenses—comes from the fact that it was the son Shechem who offended, but his father, Hamor, paid the penalty too.[6] For the Numbers narrator-lawgiver, the dramatic, total disappearance of lines of succession among the Hivites brings up for consideration the issue in some comparable situation among the Israelites that will affect their future residence in the new land—hence the rule in Num 27:1-11. It is not an unrealistic issue to raise. Jacob articulates the concern that he and his sons would face a similar fate at the hands of the Canaanites if they paid back in kind what Simeon and Levi had done to the Hivites (Gen 34:30). "I and my house will be destroyed," Jacob says in vs. 30—exactly the situation in one later Israelite household, Zelophehad's, when he died and no son existed to ensure succession.

The prominence of Jacob's daughter Dinah in the Genesis story may have been a factor in triggering the focus on later daughters of Israel. If all her brothers and father had been slaughtered by the Hivites, what would have happened to their possessions: might Dinah have inherited as closest next-of-kin? However that possibility may have played out, the reality is that she has no voice whatever in the Genesis incident (her actions are merely described), whereas the voice of Zelophehad's daughters is singularly prominent in Numbers 27. Mainly, however, the topic probably comes to the fore when the Numbers narrator contemplates the position of the surviving Hivite women and children in Genesis 35 who had been incorporated into Jacob's group. Dwelling in Israel's midst, they had been left without adult brothers and fathers. They had also lost their tribal attachment. No further reflection on their status is found in Genesis 35, for it is probably one of enslavement and hence no issue of inheritance arises for them. The point, moreover, is moot because the Israelites were to inherit (by God's decree) Hivite (Canaanite) land. The experience of the Hivites at the hands of Simeon and Levi nonetheless provides a dramatic reminder of families within the incipient nation of Jacob-Israel who have experienced the loss of fathers and sons.

Why does the narrator choose to bring up the issue of Zelophehad's sin? "Our father," the daughters complain, "died in the wilderness, and he was not in the company of them that gathered themselves together against Yahweh in the company of Korah; but died in his own sin, and had no sons" (Num 27:3). We might recall that the sins of Shechem (Genesis 34) and Korah (Numbers 16) are visited upon, respectively, the entire family of Hamor (Shechem's father), that is, the entire male Hivite population, and upon every member of Korah's family. Attached to the tribe of Joseph, Zelophehad's family, it is perceived, does not deserve the communal fate experienced by Hamor, the head of his family, nor the outcome that befell Korah, the head of his. Zelophehad's family should not be deprived of an allotment in the land of Canaan because any sin their father committed was not of the kind committed by Shechem (inferred attachment to Canaanite gods) and Korah (an inner Israelite offense against the sacred order). The communal principle of punishment might have its place, especially in the sphere of the sacred. (It is well recognized that in a theocracy God's justice is perceived as especially oppressive.)[7] The principle should not, however, apply to Zelophehad's family and its future line within a tribe of Israel—hence the justified complaint of the dead man's daughters.

Genesis	Numbers
Leadership Simeon and Levi are model leaders because they exhibit a commitment to Israel's distinctive identity in the midst of the Canaanites (Genesis 34).	*Leadership* Joshua succeeds Moses and bows to the authority of Aaron's successor, Eleazar, a Levite, who will maintain proper standards in the acquired land of Canaan (Numbers 27).

MOSES' FAILURE TO ENTER THE PROMISED LAND AND THE ISSUE OF LEADERSHIP THERE

Num 27:12–23 goes on to consider the role of leadership among the Israelites because Moses is about to die—for his own sin, we might note, like Zelophehad—and not individually inherit in the future land, a topic in keeping with the preceding concern about a loss of inheritance to Zelophehad:

> 12 And Yahweh said unto Moses, Get thee up into this mount Abarim, and see the land which I have given unto the children of Israel. 13 And when thou hast seen it, thou also shalt be gathered unto thy people, as Aaron thy brother was gathered. 14 For ye rebelled against my commandment in the desert of Zin, in the strife of the congregation, to sanctify me at the water before their eyes: that is the water of Meribah in Kadesh in the wilderness of Zin. 15 And Moses spake unto Yahweh, saying, 16 Let Yahweh, the God of the spirits of all flesh, set a man over the congregation, 17 Which may go out before them, and which may go in before them, and which may lead them out, and which may bring them in; that the congregation of Yahweh be not as sheep which have no shepherd. 18 And Yahweh said unto Moses, Take thee Joshua the son of Nun, a man in whom is the spirit, and lay thine hand upon him; 19 And set him before Eleazar the priest, and before all the congregation; and give him a charge in their sight. 20 And thou shalt put some of thine honour upon him, that all the congregation of the children of Israel may be obedient. 21 And he shall stand before Eleazar the priest, who shall ask counsel for him after the judgment of Urim before Yahweh: at his word shall they go out, and at his word they shall come in, both he, and all the children of Israel with him, even all the congregation. 22 And Moses did as Yahweh commanded him: and he took Joshua, and set him before Eleazar the priest, and before all the congregation: 23 And he laid his hands upon him, and gave him a charge, as Yahweh commanded by the hand of Moses. (Num 27:12–23)

Moses loses any forthcoming personal inheritance in the new land because he spurned God's command to produce water from the rock by failing to harness the power of the divine name (Num 20:1–13, 27:14). Joshua is to replace Moses. He must, however, seek counsel, "[Yahweh's] word," from Aaron's successor, Eleazar, who serves at the sanctuary. We might recall that in Genesis 34 and 35 Jacob, as the head of family and as the one who constructed altars (Gen 33:20, 35:1–3, 7), controlled both the political and the cultic offices. From the perspective of Numbers, however, it was Simeon and Levi who adhered to a higher standard of leadership because, much to Jacob's chagrin, they acted on their religious convictions. In Numbers, Joshua as a political and military leader has to "stand before Eleazar the priest, who shall ask counsel for him [Joshua] after the judgment of Urim before Yahweh: at his word shall they [the congregation] go out, and at his word they shall come in, both he, and all the children of Israel with him, even all the congregation" (Num 27:21). The panoply of power attaching to Joshua has to give way to priestly authority because Simeon's and Levi's stance in Genesis 34 is the proper one in governing the people's affairs. The role of the Urim in the possession of the priests ensures independent judgment in resolving disputes. In Genesis 34 the dispute between Jacob the father and his sons Simeon and Levi had no independent arbitrator when the sons' judgment, born of religious conviction, clashed with their father's diplomatic one (Genesis 34).

That both Zelophehad (through Manasseh) and Joshua (through Ephraim) are descended from Joseph will prove significant in light of the Numbers narrator's interest in the annals of Jacob-Israel, particularly in the life of Joseph (see chapter 11). For one thing, Zelophehad and Joshua, like Joseph, barely escaped loss of inheritance: Zelophehad had no sons to ensure inheritance, and Joshua (with Caleb) survived the wiping out of all other adult heads of household in the wilderness. In Numbers 36 we shall note that Joseph's tribe, not just a particular family belonging to it (Zelophehad's), is singled out for special attention because its history provides the closest parallel to the prospect of the entire Jacob group being wiped out in Genesis 34.

Genesis	Numbers
Religious commitment Anticipating Israel's future worship, Jacob builds an altar at Bethel in fulfillment of an earlier vow there (Gen 28:20–22, 35:1–7).	*Religious commitment* Moses gives an exhaustive list of the altar offerings that the Israelites are to present at the sanctuary in the new land (Numbers 28 and 29).

ELEAZAR'S ROLE

The Numbers narrator continues to take his inspiration from the first developments ever in Israelite religious matters, namely, from events in the life of Jacob and his family in Genesis 28–35. Numbers 28 and 29 present the whole array of sanctuary activity, the various sacrifices and religious feasts in which the people are to participate under the supervision, it is understood, of the priests and Levites with their leader Eleazar, Aaron's successor. The leadership role of the tribe of Levi stems from Levi's stance in Genesis 34 against perceived Canaanite influences. In Numbers, the feasts to Yahweh, the sacrifices to the Israelite god, ground Israel's communal well-being in opposition to feasts to other gods, such as those of the Hivites (potentially) in Genesis 34 and those of the Moabites (actually) in Numbers 25.

There is a further, specific reason for the presentation at this point in Numbers 28 and 29 of the calendar of public offerings at the sanctuary. With Joshua bowing to his authority, Eleazar is the person clearly responsible for establishing the role of the sanctuary in the new land. In typical fashion, the Numbers narrator relates the development to the beginnings of the cult in the nation's history, that is, to the altar-building activity of its first ancestor, Jacob. In Gen 28:20–22 Jacob made a vow at Bethel and fulfilled it in Gen 35:1, 7, when, returning there, he built an altar and offered a libation at it (Gen 35:14). The father of the nation's first involvement ever in worshiping God at an altar by presenting a libation anticipates Israel's later worship at the sanctuary. Thus according to the scheme laid out in Numbers 28 and 29 there is instruction about the giving over of various offerings—including drink offerings (Num 28:7, 14, 29:18, 24, 27, 30, 33, 34, 37, 38, 39). The occasion of Jacob's vow and the beginnings of a sacred order in his time are very relevant to the next section in Numbers 30 on vows and oaths.

Genesis	Numbers
Jacob's vow and oath Escaping the wrath of Laban and Esau, Jacob begins to fulfill his vow at Bethel. He receives a blessing of fertility, but Rachel, who earlier avoided death despite her husband's oath about her possession of her father's gods, dies in childbirth (Gen 31:32, 35:9–20).	*Vows and oaths* A man's vow or oath is comprehensively binding, as is the vow or oath of a woman. It makes a difference, however, if she is under the authority of her husband or her father (Numbers 30).

Numbers 30 takes us to the subject of vows and oaths, with special attention given to those affecting women. Why at this point in Numbers does the particular topic come up for consideration and why is there a major focus on those involving women? The story in Genesis again determines the presentation of material in Numbers 30.

The episode in Genesis 34 and 35 about the destruction of Hivite fathers and sons raised for the Numbers lawgiver issues within Zelophehad's family about women in their role as daughters in the absence of a father and a son. Hence the ruling is set down in Numbers 27 that daughters can inherit in the absence of sons at the death of the father. After the destruction of the Hivite males in Genesis, Jacob has the Hivite women in his midst put away all their gods, and he then receives a blessing assuring him of great fertility in the future (Gen 35:11). Following this blessing of fruitfulness, however, the next incident is one that seems to run counter to it: Rachel dies in childbirth (Gen 35:16–20).

VOWS

The Genesis narrator links the blessing of Jacob's fruitfulness in Gen 35:11 at Bethel, "the House of God," with the previous blessing he received in the same place after he fled from Esau to go to Aram and marry Rachel (Gen 28:1–15). The words of both blessings are similar. In response to the first one, Jacob uttered his famous vow: "And Jacob vowed a vow, saying, If God will be with me, and will keep me in this way that I go, and will give me bread to eat, and raiment to put on, So that I come again to my father's house in peace; then shall Yahweh be my God: And this stone, which I have set for a pillar, shall be God's house: and of all that thou shalt give me I will surely give the tenth unto thee" (Gen 28:20–22).

The vow began to be fulfilled when, under the deity's protection, Jacob preserved his fraught marriages to Rachel and Leah, fled the wrath of their father, Laban, and escaped Esau's murderous intent. Jacob returned to Bethel and constructed the altar to Yahweh (Gen 35:1, 7), thereby fulfilling his vow to acknowledge Yahweh as his God. The opening part of the law on vows and oaths in Num 30:2 concerns an Israelite male's vow and can be viewed as an echo of Jacob's vow at Bethel: "If a man vow a vow unto Yahweh, or swear an oath to bind his soul with a bond; he shall not break his word, he shall do according to all that proceedeth out of his mouth." Jacob did not break his word. He duly went about doing according to what he had said with his mouth.

The fulfillment of vows also comes into consideration in Numbers 28 and 29 concerning Israel's commitment to a calendar of public worship at Yahweh's altar. The concluding part of the calendar specifically concerns votive offerings: "These things ye shall do unto Yahweh in your set feasts, beside your vows, and your freewill offerings, for your burnt offerings, and for your meat offerings, and for your drink offerings, and for your peace offerings" (Num 29:39). There is, then, more than just continuity in subject matter between the vows cited in Num 29:39 and the focus on them in the immediately following rules in Numbers 30. There is also a link to the vow of the first ancestor of the nation, Jacob's, at Bethel with its commitment to presenting offerings, for example, tithes, which presumably looks ahead to those at Israel's future sanctuary. Comparable in its forward-looking orientation is God's promise in Gen 35:11 about Israel's future expansion: "And God said unto him [Jacob], I am God Almighty: be fruitful and multiply; a nation and a company of nations shall be of thee, and kings shall come out of thy loins."

OATHS

Significantly, oaths are not cited in Num 29:39 but come into focus in the rule in Numbers 30. The explanation is that whereas Jacob's vow "unto Yahweh" (Gen 28:20–22) is linked to the altar that Jacob built at Bethel, the interest in oaths comes from one that Jacob made, not with regard to that altar but with regard to Laban's stolen household gods. Whereas in the rule we have the person making a vow "to Yahweh," there is no explicit reference to Yahweh in regard to an oath: the man swears "an oath to bind his soul with a bond" (Num 30:2). I turn here to that incident.

Following Jacob's cultic activity at Bethel, the death of his wife, Rachel, in childbirth is clearly incompatible with the blessing of fertility on Jacob and his family, which he received just before she died. Rachel's death ties in much more with Jacob's previously expressed fear of losing sons because of Simeon's and Levi's action against the Hivites. To be sure, even though she dies, Rachel delivers a son, Benjamin, but she will deliver no more. Whereas Jacob had just focused on the threat to his progeny coming from outside Israel, from avenging Canaanites, with the event of Benjamin's birth there is the removal of an Israelite mother from any future child-bearing role. What we have to take particular note of is that Rachel is fortunate indeed ever to have reached the stage of giving birth to a second son (Joseph being her first).

We have to recall that when Jacob and his family were in flight from Laban and Laban caught up with them, Rachel was hiding her father's household gods. Laban demanded their return, and Jacob, not knowing that Rachel had them, swore an oath on the occasion: "With whomsoever thou findest thy gods shall not live" (Gen 31:32). The gods were not found, in a literal sense, because Rachel was sitting on them, and her father could not approach her because she claimed she was menstruating.

In his *Studies in Biblical Law*—under the heading *Summum Ius—Summa Iniuria* (utmost law, utmost injustice), the notion that by keeping the law, you can break the law—David Daube stresses the importance of the literalness of the words of an oath.[8] We have already noted just how much a role the literalness of Esau's request for the "red, red" dish played when Jacob had him swear to give over the birthright. In Jacob's flight from Laban, if Jacob had come upon, literally found, the household gods of his father-in-law with Rachel, the oath would have been upheld and her life forfeited: "With whomsoever thou findest thy gods shall not live" (Gen 31:32). No future son, Benjamin, would have been born, and there would have been no tribe of Benjamin to take up an inheritance in the new land. In Numbers 33–34 the narrator takes up the subject of Benjamin's inheritance, and Numbers 34:21 spells out his particular allotment in the land.

The rule about an oath, *šebuʿah*, explicitly brings up the aspect of a binding commitment, a feature that Levine refers to as "a type of contractual obligation known as *'issar* or *'esar* 'binding agreement,' usually executed in writing."[9] To grasp this aspect of the rule we have to note the outcome of Jacob's oath to Laban about his household gods. The result is, indeed, a contractual agreement between them. Jacob vehemently dismissed Laban's claim about the theft. The gods could not be found—Jacob did not know that his wife had them in her possession—and he entered into an angry exchange about Laban's treatment of him and his wives and children. Laban defended himself but then he proposed,

> 44 Now therefore come thou, let us make a covenant, I and thou; and let it be for a witness between me and thee. 45 And Jacob took a stone, and set it up for a pillar. 46 And Jacob said unto his brethren, Gather stones; and they took stones, and made an heap: and they did eat there upon the heap. 47 And Laban called it Jegar-sahadutha: but Jacob called it Galeed. And Laban said, 48 This heap is a witness between me and thee this day. Therefore was the name of it called Galeed; 49 And Mizpah; for he said, Yahweh watch between me and thee, when we are absent one from another. 50 If thou shalt afflict my daughters, or if thou shalt take other wives beside my daughters, no man is with us; see, God is witness betwixt me and thee. 51 And Laban said to Jacob, Behold this heap, and behold this pillar, which I have cast betwixt me and thee; 52 This heap be witness, and this pillar be witness, that I will not pass over this heap to thee, and that thou shalt not pass over this heap and this pillar unto me, for harm. 53 The God of Abraham, and the God of Nahor, the God of their father, judge betwixt us. And Jacob sware by the fear of his father Isaac. 54 Then Jacob offered sacrifice upon the mount, and called

his brethren to eat bread: and they did eat bread, and tarried all night in the mount. (Gen 31:44–54)

Although not alert to the link between the rule and the narrative, Levine's words about the rule capture the outcome of the dispute between Jacob and Laban. Levine writes, "The enactment of *šebuʿah, ʾissar* involves God in a binding agreement between parties through the words of the oath in his name. The attendant obligations occur in sequence: First, a person swears to enter into a binding agreement whose specific terms are then set forth in binding, written form. In effect, God is the guarantor of the agreement, whereas its performer, or performers are human."[10] The final agreement between Jacob and Laban is, I should emphasize, closely connected to Jacob's oath about the household gods in Rachel's possession. The sworn pact between the men comes about because, Jacob and Laban not knowing that Rachel had the gods, the oath concerning the misappropriated objects could not be fulfilled. All the ingredients for what constitutes the makeup of a man's oath in Numbers 30 are to be found in the narrative in Genesis 31.

WOMEN'S VOWS AND OATHS

Not knowing that his wife was hiding her father's household gods, Jacob supplied an example of someone swearing a sacred oath that rendered his wife subject to a death sentence (Gen 31:32): "If a man swear an oath to bind his soul with a bond; he shall not break his word, he shall do according to all that proceedeth out of his mouth" (Num 30:2). Laban accepted the validity of Jacob's oath about the household gods. That means that the life of a woman as a man's wife *and* as a man's daughter was at stake because of the oath. The rules in Numbers focus on a man and his wife and on a man and his daughter: "These are the statutes, which Yahweh commanded Moses, between a man and his wife, between the father and his daughter, being yet in her youth in her father's house" (Num 30:16). (We might have expected the sequence, father-daughter and then husband-wife, not the other way round, but Jacob's oath came after his marriage to Rachel and it related back to their recent residence in her father's house.) The gods were not found, so Rachel did not die. Her death, as indicated, occurred later when she gave birth to Benjamin. Rachel's end, however, brought back into consideration the previous time when her death seemed to be at hand because of Jacob's oath to Laban. On the occasion of the oath Rachel had claimed she was menstruating. It was a lie on her part to justify why she could not rise from the camel's saddle on which she was seated in order to conceal her father's household gods.

David Cotter states that Jacob in his ignorance inadvertently cursed Rachel and thereby predicted her death. Cotter thus affirms a direct link between her demise and the earlier oath.[11] There may, indeed, be a sense in which the oath was fulfilled with Rachel's death. The household gods were literally not found at the time of Laban's search, but they were certainly to be found on her. If we press the literal meaning of the oath—"with whomsoever thou findest thy gods shall not live" (Gen 31:32)—it came to fulfillment with her death when she gave birth to Benjamin. Jon Levenson notes that *Genesis Rabba* on 31:32 views Jacob's oath as bringing about Rachel's premature end.[12] (The deaths, actual or forthcoming, of Miriam, Aaron, and Moses have just received attention or will shortly receive attention by the Numbers narrator, Num 20:1, 12, 24–28, 27:13, 31:2.)

In the laws in Numbers 30 we first find a male vow or oath that is strictly binding. In focus are both Jacob's vow at Bethel and his oath to Laban. Next in Numbers 30 we have the case of a daughter's or a wife's vow or oath. In the story, Rachel is Laban's daughter and she is also Jacob's wife and the unwitting focus of Jacob's oath to Laban. In the law in Num 30:3–16 the concern is with a woman who makes a vow or an oath, and their binding nature is affected by her relationship to her father or husband. The topic of a woman's vow or oath brings in initially the role of a male because the matter is an outgrowth of the narrative. One issue that comes into reckoning in Numbers 30 is, should a daughter or a wife be affected if a father or a husband involves her in the vow or the oath? The answer is yes: "If a man vow a vow unto Yahweh, or swear an oath to bind his soul with a bond; he shall not break his word, he shall do according to all that proceedeth out of his mouth" (Num 30:2). It is Jacob's case exactly. That is, both Jacob's vow at Bethel and his later oath to Laban underlie the rule.

Another question, however, is, when the woman herself makes a vow or an oath, should she be held to the same level of accountability as a father or a husband when he makes one? The answer is a qualified no. In this instance the vow or oath need not be binding because a father can annul it:

> 3 If a woman also vow a vow unto Yahweh, and bind herself by a bond, being in her father's house in her youth; 4 And her father hear her vow, and her bond wherewith she hath bound her soul, and her father shall hold his peace at her: then all her vows shall stand, and every bond wherewith she hath bound her soul shall stand. 5 But if her father disallow her in the day that he

heareth; not any of her vows, or of her bonds wherewith she hath bound her soul, shall stand: and Yahweh shall forgive her, because her father disallowed her. (Num 30:3–5)

The same consideration applies to a wife's vow or oath. Her husband can void it if he moves to annul it on the day she makes it (Num 30:6–8). (The sequence is the more logical one of father-daughter and then husband-wife because the topic is not a direct outcome of the story.) The timeliness that is required to undo the vow or oath is probably linked to the recognition that, if Jacob had realized what he had done to his much-loved wife, he surely would have wanted to cancel his oath immediately because of its calamitous contents. The Numbers lawgiver would not have allowed him to do so, but there is found some limited scope in a woman's vow or oath to permit its cancellation should a husband or father—Laban was very concerned about his daughter's welfare (Gen 31:43, 44, 50)—find its contents equally calamitous. The severity involved in upholding vows and oaths in the biblical sources reflects the ancient reality that, in the absence of legal instruments, what a person said was of enormous significance in social and legal relations.

To go back to the Genesis incident: because it is understood that a male is held to his oath, Rachel would have been trapped. A question that rises naturally from hearing about the development in Jacob's history is, when might a wife not be trapped by an oath (or a vow)? The rules in Numbers 30 understandably take up the harshness of a husband's (Jacob's) oath (or vow) when he has unwittingly involved his wife. It is not likely that in the ordinary way of things a man would swear an oath that has terrible consequences for his spouse. Jacob's words on the occasion provide a major reason there is so much emphasis on the care to be exercised in making any oath (or vow). Jacob's oath cannot be undone, but there is leniency in holding a woman to hers. The atmosphere of the incidents in the life of Jacob, the father of the nation Israel, permeates the entire discussion about the subject of vows and oaths among later sons of Israel and their daughters and wives.

Genesis	Numbers
Sexual and religious seduction After the slaughter of the Hivite males on account of Shechem's seduction of Dinah, Jacob takes in the Hivite women and children. On his way to build the altar at Bethel, Jacob removes their gods (Gen 34:29, 35:2–4).	*Sexual and religious seduction* Moses exterminates the Midianite married women and their male children. Like the Moabite women in Numbers 25, the Midianite women had seduced the Israelites with their gods (Numbers 31).

The death of Rachel (following the slaughter of every adult male Hivite) triggers, we saw in discussing the preceding rules about vows and oaths, the interest in her near death because of her husband's oath. The topic is in line with Jacob's fear of losing sons and consequently losing Israel as a distinctive group when Simeon and Levi slaughtered the adult male Hivites. Each context, the flight from Laban (Genesis 31) and the incorporation of the Hivite women and children into Jacob's household (Genesis 34), involved importing foreign gods into Israel; first by the Aramean Rachel and then by the Hivite women (Gen 31:19, 34, 35:2).[13]

MIDIANITE WOMEN AND MALE CHILDREN

In Numbers 31, after every Midianite adult male has been slaughtered (Num 31:7), Moses has the married Midianite women and their male offspring killed as well because the women had seduced the Israelites into sacrificing to their gods (Num 31:16 refers back to the celebrations at Baal-Peor in Num 25:2, 3). Moses' zealousness contrasts with the laxer attitude on display by Jacob at Bethel, the "House of [Israel's] God," when Jacob was solely intent on removing the gods of the Hivite women, not the women themselves, from his encampment (Gen 35:1–4). Perhaps, too, there has been negative judgment on Jacob for not casting out the household gods that remained in Rachel's possession. No notice tells of their removal from Jacob's house.

As it happens, although Moses quickly moves to oppose it, a similarly lax attitude to Jacob's is also present in Numbers 31. In the Israelites' initial dealings with the Midianites, they kill only the Midianite adult males (which include the kings of Midian and the diviner Balaam). The judgment of the Numbers narrator appears to be that Simeon and Levi had not gone far enough in slaying only the adult male Hivites (Genesis 34). They should have destroyed the married women too. It is true that the Midianite women in Numbers are the ones who seduce the Israelite males, unlike Shechem, who seduced Jacob's daughter. There is nothing about any comparable seductive activity by a Hivite woman. Yet in Genesis 34, even if there is no awareness of seductive activity by any Hivite woman, it is Dinah who joins these foreign women, "the daughters of the land," and among them she becomes a seductress. Recall that Dinah was the one who took the initiative in visiting the Hivite women and made herself available to Shechem: "And Dinah the daughter of Leah, which she bare unto Jacob, went out to see the daughters of the land" (Gen 34:1). N. M. Sarna points out that the verb *yaṣa'* (to go out) in Gen 34:1 draws attention to Dinah's suspect behavior. Sarna comments, "Like its Akkadian and Aramaic equivalents, the verb can connote coquettish or promiscuous conduct." *Genesis Rabba* already interpreted "And Dinah went out" (Gen 34:1) as reminiscent of Gen 30:16 when "Leah went out" (to meet Jacob for her hired time of lovemaking). Like Leah, Dinah was angling. Pointing to their seductive potential, the phrase "the daughters of the land" in other texts indicates disapproval (Gen 24:3, 37, 27:46, 28:1, 6, 8).[14]

There is no mention again of the nonvirginal Dinah. The fact that she showed initiative in visiting the foreign group and had intercourse with the Canaanite Shechem suggests a negative evaluation of her by the Genesis narrator.[15] In any event, the Numbers narrator has Moses express anger against the nonvirginal Midianite women consistent with the ferocious antagonism to the Hivite males shown by Simeon and Levi. Thus Moses declaims, "Have ye saved all the women alive? Behold, these caused the sons of Israel, through the counsel of Balaam, to commit trespass against Yahweh in the matter of Peor.... Now therefore kill every male among the little ones, and kill every woman that hath known man by lying with him. But all the women children that have not known a man by lying with him keep alive for yourselves" (Num 31:15–18).

An even fiercer spirit than Simeon's and Levi's prevails in Numbers 31, as it did with Phinehas in Num 25:1–13. But even for Phinehas, zeal for Israelite purity was directed only at those Israelite men "who were joined unto Baal-peor," plus the Midianite woman, Cozbi, whom Zimri, the Simeonite, had brought into the camp, and Zimri himself (Num 25:5–8). The judgment emerging from Numbers 31 is that Jacob should have shown a comparable ferocity in Genesis 34 and not incorporated Hivite women and children into his household. The judgment may also prevail that the slaughter of those Israelites involved with the Moabites in Numbers 25 should have extended not just to the one Midianite woman, Cozbi, but also to the daughters of Moab with whom the Israelite men committed whoredom (Num 25:1). To be sure, the continuation of the story in Numbers 31 may cover this aspect of Numbers 25.

When Israel incorporates into its camp the virginal Midianite girls who are spared death, these women will doubtless enter into marriages with Israelite men. The reasoning is, presumably, that in mating with them there will be an increase in numbers of Israelite offspring. The increase will be in line with the blessing of many descendants that Jacob received at Bethel in Gen 35:11: "And God said unto him, I am God Almighty: be fruitful and multiply; a nation and a company of nations shall be of thee, and kings shall come out of thy loins." "Thy loins"—not from those of the Midianite kings, "Evi and Rekem, and Zur, and Hur, and Reba, five kings of Midian" (Num 31:8), but future Israelite kings, that is, in the monarchical period as recounted in their history in 1 Samuel through 2 Kings.

Zealous conduct in the interests of purity shows up too in the instruction to use the water of separation containing the ashes of the Red Heifer for those Israelite warriors who have been in contact with the slain among the Midianites. Recall that the background for the Red Heifer institution (Numbers 19) is Jacob (who becomes Israel) attaining the birthright from Esau (who becomes Edom), in return for Esau being saved from dying because of his failure to obtain his habitual blood dish. The background model for the treatment of the Midianites, in turn, is Simeon's and Levi's slaughter of the Hivite males, that is, the development just after Jacob feared that Esau would avenge himself for losing his birthright to Jacob. Instead, Esau was welcoming, and Jacob then purchased land from the Hivites and built an altar on it (Gen 33:18–20).

The booty from both the Hivites in Gen 34:28, 29 and the Midianites in Num 31:21–24 is divided among the Israelites. Numbers 31 goes into much detail about its impurity, in line again with the attitude expressed in Gen 35:2: "Then Jacob said unto his household, and to all that were with him, Put away the strange gods that are among you, and be clean, and change your garments." The concern with defilement is extended in Numbers 31 to cover all of the acquired Midianite possessions. Fire, for example, is used to purify the metals the Israelites take from the Midianites and water to purify those objects not suitable for exposure to fire. From the Numbers perspective, in Gen 35:2, water would have been used in purifying the people and possibly fire in disposing of the cast-off clothes. Or perhaps Numbers is critical of what transpired in Gen 35:4 when Jacob merely buried the earrings of the Hivite women—he should have had them purified with fire. The Levites in Numbers 31 play a major role in religious affairs because of their ancestor Levi's praiseworthy attitude in Genesis 34, and they too receive a share of the booty (Num 31:29, 30).

In Gen 35:4 Jacob's household gives over to him "all the strange [Hivite] gods which were in their hand, and all their earrings which were in their ears; and Jacob hid them under the oak which was by Shechem." Jacob at the time was on the way to Bethel to build an altar to God, so there is an accompanying aura of holiness (Gen 35:1–3). Presumably, the oak at the place Shechem with the jewelry under it serves as a geographical pointer to recall the historical destruction of the Hivites and to indicate also freedom from defilement. A similar development takes place after the destruction of the Midianites in Num 31:49–54. Just as no man of Jacob's house loses his life in the action against the Hivites in Genesis 34 despite Jacob's fear that he would lose all the males, so too those who destroy the Midianites all remain alive: "And there lacketh not one man of us" (Num 31:49). In gratitude and to remember this fortunate outcome, but also as a marker of a higher order of holiness than prevails in Gen 35:4, the warriors bring to the sanctuary "jewels of gold, chains, and bracelets, rings, earrings, and tablets, to make an atonement." Moses and Eleazar take the jewelry and place it in the sanctuary as "a memorial for the children of Israel before Yahweh" (Num 31:50, 54).

11

REUBEN'S LEGACY (NUMBERS 32-36)

Throughout Numbers there is allusion to events in Genesis because the later era links up with the earlier, legendary time of the nations' founding fathers. Numbers 32–36 look back to significant events in the lives of Reuben and Joseph as described in Genesis 35–50. There is a negative view of Reuben's loss of firstborn status (revealed in the allotment of Reuben's tribal inheritance in Numbers 32–34) and a positive view of Reuben saving Joseph's life from the threat of his murderous brothers (revealed in the establishment of the cities of asylum and the homicide laws in Numbers 35). Events after Israel leaves Egypt on the way to acquiring the land of Canaan mirror preceding patriarchal history. In Numbers, then, patriarchal as well as post-Exodus incidents receive scrutiny.

The writing-up of Genesis to be followed by the composition of Exodus through 2 Kings will have been a process intertwined from the outset in the overall preparation of Genesis–2 Kings. Gen 35:11 ("a nation and a company of nations shall be of thee, and kings shall come out of thy loins") thinks forward, we noted, to the monarchical period of Israelite history contained in 1 Samuel through 2 Kings. So many events in the lives of the Genesis patriarchs occurred in Egypt and Canaan. Developments were often morally troubling, with much unsatisfactory conduct committed by the patriarchs themselves. Aside from exhibiting craftiness of a decidedly dubious character, some of them also contracted incestuous unions: those of Abraham with his half sister, Jacob with two women who were sisters, Judah with his daughter-in-law, and Amram, Moses' father, with his father's sister. Moses in Leviticus 18 and 20 prohibits such unions because they came about in Egypt or Canaan (Gen 20:12, 29:21–30, 38:15–26; Lev 18:11, 12, 15, 18, 20:12, 17, 19, 20; Num 26:59). The seeming contradiction that these unions are condemned because the Egyptians and the Canaanites entered into them (Lev 18:3, 24–30, 20:23)—yet we find that the patriarchs also undertook them—is resolved precisely on account of the fact that the patriarchs contracted the unions while living among these foreigners. The lawgiver on some level excuses the fathers of the nation because, although he views milieu as exercising a baneful influence, he also sees it as a mitigating factor in the lives they lived there. The implied judgment is that the patriarchs could not escape their deplorable environment.[1]

In outline, the following sketch of the lives of Jacob-Israel, Reuben, and Joseph in Genesis 35–45 is relevant to the write-up in Numbers 32–36 of Israel's history just before the conquest of Canaan, particularly events affecting the descendants of Reuben and Joseph.

Genesis 35–45	Numbers 32–36
Inheritance and cattle Israel is in transit, and Reuben has intercourse with his father's concubine, an act that will affect his inheritance. In the listing of Jacob's twelve sons, Reuben is cited as firstborn. Esau and Jacob bury their father, Isaac, whose firstborn, Esau, has his future lineage listed. Jacob and Esau are not able to dwell in the same land because each has many cattle. Esau travels to Mount Seir, which has good cattle land, and settles there. His brother Jacob-Israel's journey to Egypt is about to begin (Gen 35:22–36:43).	*Inheritance and cattle* The Reubenites and Gadites journey east of the Jordan with many cattle and petition to secure their inheritance there because it is good cattle land. In return, to assuage Moses' anger at their request, they promise to assist their brother tribes to settle west of the Jordan. There is also recall of Israel's transit from Egypt to their final encampment east of the Jordan as they prepare to destroy the religious objects of the Canaanites, possess their land, and arrange for each tribe's allotted portion in it (Numbers 32–34).
Manslaughter Under threat of murder by his brothers, Joseph ends up in Egypt lost to Jacob-Israel's family (Genesis 37).	*Manslaughter* The Levites acquire cities of asylum for manslayers, and there are laws about homicide (Numbers 35).
Loss of inheritance Joseph's removal to Egypt held out the prospect of permanent loss of his patrimony (Genesis 37–45).	*Loss of inheritance* Descendants of Joseph face permanent loss of their tribal inheritance (Numbers 35 and 36).

An aim of the Numbers narrator is to ensure that when Canaan is acquired as Israelite land the ideal rules that Moses constructs on the basis of contemporary and past conduct can apply there so that Israelite behavior will change for the better. When in Numbers 32 the two tribes, Reuben and Gad, seek to acquire land east of the Jordan, Moses views their request as discouraging the other tribes from acquiring land west of the Jordan. Moses tells them that they are repeating the mistakes of their fathers, who, listening to the spies' report about the fearful inhabitants of Canaan, discouraged them from going forward (Num 32:8 referring back to the spies in Numbers 13). Moses nonetheless reaches a compromise with them. Leveen states, "The past must be recalled in specific and polemically useful ways."[2] Her statement about how past events in Numbers and Exodus are sometimes singled out for special attention is also true for incidents going back to Genesis. At the same time, corrections have to be made and are made. Moses comes to an agreement with the Reubenites and Gadites, who arrange to settle in good cattle land east of the Jordan in return for their military assistance. In earlier times Esau and Jacob, too, had separated amicably and, after burying their father, Esau settled in good cattle land in the hill country of Seir (Gen 36:8).

Genesis	Numbers
Inheritance and cattle Israel is in transit and Reuben has intercourse with his father's concubine, an act that will affect his inheritance. In the listing of Jacob's twelve sons, Reuben is cited as firstborn. Esau and Jacob bury their father, Isaac, whose firstborn, Esau, has his future lineage listed. Jacob and Esau are not able to dwell in the same land because each has many cattle. Esau travels to Mount Seir, which has good cattle land, and settles there. His brother Jacob-Israel's journey to Egypt is about to begin (Gen 35:22–36:43).	*Inheritance and cattle* The Reubenites and Gadites journey east of the Jordan with many cattle and petition to secure their inheritance there because it is good cattle land. In return, to assuage Moses' anger at their request, they promise to assist their brother tribes to settle west of the Jordan. There is also recall of Israel's transit from Egypt to their final encampment east of the Jordan as they prepare to destroy the religious objects of the Canaanites, possess their land, and arrange for each tribe's allotted portion in it (Numbers 32–34).

THE FUTURE LIVELIHOODS OF THE REUBENITES AND THE GADITES; ALSO OF THE OTHER TRIBES

In Numbers 32, after slaughter is visited upon the Midianites a second time, when Moses orders that Midianite women who have experienced sexual intercourse must be killed (Numbers 31), focus falls on the future life of the Reubenites (and Gadites). It is not surprising that the interest at this point in Reuben's tribal inheritance is tied to the fact that in Gen 35:22 Reuben's wrongful intercourse with his father's concubine Bilhah, caused Jacob to alter how Reuben's future inheritance would play out in relation to those of his brothers (Gen 49:3, 4). One outcome is given concrete expression in Numbers 32: in keeping with the twist in Reuben's fortunes in Genesis, his descendants' inheritance also takes an unexpected turn. To Moses' initial, intense anger, they seek to settle separately from the other tribes on the east side of the Jordan on account of their many cattle.

The links between Reuben in Genesis and the Reubenites in Numbers can be reinforced, but first it is helpful to take stock of the wider picture in Genesis 25 through Genesis 36. In this part of the overall Genesis narrative, we have intertwined accounts of the lives of Jacob and Esau, from the struggle in their mother's womb to each receiving a paternal blessing (Gen 27:29, 40), to Esau settling permanently in Edom and Jacob dwelling in Canaan but soon to leave for Egypt. In Genesis 36, just after Jacob and Esau bury their father, Isaac, the descendants of Esau are listed. David Cotter states, "The intention seems to be to sum up the life and inheritance of the non-chosen son before moving on to an extended treatment of what happened to the favored son."[3] We learn that Esau settled in the hill country of Seir on account of its suitability for cattle (Gen 36:6–8).

In Genesis, the firstborn of Isaac, Esau, loses out to Jacob as primary son, and in the next generation the firstborn of Jacob, Reuben, loses out to Joseph as primary son because he lay with Jacob's concubine (Gen 35:22).[4] Just as the descendants of the demoted Esau separated from the descendants of his brother Jacob because they possessed many cattle (Genesis 36), so in Numbers the descendants of the demoted Reuben separate from their relatives and seek to settle east of the Jordan because they possess many cattle (Num 32:1, 4). Moses initially protests vehemently to the Reubenites about their request on the grounds that they are jeopardizing the other tribes' inheritance because they will not be available to aid their brother tribes in capturing the land west of the Jordan. Moses desists once the Reubenites (and Gadites) agree to contribute to the military effort. A noteworthy contrast is that between Moses' immediate, outspoken objection to the Reubenites' proposal and Jacob's silence in reaction to Reuben's seduction of his concubine (Gen 35:22). As we saw, Moses, in dealing with the Midianite women's sexual experience (Numbers 31), is a much more aggressive leader than Jacob when he had to deal with Shechem's sexual violation of Dinah. Moses is zealous in a way that Jacob was not in affirming the nation's unique identity, one often bound up with sexual conduct.

OVERVIEW OF NUMBERS 32–36 IN RELATION TO GENESIS 35–37

Numbers 33 recounts Israel's travels and looks back at the Exodus from Egypt from a point in time when preparations are being made to establish final camp east of the Jordan in anticipation of permanent settlement west of the Jordan. The Israelites are to destroy Canaanite religious icons, aim to possess Canaan, and arrange for each tribe's future allotment in it. The anti-Canaanite bias at this point in Numbers may owe its inspiration to the account in Genesis of Esau's earlier migration to the southeast of Canaan (Seir), specifically, to the involvement of Esau with Canaanite wives: "Esau took his wives of the daughters of Canaan; Adah the daughter of Elon the Hittite. . . . And Adah bare to Esau Eliphaz" (Gen 36:1–5). Canaanite wives were, after all, of much concern to Isaac and Rebekah. At one point, Esau married two (Canaanite) Hittite women who made "life bitter for Isaac and Rebekah" (Gen 26:35). When Rebekah complained to Isaac that her life was no good to her should Jacob take unacceptable foreign women, Isaac "called Jacob, and blessed him, and charged him, and said unto him, Thou shalt not take a wife of the daughters of Canaan" (Gen 27:46–28:1). In any event, Numbers 34 lays out boundaries and selects chieftains from each Israelite tribe to apportion future towns and allotments in a conquered Canaan. Like Esau-Edom settling in Seir in Genesis (and taking Canaanite wives), Jacob-Israel looks forward in Numbers to settling in Canaan (but, in contrast, is ordered to avoid contact with Canaanite culture).

In Israel's earlier journeying in Gen 35:22–29, Reuben, we noted, seduced his father's concubine Bilhah. We are then given the list of the twelve sons of Jacob, with Reuben cited as firstborn and Bilhah mentioned with the other mothers of Jacob's sons. Esau and Jacob bury their father, Isaac, and with that event we have the passing of a previous generation and a looking ahead to the future generations of Esau and Jacob. The historian Josephus breaks off his retelling of the contents of the Book of Genesis at the end of Genesis 35, and H. St. J. Thackerey wonders if the Greek Genesis was once divided at this point.[5]

Whether that is so or not, it is an understandable division, as the treatment of Genesis by the Numbers narrator shows.

Genesis 36 enumerates Esau's sons and grandsons, and Genesis 37 switches to the history of Jacob's sons, in particular, to the infighting among them when Reuben plays a critical role in keeping Joseph safe from his murderous brothers. Attention will also focus, in Genesis 48, on two grandsons of Jacob, Joseph's Ephraim and Manasseh. Numbers 35, in turn, addresses issues arising from the hostility to Joseph that dominates Genesis 37, a hostility among brothers that certainly has its precedent in Jacob's relationship with Esau and one in which the Numbers narrator has already shown a considerable interest (see chapter 8). Numbers 36, in turn (and as the last topic in the Book of Numbers), addresses a problem of inheritance that arose for Jacob's descendants through his grandson, Manasseh, Joseph's son.

MURDER AND MANSLAUGHTER

How do we account for the not at all obvious move from the topic of possessing land to the topic of homicide in Numbers 35? We might take stock of the following lineup. Both Reuben's history in Numbers 32 (place of final settlement and possession of cattle) and Jacob-Israel's in Numbers 33–34 (anticipation of final settlement in the land of Canaan) mirror matters in Esau's history in Genesis 36 (place of final settlement and possession of cattle). Numbers 35 (about homicide), in turn, pays attention to Genesis 37, especially Reuben's actions in saving Joseph from being murdered by his brothers.

The narrator in Numbers 35 first continues his interest in the topic of possessing land by singling out the special possession that the Levites in Canaan are to receive. They are to settle in certain cities with attached pastureland for their cattle. Six of these cities are to be places of refuge for manslayers, three of them, we might note, in Reubenite and Gadite territory. The role of the Levites proves to be important because of notions of impartiality in judgment and its lack in Genesis 37. Numbers 35, then, looks back, through the prism of the homicide laws, at the history of Jacob's family as recounted in Genesis 37, with Reuben looming large in the concerns the Numbers narrator-lawgiver takes up. Recall again that a number of Joseph's brothers seek to slay him but do not carry out their plan because Reuben intervenes. Reuben causes them to waver between their wish to kill Joseph and their uncertainty as to whether or not to do so. In the end, the aims of those brothers set on killing Joseph are thwarted because he disappears.

Genesis	Numbers
Manslaughter Under threat of murder by his brothers, Joseph ends up in Egypt lost to Jacob-Israel's family (Genesis 37).	*Manslaughter* The Levites acquire cities of asylum for manslayers, and there are laws about homicide (Num 35:9–34).

Underlying Numbers 35 is the question, what if Joseph had died, either in the pit or after he disappeared from it? Would the offense done to him be murder or manslaughter, and how is the matter to be judged? In Gen 37:18, we learn that the brothers of Joseph "conspired to kill him." (The rare verb *hithnakal*, "to deal deceitfully, in wily fashion," is employed, one that Num 25:18 uses of the Midianites at Baal Peor, who deal in wily fashion with the later sons of Israel to lure them into idolatry.) Seeing Joseph approaching from a distance, nine of his brothers decide to kill him, throw his body into a pit, and cover up the murder so that it would be difficult to determine what actually caused his death. They would put it about that he was the victim of a wild beast. Reuben, however, urges them "not to strike him to the life," not to "shed any blood" (Gen 37:20, 21). They should simply cast him alive into the pit before making any final decision about him. Reuben's commendable intention was to stall in the hope that he could rescue Joseph from the murderous brothers and restore him to his father. Responding to Reuben's counsel, the brothers assault Joseph, remove the coat that marked him as special, and cast him alive into a pit until such time as they make up their minds what to do with him. The attitudes and actions on display prompt the Numbers lawgiver to come up with criteria for innocence and guilt should Joseph have died. If Joseph had succumbed in the pit, Reuben would be innocent of murder because he had no intention of killing Joseph. The nine other brothers, however, would be guilty.

The rules in Num 35:10–34 about the cities of refuge and the laws of homicide read as follows:

> 10 Speak unto the sons of Israel, and say unto them, When ye be come over Jordan into the land of Canaan; 11 Then ye shall appoint you cities to be cities of refuge for you; that the slayer may flee thither, which killeth any person at unawares. 12 And they shall be unto you cities for refuge from the avenger; that the manslayer die not, until he stand before the congregation in judgment. 13 And of these cities which ye shall give six cities shall ye have for refuge. 14 Ye shall give three cities on this side Jordan, and three cities shall

ye give in the land of Canaan, which shall be cities of refuge. 15 These six cities shall be a refuge, both for the sons of Israel, and for the stranger, and for the sojourner among them: that every one that killeth any person unawares may flee thither. 16 And if he smite him with an instrument of iron, so that he die, he is a murderer: the murderer shall surely be put to death. 17 And if he smite him with throwing a stone, wherewith he may die, and he die, he is a murderer: the murderer shall surely be put to death. 18 Or if he smite him with an hand weapon of wood, wherewith he may die, and he die, he is a murderer: the murderer shall surely be put to death. 19 The revenger of blood himself shall slay the murderer: when he meeteth him, he shall slay him. 20 And if he thrust him of hatred, or hurl at him by laying of wait, that he die; 21 Or in enmity smite him with his hand, that he die: he that smote him shall surely be put to death; for he is a murderer: the revenger of blood shall slay the murderer, when he meeteth him. 22 But if he thrust him suddenly without enmity, or have cast upon him any thing without laying of wait, 23 Or with any stone, wherewith a man may die, seeing him not, and cast it upon him, that he die, and was not his enemy, neither sought his harm: 24 Then the congregation shall judge between the slayer and the revenger of blood according to these judgments: 25 And the congregation shall deliver the slayer out of the hand of the revenger of blood, and the congregation shall restore him to the city of his refuge, whither he was fled: and he shall abide in it unto the death of the high priest, which was anointed with the holy oil. 26 But if the slayer shall at any time come without the border of the city of his refuge, whither he was fled; 27 And the revenger of blood find him without the borders of the city of his refuge, and the revenger of blood kill the slayer; he shall not be guilty of blood: 28 Because he should have remained in the city of his refuge until the death of the high priest: but after the death of the high priest the slayer shall return into the land of his possession. 29 So these things shall be for a statute of judgment unto you throughout your generations in all your dwellings. 30 Whoso killeth any person, the murderer shall be put to death by the mouth of witnesses: but one witness shall not testify against any person to cause him to die. 31 Moreover ye shall take no satisfaction [ransom] for the life of a murderer, which is guilty of death: but he shall be surely put to death. 32 And ye shall take no satisfaction [ransom] for him that is fled to the city of his refuge, that he should come again to dwell in the land, until the death of the priest. 33 So ye shall not pollute the land wherein ye are: for blood it defileth the land: and the land cannot be cleansed of the blood that is shed therein, but by the blood of him that shed it. 34 Defile not therefore the land which ye shall inhabit, wherein I dwell: for I Yahweh dwell among the sons of Israel.

PREMEDITATED HOMICIDE

Num 35:16–21 provide criteria for what constitutes intentional and unintentional homicide. The first example that comes under scrutiny is where the victim is struck in such a way that he dies from the blow. If, in Reuben's language (Gen 37:21), the striking "to the life" consists of a blow with iron, stone, or wood it is objective proof that the one doing the striking is a murderer (Num 35:16–18). This part of the rule can be viewed as a response to Reuben's clear-cut statement that his brothers should not strike down Joseph so as to kill him. In a situation like Joseph's, where the victim is found in a pit, the issue has to turn on the role of prior malice, which certainly showed up in the brothers' attitude. To be sure, if the brothers had killed Joseph, as was their initial intention, the testimony of Reuben—more sensible and ethical than the brothers in the stand he took—would not have counted according to Num 35:30 because he would have been the only witness ("one witness shall not testify against any person to cause him to die"). Reuben's exceptional stance prompts the lawgiver in Numbers to raise the problem of testimony in the absence of more than one witness.

Num 35:20 next speaks of intentional killing in terms of how the murderer "pushed him in hate or hurled [*Hiphil šalak*] at him when lying in wait." The description is close to what the brothers intended to do: "When they saw him [Joseph] afar off, even before he came near unto them, they conspired against him to slay him . . . and throw [*Hiphil šalak*] him into some pit" (Gen 37:18, 20). They did indeed lie in wait with malicious intent. Num 35:21 then speaks of the murderer striking "with his hand in enmity," and again the criterion is close to the brothers' action against Joseph. They forcefully take hold of him, strip off his coat, and cast him into the pit. They are still intent on killing him. Only Reuben's plea causes them to postpone the moment.

UNINTENDED HOMICIDE

Num 35:22, 23 proceed to consider criteria for unintentional killing, where the slayer has acted "without malice" but the person dies: "But if he thrust him suddenly without enmity, or have cast upon him any thing without laying of wait, Or with any stone, wherewith a man may die, seeing him not, and cast it upon him, that he die, and was not his enemy, neither sought his harm." If Reuben helped to cast Joseph into the pit, as he probably did—Reuben's actual words are "do not strike him to the life," so they may be construed as giving license to assault Joseph—Reuben would come under this description of not seeking to deliver a fatal blow because his intention was to take him back to his father, not to kill him. He was not Joseph's mortal enemy but recognized that some physical action was required to appease his brothers and possibly, up to a point, some animosity to Joseph on his part.

The rule may also have focused on absence of malice because the brothers' malice is so prominent. Theirs raises the issue of its lack. If the brothers had assaulted Joseph in line with their initial intention, it is hard to believe they would not have killed him (nine to one were dangerous odds). In terms of how the story plays out, however, the only unwitting aspect of the brothers' behavior is that by casting Joseph into the pit they ended up actually saving him from their murderous intent because passing traders removed him from it.

It is striking that Numbers 35 has nothing on the far-from-uncommon offense of intentional but unpremeditated homicide, as in a sudden, deadly quarrel. If the lawgiver wished to respond to the social problems of ancient Israelite society, the gap is a serious omission.[6] The surprising silence can be accounted for by noting that this kind of offense does not arise in Genesis 37. Premeditated action is very much the pattern in the brothers' stance toward Joseph, but sudden enmity is not a feature.

THE AVENGER OF BLOOD

In the narrative in Genesis 37 Joseph does not die, but the circumstances are such that his death very much comes into consideration. The brothers are initially intent on murdering him and covering up the deed. When they last see him, he is alive in the pit, having been assaulted and thrown into it by them. Eventually, however, they discover that he has disappeared. There is no body but, given the wilderness setting, they have reason to believe he is dead. (I agree with Ron Pirson's assessment that since the brothers were not staying in the area of the pit, they "cannot have pulled Joseph out of the pit, or have sold him.")[7] To escape their father's vengeance for Joseph's seeming end, they persuade Jacob that Joseph has died by *force majeure,* the victim of a wild beast. Yet, equally to the point, the brothers know that their initial hostility against Joseph has, to all appearances, led to a terrible result.

We should take stock of another feature of the Numbers rule in light of the fact that the brothers felt constrained to produce evidence (the blood-stained garment) to their father that they had no hand in Joseph's disastrous disappearance. One implication of their action is the recognition that Jacob was duty bound to find out who was responsible had he concluded that there had been a murder and then to avenge it. No other legislative authority existed at the time to which the person could be handed over. We should not read the rule in Numbers as representing an early stage of Hebrew law, as is commonly done, but see it as formulated in response to the narrator-lawgiver looking back on the patriarchal age. It is he who adduces a law or custom whereby Jacob was bound to seek out the person or persons responsible for Joseph's death. Thus I do not think that Hans Jochen Boecker is correct to state a widely held view that "local courts [in the time when Numbers was composed] could evidently neither eliminate nor integrate into their own legal competence an important legal institution [the role of the avenger of blood]." No such easy correlation can plausibly be made between law and society in dealing with biblical sources.[8] The blood-stained garment that was given to Jacob, however, obviated the need for him to pursue the matter further. In the law, the carrying out of the death sentence is the responsibility of the avenger of blood, that is, a relative of the victim, and much emphasis is given to the blood: "Ye shall not pollute the land wherein ye are: for blood it defileth the land: and the land cannot be cleansed of the blood that is shed therein, but by the blood of him that shed it" (Num 35:33). The shed blood of Joseph is a much-highlighted feature of his alleged death, and Jacob, his close relative, had to accept that the evidence furnished him did not in this instance warrant vengeance for the bloodshed.

FORMAL ADJUDICATION

In the Numbers rule there has to be adjudication by the congregation in deciding whether the avenger of blood can act against the killer as murderer or whether the avenger must refrain because the killer is entitled to seek residence in a city of refuge as a manslayer (Num 35:24). Features of the Joseph narrative may also be relevant to this part of the rule. A disturbing aspect of the story is the poor judgments being made. As head of the family Jacob groundlessly downgrades Joseph's brothers by favoring Joseph with a special garment. The brothers, in turn, unilaterally condemn Joseph and wrongfully take matters into their own hands (Gen 37:2). Further flawed judgment follows when Jacob is misled into the error of pronouncing Joseph's death because of the blood on his garment. The Numbers rule, in contrast, carefully spells out a need for proper adjudication: the manslayer may not die "until he stands before the congregation in judgment" (Num 35:12). All aspects of the relationship between victim and accused are to be properly assessed by an impartial inquiry.

THE LEVITICAL CITIES OF ASYLUM

A manslayer cannot leave a city of refuge before the death of the high priest (Num 35:25). If he does, he can be killed by the victim's relative in his role as avenger of the blood that has been shed. The guilt for the manslayer's death at the hands of the avenger attaches not to the latter, but to the manslayer because he irresponsibly left the city. I am not so sure that Pamela Barmash is correct when she states that "any killer of a human being, even accidentally, was considered guilty." She sees the problem when she asks, "If he [a killer] is found to have killed accidentally, why should he be forced to remain in the city of refuge?"[9] I wonder whether the assumption in Numbers 35 is that, although the asylum resident has been involved in someone's death, culpability for it has proved difficult to determine except in clear-cut cases where it is indeed wholly accidental. Joseph's situation raises the issues. The brothers see themselves as responsible for his disappearance. They had sought to kill him but did not accomplish the deed. Even they saw that culpability for his presumed death lay with them. The problem points to the need to offer persons like them a place of refuge from an avenger of blood. The law's major concern with blood mirrors the central role of Joseph's blood in the story. In short, it makes sense that actors like the brothers should have restricted freedom and remain in a city of asylum, potentially for a long time.

Even more to the point is Reuben's role in the story. If we ask why the six Levitical cities of refuge come into the rule at all, we might recall Reuben's distraught remark on finding that Joseph was no longer in the pit, "The child is not; and I, whither shall I go?" (Gen 37:30). Reuben himself brings up the idea that, if Joseph is dead, he has to flee. He expresses the notion that, although he did not kill Joseph, he bears the moral responsibility for his disappearance and presumed death. Further, to repeat, he expresses the concern that because he is guilty he must flee to somewhere. Reuben's remark is a precursor to the idea of the city of refuge, the place to which someone bearing the moral onus of death without actually having murdered must go.

An answer to Reuben's dilemma, then, about where to go in some comparable situation occurring among Israelites after they settle in the land of Canaan might be, to a city of refuge. These cities belong to the Levites, but three of them, that is, no less than half of them, are to be located in the geographical area east of the Jordan, where the Reubenites (with the Gadites and the half tribe of Joseph's Manasseh are to settle). This is a puzzling division. As Milgrom points out, "The two and a half tribes east of Jordan are to have the same number of asylums as the more numerous—and more populous—tribes in Cisjordan."[10] The curious, imbalanced division may reflect Reuben's original situation. Even if in the end he contributed to Joseph's fate of being sold to Egypt as a slave, Reuben deserved recognition for the stance he had taken against his murderous brothers: "And Reuben answered them [his brothers], saying, Spake I not unto you, saying, Do not sin against the child; and ye would not hear? therefore, behold, also his blood is required" (Gen 42:22). Reuben includes himself in the culpability for the crime. The justness he exhibited in the matter, however, is rewarded, we might infer, with three cities of refuge east of the Jordan because such cities stand for rescue from vengeance for someone like Reuben who is not fully implicated in a homicide. Practical considerations appear not to be relevant to the three cities being awarded to those living east of the Jordan. Instead, Reuben's virtuous role in rescuing Joseph from death at the hands of his brothers may be because his situation highlights the need for such cities.

One of the western cities of refuge is, we learn from Josh 20:7, Shechem, the very place in Gen 37:12–14 from which Joseph set out to meet up with his brothers and confront their murderous intent. In Josh 20:7 Shechem is attributed to the tribe of Ephraim, while in Josh 17:2, 7 it is attributed to Manasseh. Both Ephraim and Manasseh are sons of Joseph. Shechem is also the place where Joseph is buried (Josh 24:32). The connection between the Joseph story in Genesis 37 and the laws about homicide in Numbers 35 may be relevant to the inclusion of Shechem as a city of refuge. The issue of protecting a manslayer in Numbers 35 had its beginnings in that city.

Why are the cities of asylum under the charge of the Levites? In the story, Jacob's favoritism toward Joseph ruled him out as a source of justice for dealing with his sons' hatred of their brother. Yet, having *patria potestas*, Jacob held sway over the *iudicium domesticum*. Levi was one of the brothers originally set on getting rid of Joseph, but his descendants later proved to be loyal to Yahweh in the matter of the Golden Calf. On the occasion, they even carried out executions on Yahweh's behalf. The Levites are thus seen as capable of demonstrating proper partiality in judging capital cases among the Israelites (Exod 32:26–29; Deut 33:8–11). Cities of asylum stand precisely for this lack of bias in judgment, and the Levites, fittingly, are those who oversee the administration of justice for the wider family of the later sons of Jacob-Israel.

PAYMENT OF MONEY

The law prohibits the payment of a ransom (satisfaction) either in return for freeing someone who has been found guilty of murder or for releasing a manslayer from a city of asylum before the high priest's death. (With the latter's death the manslayer is freed both from the city of asylum and from the victim's avenging relative.) Why should the issue of payment arise? Again, the narrative proves illuminating. Although the notion of ransom for release from a sentence of death might well be familiar to the actual world of the compiler of Numbers—we just do not know—it is nonetheless telling that the equation between money and killing a person turns up in Genesis 37.

Invoking a ghastly quibble about not getting rid of their own flesh, Judah persuades his brothers—with the exception of Reuben—to refrain from killing Joseph and to sell him instead (Gen 37:26). It is money for a life. Theirs is a quasi-judicial attempt at some kind of justice: they will not spill the blood of their "own brother and our flesh" (Gen 37:27). They will, however, save his life by receiving money instead. Numbers 35 considers the proper and much more impartial juridical side of the matter that should prevail among later Israelites. There should be no equating of a man's life with money.

What should be done if the victim has, in fact, unlike Joseph, died? should there be scope for releasing the manslayer for payment of money? Just as the brothers were not, in fact, successful in their self-serving and quite unjust aim of substituting money for killing, so there should be no comparable exchange when the issue of a killer's release from his fate comes up for consideration. The brothers equate payment with not killing Joseph. The juridical position is that should the victim die, monetary compensation cannot serve as a substitute either for relief from a sentence of death or for early release from a city of refuge. The rule constitutes a quite specific reaction against the nefarious attempt by these first sons of Israel to achieve what they judged to be a satisfactory substitution of money for a person's life.

Milgrom salutes the higher standards in the biblical rule, with its rejection of ransom, in contrast to the supposedly inferior role of ransom to be found among Near Eastern neighbors. But we are simply not comparing like with like. It is wholly understandable why the dismissal of a ransom payment is ruled out in Numbers 35 because of the intense and quite particular interest in the nation's first family. The refusal of ransom cannot automatically be understood as a rejection of a practice in the society to which the Numbers narrator belonged or in another society known to him. The Numbers rule is an ideal construction and may well be contrary to the realities of the world in which Numbers was composed. There are many examples in Near Eastern law codes of the payment of ransom in lieu of a death sentence (for example, HL 1–5; MAL A10 and B2) and one example in Exod 21:28–32: the owner of an ox that has been known to gore can pay a ransom instead of being put to death if the ox has killed a person. The offender in Numbers 35 is singled out as an instance in which ransom is not acceptable because of the role of money in the brothers' decision to obtain some for Joseph instead of killing him.

DEATH OF THE HIGH PRIEST

A most puzzling aspect of the rule about the manslayer is that he has to remain in a city of refuge until the death of the high priest. The time spent could be two days or twenty years, an astonishing disparity however we reckon it. The problem is slurred over by commentators in their assumption that somehow the sacred official's (natural) death atones for the blood-guilt attaching to the manslayer. Why could the arrangement for release not be some sacrificial ritual involving animal blood, which takes place after a certain specified time?

The guilt attaching to Joseph's brothers for their offense against him may again provide illumination because they fear vengeance from Joseph after their father dies. Jacob is the person who, according to Gen 50:15–20, commanded the brothers to seek forgiveness from Joseph for their offense. Joseph responded to their request, however, by telling them that only God could forgive them:

> 15 And when Joseph's brethren saw that their father was dead, they said, Joseph will peradventure hate us, and will certainly requite us all the evil which we did unto him. 16 And they sent a messenger unto Joseph, saying, Thy father did command before he died, saying, 17 So shall ye say unto Joseph, Forgive, I pray thee now, the trespass of thy brethren, and their sin; for they did unto thee evil: and now, we pray thee, forgive the trespass of the servants of the God of thy father. And Joseph wept when they spake unto him. 18 And his brethren also went and fell down before his face; and they said, Behold, we be thy servants. 19 And Joseph said unto them, Fear not: for am I in the place of God? 20 But as for you, ye thought evil against me; but God meant it unto good, to bring to pass, as it is this day, to save much people alive.

After the cult has been established, the request for forgiveness in Genesis 50 elicits in Num 35:26–28 the concern with what is required to free a manslayer from the guilt of bloodshed. Just as the death of Jacob, the father of the nation, triggered the issue of amnesty within his family because of the brothers' fear that Joseph would seek vengeance, so the signal for the release of a manslayer is the death of the high priest, the nation's preeminent sacred authority. His demise signals God's amnesty and the removal of any requital for a manslayer's act of bloodshed. When Jacob died his concern about the brothers' actions against Joseph came to an end. Equally to the point, the notion of forgiveness arose at his death. The death of the high priest, in turn, signifies closure for a son of Israel who has shed blood. In sum, in response to Joseph's acknowledging, after Jacob's death, that he is not in the place of God to forgive his brothers their misdeed, the lawgiver in Numbers has the institute of the cult take on that function and grant release from guilt.

JOSEPH'S LOSS OF INHERITANCE AND HIS DESCENDANTS' LOSS

Numbers 36, which comes after the seemingly unrelated subject of homicide in Numbers 35, brings about a change in the new inheritance law that had been introduced in Numbers 27. The latter rule had altered an existing notion that daughters could not inherit in the absence of sons. The reason for the introduction of the amendment in Numbers 36 is that the change to the law permitting daughters to become heirs has the potential to bring about another instance of unjust enrichment, "a benefit obtained from another, not intended as a gift and not legally justifiable."[11]

Genesis	Numbers
Loss of inheritance Joseph's removal to Egypt held out the prospect of permanent loss of his patrimony (Genesis 37–45).	*Loss of inheritance* Descendants of Joseph face permanent loss to their tribal inheritance (Numbers 35 and 36).

Numbers 36 reads as follows:

1 And the chief fathers of the families of the children of Gilead . . . of the families of the sons of Joseph, came near, and spake before Moses, and before the princes, the chief fathers of the children of Israel: 2 And they said, Yahweh commanded my lord to give the land for an inheritance by lot to the children of Israel: and my lord was commanded by Yahweh to give the inheritance of Zelophehad our brother unto his daughters. 3 And if they be married to any of the sons of the other tribes of the children of Israel, then shall their inheritance be taken from the inheritance of our fathers, and shall be put to the inheritance of the tribe whereunto they are received: so shall it be taken from the lot of our inheritance. 4 And when the jubilee of the children of Israel shall be, then shall their inheritance be put unto the inheritance of the tribe whereunto they are received: so shall their inheritance be taken away from the inheritance of the tribe of our fathers. 5 And Moses

commanded the children of Israel according to the word of Yahweh, saying, The tribe of the sons of Joseph hath said well. 6 This is the thing which Yahweh doth command concerning the daughters of Zelophehad, saying, Let them marry to whom they think best; only to the family of the tribe of their father shall they marry. 7 So shall not the inheritance of the children of Israel remove from tribe to tribe: for every one of the children of Israel shall keep himself to the inheritance of the tribe of his fathers. 8 And every daughter, that possesseth an inheritance in any tribe of the children of Israel, shall be wife unto one of the family of the tribe of her father, that the children of Israel may enjoy every man the inheritance of his fathers. 9 Neither shall the inheritance remove from one tribe to another tribe; but every one of the tribes of the children of Israel shall keep himself to his own inheritance. 10 Even as Yahweh commanded Moses, so did the daughters of Zelophehad: For Mahlal, Tirzah, and Hoglah, and Milcah, and Noah, the daughters of Zelophehad, were married unto their father's brothers' sons: 12 And they were married into the families of the sons of Manasseh the son of Joseph, and their inheritance remained in the tribe of the family of their father. 13 These are the commandments and the judgments, which Yahweh commanded by the hand of Moses unto the children of Israel in the plains of Moab by Jordan near Jericho.

Zelophehad's clan objects to the ruling in Numbers 27 because its members note that should an heiress marry outside her tribe there would be a loss of land to them and a gain for the tribe into which she marries. Moses sustains the objection and rules that, although a daughter can inherit where there is no son, she has to marry within her tribe (Numbers 36). The same standard is applied as when Moses upheld the objection of the daughters in Numbers 27: "Right speak the tribe of the sons of Joseph" (Num 36:5). What is right, Hebrew *ken*, "straight and honest," can in fact prove problematical. A concession made in the name of equity leads to a fresh injustice, and a further balancing of rights is required. Any form of law is inherently indeterminate. A law can be both just and oppressive, and Moses' judgment in favor of the daughters in Numbers 27 furnishes a fine example.[12]

Why is the ruling about the daughters of Zelophehad in Numbers 36 not given immediately after the one in Numbers 27? The standard stab at the problem is to claim that the amendment constitutes an alteration in the practice and that it has been added at some point after the law in Numbers 27 came into effect and after an earlier version of the Book of Numbers circulated. This view of the matter then permits critics to explain why the Book of Numbers ends on a rather insignificant note, "in such a legalistic and dry fashion," in the words of

Leveen.[13] To counter this inconsequentiality she suggests that the reform points to an important hope for the future nation that it will be governed by law, with the rules subject to alteration. This benign perspective may prevail at some level, but nothing in the account of Numbers 36 suggests that the expression of this hope is the intent of the narrator-lawgiver.

Leveen's view fails to take into account how, as we have seen, the Numbers narrator proceeds in setting out his material. The modification in Numbers 36 of the previous law about Zelophehad in Numbers 27 is not an addendum to be attributed to a literary history of the Book of Numbers. The important observation is that Zelophehad is in the line of Joseph (through Manasseh), and the Joseph story has been a dominant interest in the preceding texts in Numbers. The shaping of the material, whether law or legend, comes not in terms of one topic following logically from the one before—certainly not true in this instance, in which the topic of inheritance comes after the topic of homicide—but is mainly inspired by issues arising in Genesis. The climactic feature of the Joseph story is that the brothers ended up a united band, the ancestors of the future twelve tribes. The concluding part of the Book of Numbers is about preserving intact that unity, unaltered by enhancement or diminution of inheritable property among the tribes. This is an altogether loftier and fundamentally more important concern than Leveen's idea.

The daughters of Zelophehad belong to the tribe of Joseph (Num 36:1), and it is this tie that is crucial for understanding the placement of the ruling at this point in Numbers. Following his near homicide, Joseph's fate in Genesis 37 is that, unknown to his family, he is lost to Egypt, to a new land and a new way of life. A future life in Canaan—the topic dominates the presentation of the material in Numbers 32–36—would never have materialized for Joseph in the ordinary way of things because if a man is sold abroad as a slave, any acquisition of land or property is out of the question because of his status as a slave. Moreover, he is likely to disappear from the community without trace to a foreign land, never to return. If Joseph had been killed or permanently cut off from his family, there would have been no tribe of Joseph—his descendants would have been obliterated by never having been born. If, in Numbers 36, the women can take what they inherit from their father to the tribe into which they marry, Joseph's tribe would have experienced another kind of elimination.

The rule in Numbers 36 deals with a much less dire situation in which an inheritance might be lost to a family of the tribe of Joseph. Significantly, however, the spotlight falls not just on the family within the tribe but on the whole tribe. The underlying concern is with the transfer of ancestral tribal land from that family to another tribe and hence a loss of land to the transferring tribe.

Num 36:5 speaks of "the tribe of the sons of Joseph," that is, the entire tribe is considered. When Num 36:8 rules that an heiress must marry into a family of her father's tribe, it is to the end "that the sons of Israel enjoy every man the inheritance of his fathers." Each tribe must fully benefit from its inheritance, and that includes what is owing to Joseph, the ancestor and first father of Zelophehad's family.[14]

JOSEPH AND THE YEAR OF JUBILEE

Num 36:1–12 has the one other reference outside the Book of Leviticus to the Year of Jubilee, and critics regard it as an odd reference because they state that the Jubilee concerns land that is sold before the Jubilee comes about and is not about land that has been inherited. They view it as an addition, even as an "irrelevant addition."[15] The background focus on the history of Joseph in Genesis again proves illuminating, however. In Numbers 36 the heads of households of the Josephite tribe bring to Moses the problem about their loss of inheritance to another tribe at the Jubilee should the daughters of Zelophehad marry men from outside their own tribe. Num 36:1, 5, 12 expressly state that the households in question are those of the sons of Joseph. The initial issue of the loss of inherited land, about which the Year of Jubilee is indeed set up to handle for Israelites—"In the year of this jubilee ye shall return every man unto his possession" (Lev 25:13)—arose because of Joseph's original policy in Egypt when he arranged for the inherited lands of the Egyptians to be given over permanently to Pharaoh.[16] We are focused not just on land that is sold at some point before the Year of Jubilee but also on inheritance, a notion that evokes the ancestor, Joseph, whose action prompted the topic.

The establishment of the Year of Jubilee is an example of how the Israelites are not to do as the Egyptians did (Lev 18:3). It is ironic that it is Joseph's future family that faced permanent loss of inherited lands in Canaan because it was he who had caused all Egyptian families to experience that fate in Egypt. In this light there is a sense in which mirroring retribution came to hang as a threat over his descendants. The coin Joseph had paid out in Egyptian currency, his descendants almost had to pay out in native currency. We have perhaps further indication of the negative portrayal of Joseph that Pirson and Wildavsky pick up in the story about him (see chapter 6) and that is a feature of the rules in Numbers 15 and of the Book of Daniel.

So concludes my study of the Book of Numbers, which I claim is largely a critique of the lives of the nation's patriarchs in the Book of Genesis. Numbers is a thoroughly integrated work that reflects the writer's acute awareness of his nation's history and prehistory, particularly as relayed in Genesis. It is the Numbers author's sense of history that we must pay attention to, not the sense generated by the historical-critical school of recent centuries. The bewildering interruptions in the flow of material that this school detects in fact constitute the author's idiosyncratic mode of expressing detailed reflections on issues that mainly arise in Genesis. The exploration of these concerns is at the heart of the work. The narration of the post-Exodus wandering in the wilderness is a vehicle for Numbers to probe further the story of the nation's fathers. Understandably, the author of Numbers did not have access to the kind of historical knowledge available today. But his extraordinary ability to draw out subtle and multifaceted issues from the traditions that were available to him more than made up for the lack.

Abbreviations

AB	Yale Anchor Bible
ABD	*Anchor Bible Dictionary* (New York, 1992)
ANET	*Ancient Near Eastern Texts Relating to the Old Testament* ed. J. B. Pritchard (3d ed., Princeton, 1969)
AV	Authorized Version
BDB	F. Brown, S. R. Driver, and C. A. Briggs, A *Hebrew and English Lexicon of the Old Testament* (Oxford, 1906)
BLL	*Studies in Comparative Legal History: Collected Works of David Daube*, volume 3, *Biblical Law and Literature*, ed. Calum Carmichael (Berkeley, 2003)
BZAR	Beihefte zur Zeitschrift für altorientalische und biblische Rechtsgeschichte
BZAW	Beihefte zur Zeitschrift für die alttestamentliche Wissenschaft
CB	Century Bible
CBSC	Cambridge Bible for Schools and Colleges
CH	Code of Hammurabi
CKLR	*Chicago-Kent Law Review*
CLR	*California Law Review*
D	The Deuteronomic literary strand in the Pentateuch
EOW	*Studies in Comparative Legal History: Collected Works of David Daube*, volume 4, *Ethics and Other Writings*, ed. Calum Carmichael (Berkeley, 2006)
H	The Holiness Code of Leviticus 17–26
HL	Hittite Laws
HTR	*Harvard Theological Review*
ICC	International Critical Commentary
JBL	*Journal of Biblical Literature*
JBQ	*Jewish Bible Quarterly*
JE	The Y(J)ahwistic and Elohistic literary strand in the Pentateuch

JHS	*Journal of Hebrew Scriptures*
JPS	Jewish Publication Society
JPSTC	Jewish Publication Society Torah Commentary
JSB	*Jewish Study Bible*
JSOT	*Journal for the Study of the Old Testament*
JSOTSS	Journal for the Study of the Old Testament Supplement Series
LXX	The Septuagint
MAL	Middle Assyrian Laws
MLR	*Modern Law Review*
MT	The Massoretic Text
NAC	New American Commentary
NCBC	New Century Bible Commentary
NEB	New English Bible
NICOT	New International Commentary on the Old Testament
NTJ	*Studies in Comparative Legal History: Collected Works of David Daube*, volume 2, *New Testament Judaism*, ed. Calum Carmichael (Berkeley, 2000)
OTL	Old Testament Library
P	The Priestly literary strand in the Pentateuch
RBL	*Review of Biblical Literature*
RIDA	*Revue Internationale des Droits de l'Antiquité*
RJ	*Rechtshistorisches Journal*
RSV	Revised Standard Version
RV	Revised Version
SBLDS	Society of Biblical Literature Dissertation Series
SLR	*Stanford Law Review*
SVT	Supplement *Vetus Testamentum*
TDOT	*Theological Dictionary of the Old Testament*, ed. G. J. Botterweck and H. Ringgren (Grand Rapids, MI, 1980)
TOTC	Tyndale Old Testament Commentaries
VT	*Vetus Testamentum*
WBC	Word Bible Commentary
YLJ	*Yale Law Journal*
ZAW	*Zeitschrift für die alttestamentliche Wissenschaft*
ZSS	*Zeitschrift der Savigny-Stiftung für Rechtsgeschichte*

NOTES

CHAPTER 1. GENESIS EXTENDED

1. See D. N. Freedman, "The Earlier Bible," M. P. O'Connor and D. N. Freedman, eds., *Backgrounds for the Bible* (Winona Lake, Ind., 1987).
2. See Moshe Garsiel, *The First Book of Samuel: A Literary Study of Comparative Structures, Analogies and Parallels* (Ramat-Gan, Israel, 1989), 130–31; S. McDonough, "'And David was old, advanced in years': 2 Samuel xxiv 18–25, 1 Kings i, and Genesis xxiii–xxiv," VT 49 (1999), 128–31; Craig Y. S. Ho, "The Stories of the Family Troubles of Judah and David: A Study of Their Literary Links," VT 49 (1999), 514–31; John Harvey, "*Tendenz* and Textual Criticism in 1 Samuel 2–10," JSOT 96 (2001), 71–81; Dominic Rudman, "The Patriarchal Narratives in the Books of Samuel," VT 54 (2004), 239–49; Calum Carmichael, *Law and Narrative in the Bible* (Ithaca, 1985), 270–76; F. V. Greifenhagen, *Egypt on the Pentateuch's Ideological Map: Constructing Biblical Israel's Identity*, JSOTSS 361 (Sheffield, 2002), 265; and Thomas Römer, *Israels Väter: Untersuchungen zur Väterthematick im Deuteronomium und in der deuteronomistischen Tradition* (Göttingen, 1990).
3. Christophe Nihan, *From Priestly Torah to Pentateuch*, Forschungen zum Alten Testament 2 Reihe 25 (Tübingen, 2007), 608.
4. Römer, *Israels Väter*, and John Van Seters, "Confessional Reformulation in the Exilic Period," VT 22 (1972), 448–59. David Cohen has noted that classicists have long moved beyond the kind of source criticism still adhered to by biblical scholars, "Greek Law: Problems and Methods," ZSS (1989), 81–105.
5. Nihan, *From Priestly Torah*, 610; Montesquieu, *My Thoughts*, trans. Henry C. Clark (Indianapolis, 2007), no. 190.
6. Nihan, *From Priestly Torah*, 473.
7. For details, see Calum Carmichael, *Law, Legend, and Incest in the Bible* (Ithaca, 1997), 74–75.

8. Isaak Heinemann's (unfair) comment about Philo's work, *Schriften der Jüdisch-hellenistischen Literatur (Die Werke Philos von Alexandria in deutscher Übersetzung)*, ed. Leopold Cohn (Breslau, 1909), 2:8.
9. Thomas Brodie, *Genesis as Dialogue: A Literary, Historical and Theological Commentary* (Oxford, 2001), 48.
10. J. L. Barton, "Nullity of Marriage and Illegitimacy in the England of the Middle Ages," *Legal History Studies*, ed. Dafydd Jenkins (Cardiff, 1975), 40; Calum Carmichael, *The Laws of Deuteronomy* (Ithaca, 1974), 159–63.
11. See Frank Polak's review of David Wright, *Inventing God's Law: How the Covenant Code of the Bible Used and Revised the Laws of Hammurabi* (Oxford, 2009) in *RBL*, 5/10/2010.
12. Calum Carmichael, *Illuminating Leviticus: A Study of Its Laws and Institutions in the Light of Biblical Narratives* (Baltimore, 2006), 33–34. Note James Bruckner's view that in contrast to Sinaitic law, in which narrative is interrupted by the presentation of laws, pre-Sinaitic rules tend to be embedded or implied in the narratives, *Implied Law in the Abraham Narrative: A Literary and Theological Analysis* (Sheffield, 2001), 68.
13. David Daube, *He That Cometh* (London, 1966), 1 [*NTJ*, 157].
14. See Ron Pirson's analysis underlining that the brothers did not succeed in selling Joseph, *The Lord of the Dreams. A Semantic and Literary Analysis of Genesis 37–50*, JSOTSS 355 (Sheffield, 2002), 69–79.
15. Plutarch, *Moralia* 21.404 Df.
16. For details, see Carmichael, *Illuminating Leviticus*, 122–38.
17. See Karl Llewellyn, *The Bramble Bush: On Our Law and Its Study* (Dobbs Ferry, N.Y., 1960), 116, 152; David Daube, "Greek Forerunners of Simenon," *CLR* 68 (1980), 301–5; [*EOW*, 193–202]; and Assnat Bartor, *Reading Law as Narrative: A Study in the Casuistic Laws of the Pentateuch* (Atlanta, 2010).
18. Charles Foster Kent, "A Tentative Codification of the Old Testament Laws," *YLJ* 15 (1906), 284. I am indebted to Austin Blum for drawing my attention to and commenting on Kent's article in a Law Note prepared under my supervision for the *Cornell Law Review*.
19. N. H. Snaith, *Leviticus and Numbers*, CB (London, 1967), 137. "A book of laws obviously without much plan, and brought into being by loosely stringing together existing complexes of precepts," Martin Noth, *Leviticus*, OTL (Philadelphia, 1965), 146.

CHAPTER 2. PHARAOH AND YAHWEH AS GOD-KINGS (NUMBERS 1–4)

1. Indeed, the peculiar knowing of past and present on the part of Moses (especially in the laws attributed to him) shows up in New Testament sources in interesting ways. One example is when Jesus knows, without being present, the contents of a conversation Peter has had with a tax collector about payment of the temple tax. Jesus also knows that the first fish he tells Peter to catch will have the requisite payment in its

mouth (Matt 19:24–27). Similar examples show up in rabbinic sources (*t. Pes.* 1:27; *y. A. Zar.* 40a; *b. Erub.* 64b; *Lev. Rab.* on 27:2). See David Daube, "Temple Tax," *Jesus, the Gospels, and the Church: Essays in Honor of William R. Farmer*, ed. E. P. Sanders (Macon, Ga., 1987), 121–34 [*NTJ*, 771–81].

2. For details of the Egyptian–Israelite contrast, see Calum Carmichael, *Illuminating Leviticus: A Study of Its Laws and Institutions in the Light of Biblical Narratives* (Baltimore, 2006), 134–36.
3. F. V. Greifenhagen, *Egypt on the Pentateuch's Ideological Map: Constructing Biblical Israel's Identity*, JSOTSS 361 (Sheffield, 2002), 92; C. Keil and F. Delitzsch, *Biblical Commentary on the Old Testament* (Edinburgh, 1869), 1:380.
4. Jacob Milgrom, *Leviticus 23–27*, AB 3B (New York, 2000), 1958, 2380.
5. John Griffith, "The Political Constitution," *MLR* 42 (1979), 19; Bruce Wells, *The Law of Testimony in the Pentateuchal Codes* (Wiesbaden, 2004), 3, 5–6.
6. Matthew Rindge, "Jewish Identity under Foreign Rule: Daniel 2 as a Reconfiguration of Genesis 41," *JBL* 129 (2010), 100; T. E. Fretheim, "The Plagues as Ecological Signs of Historical Disaster," *JBL* 110 (1991), 385–96. On Fretheim's analysis, see my comments in *The Story of Creation: Its Origin and Its Interpretation in Philo and the Fourth Gospel* (Ithaca, 1996), 18–25; Greifenhagen, *Egypt on the Pentateuch's Ideological Map*, 60 n. 59; David Cotter, *Genesis, Berit Olam, Studies in Hebrew Narrative and Poetry* (Collegeville, Minn., 2003), 236–37; David Daube, *The Exodus Pattern in the Bible* (London, 1963), 62–72 [*BLL*, 136–43]; on Moses as a counter-Joseph in Exodus, see Calum Carmichael, "Joseph, Moses, and the Institution of the Israelite Judicature," *Studies in Honor of Dwight W. Young*, eds. J. E. Coleman and V. H. Matthews (Winona Lake, Ind., 1996), 15–25, and *The Origins of Biblical Law: The Decalogues and the Book of the Covenant* (Ithaca, 1992), 181–203.
7. See Timothy Ashley, *The Book of Numbers*, NICOT (Grand Rapids, 1993), 76.
8. Mary Douglas, *In the Wilderness* (Sheffield, 1993), 98–101, 176.
9. Gordon Wenham, *Numbers: An Introduction and Commentary*, TOTC (Leicester, 1981), 119; Devora Steinmetz, *Punishment and Freedom. The Rabbinic Construction of Criminal Law* (Philadelphia, 2008), 56; Adriane Leveen, *Memory and Tradition in the Book of Numbers* (Cambridge, Mass., 2007), 9; Jon Levenson's note on Gen 50:10–13 in his translation of Genesis, *JSB*, 99–100.
10. Leveen, *Memory and Tradition*, 1, 44.
11. Ibid., 34, 36.
12. G. B. Gray, *Numbers*, ICC (Edinburgh, 1903), 39. Not alert to the connections with Genesis on his part or on the part of the critics he lists, Reinhard Achenbach provides an extensive survey of research that emphasizes Numbers' overall lack of unity, *Die Vollendung der Tora: Studien zur Redactionsgeschichte des Numeribuches im Kontext von Hextateuch und Pentateuch*, BZAR 3 (Wiesbaden, 2003), 1–36.
13. Jacob Milgrom, *Leviticus 1–16*, AB 3A (New York, 1991), 711.
14. *JSB*, 76.

CHAPTER 3. THE SUSPECTED ADULTERESS AND THE NAZIRITE
(NUMBERS 5 AND 6)

1. So Roland de Vaux, *Ancient Israel* (New York, 1961), 1:158. Tikva Frymer-Kensky is correct to point out that the term "ordeal" is not the appropriate one for what the woman experiences, "The Strange Case of the Suspected Adulteress (Numbers V 11–31)," *VT* 34 (1984), 24. For a discussion of some elements that may reflect Near Eastern background, see Baruch Levine, *Numbers 1–20*, AB 4A (New York, 1993), 210–11, and Frymer-Kensky, 25.
2. Levine, *Numbers 1–20*, 215.
3. G. B. Gray, *Numbers*, ICC (Edinburgh, 1903), 39, 57.
4. See G. R. Driver and J. C. Miles, *The Babylonian Laws* (Oxford, 1952), 1:283–84.
5. See Levine, *Numbers 1–20*, 198, 201.
6. Levine, *Numbers 1–20*, 201. As Gray points out, the phrase *wenizreʿah zaraʿ* is similar to the one in Lev 12:2, where the meaning is to bring forth seed (*hizriʿah*), *Numbers*, 55. Some translations avoid the concrete sense and give the meaning as retaining a capacity to bear children.
7. Meir Sternberg suggests that Uriah might be aware of his wife's adultery with David, *The Poetics of Biblical Narrative: Ideological Literature and the Drama of Reading* (Bloomington, Ind., 1985), 201–9. However, Uriah did not proceed against his wife—when Judah suspected Tamar, he took action against her.
8. David Daube, "Error and Accident in the Bible," *RIDA* 2 (1949), 198 [*BLL*, 365].
9. Esther Marie Menn, *Judah and Tamar (Genesis 38) in Ancient Jewish Exegesis* (Leiden, 1997), 59, 342.
10. See Assnat Bartor, *Reading Law as Narrative: A Study in the Casuistic Laws of the Pentateuch* (Atlanta, 2010), 147.
11. As to what exactly is to happen to the woman's body is more problematic. See Levine's discussion, *Numbers 1–20*, 198, 201.
12. Robert Alter, *Genesis: Translation and Commentary* (New York, 1996), 221.
13. Menn notes Tamar's silence, *Judah and Tamar*, 27.
14. See the comments of Victor P. Hamilton, *Book of Genesis 18–50*, NICOT (Grand Rapids, 1995), 441–43.
15. Levine, *Numbers 1–20*, 193, also stresses that the husband has reason to proceed against his wife because of confusion over his wife's pregnant state.
16. On being answerable before the deity if valuables that a person has deposited with a neighbor disappear, see Carmichael, *Origins of Biblical Law*, 149–53.
17. Menn, *Judah and Tamar*, 96.
18. On gender, Levine, *Numbers 1–20*, 187, 218, and Karel Van Der Toorn, "Female Prostitution in Payment of Vows in Ancient Israel," *JBL* 108 (1989), 196; on grape products, Timothy Ashley, *The Book of Numbers*, NICOT (Grand Rapids, 1993), 142; on uncleanness, Jacob Milgrom, *Numbers*, JPSTC (Philadelphia, 1990), 46, 304 n. 18.
19. Alter, *Genesis*, 219.
20. For the role of wordplays in Genesis 49, see A. H. J. Gunneweg, "Uber den Sitz im Leben der sogenannte Stammessprüche," *ZAW* 76 (1964), 248–55.

21. Gray, *Numbers*, 69; Levine, *Numbers 1–20*, 229.
22. On Hos 3:1, C. Keil and F. Delitzsch, *Biblical Commentary on the Old Testament* (Edinburgh, 1869), *Numbers*, 4:35. Marvin Pope has an extensive discussion of the erotic associations of the "raisin cakes" (*'ašišot*) of Hos 3:1 and Cant 2:5 and views them as aphrodisiacs for both sexes. He notes that the "custom of baking cakes in the shape of the genitalia was widespread in antiquity," *Song of Songs*, AB (New York, 1977), 379.
23. See *Apocrypha and Pseudepigrapha of the Old Testament*, ed. R. H. Charles (Oxford, 1913), 2:319. On how the *Testament of Judah* interpreted Genesis 38, see C. E. Hayes, "The Midrashic Career of the Confession of Judah (Genesis xxxviii 26)," pt. 1, *VT* 45 (1995), 68; and on how, I might point out, like the official trial of the suspected adulteress in Numbers 5, the Targums Pseudo-Jonathan and Neofiti transformed Tamar's offense into a scene from a public courtroom, see 77, 78.
24. Milgrom, *Numbers*, 356; Levine, *Numbers 1–20*, 221. Other commentators also suggest that the term for the priestly crown or diadem, *nezer*, "consecration," is used of the nazirite's uncut hair (Lev 8:9, 21:12), Gordon Wenham, *Numbers: An Introduction and Commentary* (Leicester, 1981), TOTC, 86; Ashley, *Book of Numbers*, 143.
25. Keil and Delitzsch, *Numbers*, 4:36.
26. Milgrom thinks that the only link between the two laws is the role of the priest in each and possibly the shared use of the term *para'*, "let loose" (the hair); *Numbers*, 43.
27. Levine, *Numbers 1–20*, 221.
28. Joan G. Westenholz, "Tamar, *qedešah*, *qadištu*, and Sacred Prostitution in Mesopotamia," *HTR* 82 (1989), 252–54, 258–59.
29. Gray, *Numbers*, 67.
30. A. H. McNeile, *Book of Numbers*, CBSC (Cambridge, Eng., 1911), 36. Cf. Gray, *Numbers*, 71.
31. Milgrom, *Numbers*, 202.

CHAPTER 4. A TEST CASE FOR THE STUDY OF BIBLICAL LAW
(LEV 6:2–7 [5:20–26] AND NUM 5:6–10)

1. Jacob Milgrom, *Numbers*, JPSTC (Philadelphia, 1990), 302 n. 5, and *Leviticus 1–16*, AB 3A (New York, 1991), 367–69.
2. Z. W. Falk, *Hebrew Law in Biblical Times* (Jerusalem, 1964), 60–61; Bruce Wells, *The Law of Testimony in the Pentateuchal Codes* (Wiesbaden, 2004), 139. Note also Baruch Levine: "The provisions of cultic law were extended to include the criminal misappropriation of another's property, through fraud, embezzlement, and misuse of belongings entrusted to one's keeping," *Numbers 1–20*, AB 4A (New York, 1993), 187.
3. See Milgrom, *Leviticus 1–16*, 337, 365–73; Wells, *The Law of Testimony*, 138, 139; Christophe Nihan, *From Priestly Torah to Pentateuch*, Forschungen zum Alten Testament 2 Reihe 25 (Tübingen, 2007), 250.
4. Milgrom, *Leviticus 1–16*, 337.
5. The version of Theodoret of Cyr, *Historia ecclesiastica* 3.5, appears to be the main source of the legend and this particular variant.

6. Erhard Gerstenberger, *Leviticus*, trans. D. W. Stott, OTL (Louisville, 1996), 66, 67.
7. J. E. Hartley, *Leviticus*, WBC 4 (Dallas, 1992), 75, 76.
8. See Milgrom, *Leviticus 1–16*, 369. He rightly translates Numbers 5:5 as "feels guilty" (339, 368).
9. G. B. Gray, *Numbers*, ICC (Edinburgh, 1903), 41.
10. "It can be assumed that . . . the original injured party died between the crime and the reparation," Timothy Ashley, *The Book of Numbers*, NICOT (Grand Rapids, 1993), 115.
11. Levine, *Numbers 1–20*, 190, expresses surprise about the law's narrow focus: "No relatives, no heirs at all!" Eryl Davies writes, "Since there was no shortage of people who could act as *go'el*, the situation envisaged . . . where the victim had no kinsman to whom reparation could be made, must have been comparatively rare," *Numbers*, NCBC (Grand Rapids, 1995), 48.
12. See *TDOT*, entry *ma'al*, 8:460.
13. In Num 5:6, the unique language about the wrong done to the person, *mikkol-ḥaṭṭo't ha'adam*, the reference to *ha'adam* (man and woman) may be influenced by the nature of the promise Judah made to Tamar and hence to Er, namely, that in line with God's original blessing of procreation on the man and the woman in Gen 1:27, 28 increase of seed would be forthcoming. The use of *ha'adam* suggests some fundamental, universal matter such as procreation.
14. Levine, *Numbers 1–20*, 190.
15. Milgrom, *Leviticus 1–16*, 368, 369.

CHAPTER 5. JOSEPH AND MOSES AS SOURCES OF DISCORD (NUMBERS 7–14)

1. See F. V. Greifenhagen, *Egypt on the Pentateuch's Ideological Map: Constructing Biblical Israel's Identity*, JSOTSS 361 (Sheffield, 2002), 37.
2. Claus Westermann, *Genesis 37–50* (Minneapolis, 1986), 160.
3. A later expression of the notion of God as the temple's sovereign is well brought out in the syllogism that Jesus addresses to Peter about payment of the temple tax: "What thinkest thou, Simon? of whom do the kings of the earth take custom or tribute? of their own sons, or of strangers? Peter saith unto him, Of strangers. Jesus saith unto him, Then are the sons free" (Matt 17:25, 26). That is, Jesus and his disciples claim exemption as sons of the temple's sovereign, priests in some exalted sense.
4. See Calum Carmichael, *Illuminating Leviticus: A Study of Its Laws and Institutions in the Light of Biblical Narratives* (Baltimore, 2006), 122–38; also chapter 1.
5. Esther Marie Menn, *Judah and Tamar (Genesis 38) in Ancient Jewish Exegesis* (Leiden, 1997), 37, 38.
6. Adriane Leveen, *Memory and Tradition in the Book of Numbers* (Cambridge, Mass., 2007), 147.
7. See David Daube, *Sons and Strangers*, Institute of Jewish Law, Boston University School of Law (1984), 30 [BLL, 177], and *The Exodus Pattern in the Bible* (London, 1963), 42 [BLL, 123].
8. See G. B. Gray, *Numbers*, ICC (Edinburgh, 1903), 115.

9. Leveen, *Memory and Tradition*, 87; on *dibbah*, see Baruch Levine, *Numbers 1–20*, AB 4A (New York, 1993), 358.
10. Eryl Davies, *Numbers*, NCBC (Grand Rapids, 1995), 140; Timothy Ashley, *The Book of Numbers*, NICOT (Grand Rapids, 1993), 243.
11. Gray, *Numbers*, 153.
12. See David Daube's discussion of the problem in *The Deed and the Doer in the Bible: David Daube's Gifford Lectures*, vol. 1, compiled and edited by Calum Carmichael (West Conshohocken, Penn., 2008), 167–73.
13. Ashley, *Book of Numbers*, 243.

CHAPTER 6. JOSEPH'S DREAMS AND THE LAWS OF NUMBERS 15

1. Eryl Davies, *Numbers*, NCBC (Grand Rapids, 1995), 150; G. B. Gray, *Numbers*, ICC (Edinburgh, 1903), 168, also states that the third rule about inadvertent offenses presupposes the first rule about the grain offering only in a quite incidental way (because of Num 15:24). It is, we shall see, not at all incidental; Gordon Wenham, *Numbers: An Introduction and Commentary* (Leicester, 1981), TOTC, 126; and Baruch Levine, *Numbers 1–20*, AB 4A (New York, 1993), 386. Timothy Ashley notes how the vocabulary employed throughout Numbers 15 is largely consistent and indicates unity of composition, *The Book of Numbers*, NICOT (Grand Rapids, 1993), 277.
2. See Calum Carmichael, *Illuminating Leviticus: A Study of Its Laws and Institutions in the Light of Biblical Narratives* (Baltimore, 2006), 122–38.
3. Levine, *Numbers 1–20*, 386, 388.
4. Ibid., 391, 385.
5. Ron Pirson, *The Lord of the Dreams: A Semantic and Literary Analysis of Genesis 37–50*, JSOTSS 355 (Sheffield, 2002), 48, 49.
6. Pirson, *Lord of the Dreams*, 117; on Joseph's first words and the lack of any role for Yahweh in the dreams, 41; also on Joseph's idolatry, 141 nn. 64, 65. Gerhard von Rad, *Genesis* (London, 1972), 351, 352; Robert Alter, *Genesis: Translation and Commentary* (New York, 1996), 208.
7. See F. V. Greifenhagen, *Egypt on the Pentateuch's Ideological Map: Constructing Biblical Israel's Identity*, JSOTSS 361 (Sheffield, 2002), 37.
8. Aaron Wildavsky, *Assimilation and Separation: Joseph the Administrator and the Politics of Religion in Biblical Israel* (New Brunswick, 1993), 98, 116 n. 18, quoted by Pirson, *Lord of the Dreams*, 115.
9. A. D. H. Mayes, NCBC, *Deuteronomy* (London, 1971), 327.
10. S. Talmon, "Wisdom in the Book of Esther," VT 13 (1963), 419–55, cites many parallels.
11. *The HarperCollins Study Bible* (New York, 1993), 1308.
12. "Jewish Identity under Foreign Rule: Daniel 2 as a Reconfiguration of Genesis 41," JBL 129 (2010), 85–104. He does not comment on Nebuchadnezzar's act of worship before Daniel.
13. See Pirson, *Lord of the Dreams*, 61.

14. Wenham, *Numbers*, 37.
15. Levine, *Numbers 1–20*, 388; Wenham, *Numbers*, 127.
16. For example, Wenham, *Numbers*, 129–30.
17. Jacob Milgrom, *Numbers*, JPSTC (Philadelphia, 46), 125.
18. Wenham, *Numbers*, 129.
19. Meir Malul, *Knowledge, Control, and Sex: Studies in Biblical Thought, Culture and Worldview* (Tel Aviv, 2002), 469–70.
20. See Pirson, *Lord of the Dreams*, 61.
21. See Levine, *Numbers 1–20*, 398–99. The Egyptian masters forced the Israelite slaves to gather straw (*mqošeš*) for themselves (Exod 5:7).
22. See Calum Carmichael, *Sex and Religion in the Bible* (New Haven, 2010), 85–96.
23. "'What Shall We Do with the Sabbath-Gatherer?' A Narrative Approach to a 'Hard Case' in Biblical Law (Numbers 15:32–36)," VT 60 (2010), 45–62.
24. In commenting on the rule in Exod 35:3 against kindling a fire on the Sabbath, William Propp states that "making light is the first and quintessential act of Creation. To desist from making light would then be the opposite of Creation." What he seems to mean is that the offense has, indeed, to do with the idolatrous use of fire by way of claiming divine powers, *Exodus 19–40: A New Translation with Introduction and Commentary*, AB 2A (New York, 2006), 660. Gnana Robinson points out that the verb *bʿr*, "to kindle a fire," in Exod 35:3 is elsewhere used of idolatrous offenses: "Such kindling of sacrificial fire for foreign deities seems to have been closely linked with the pre-exilic Sabbath practices," and she notes in this context Jer 7:18, which cites together the gathering of wood and the kindling of fire, "The Prohibition of Strange Fire in Ancient Israel," VT 28 (1978), 306, 307.
25. Carmichael, *Sex and Religion*, 54–56.
26. Levine, *Numbers 1–20*, 401.
27. David Cotter, *Genesis, Berit Olam, Studies in Hebrew Narrative and Poetry* (Collegeville, Minn., 2003), 272; note J. H. Hertz, ed., *The Pentateuch and Haftorahs: Genesis* (London, 1929), 310 (supporting the translation from LXX, Targum Jonathan, and Kimchi): "We now know from the painted Tombs of the Bene Hassain in Egypt that, in the Patriarchal age, Semitic chiefs wore coats of many colours as insignia of rulership," cited in Bernard Jackson, "Law, Narrative, and Theology: Daube on the Prodigal Son," *David Daube: A Centenary Celebration*, ed. Ernest Metzger (Glasgow, 2010), 85.
28. Gray, *Numbers*, 185; Milgrom, *Numbers*, 128.
29. *Genesis*, 285.
30. For some examples out of many, see Calum Carmichael, *The Origins of Biblical Law: The Decalogues and the Book of the Covenant* (Ithaca, 1992), 109–39.

CHAPTER 7. THE STATUS OF FIRSTBORN (NUMBERS 16–18)

1. Baruch Levine, *Numbers 1–20*, AB 4A (New York, 1993), 405–6. On the inevitably speculative detection of sources (JE and different P layers) that have gone into the

final text, Timothy Ashley is probably correct to claim that "this view of the origin of the text, although common, seems artificial and based on the cleverness of the interpreter rather than on the text itself," *The Book of Numbers,* NICOT (Grand Rapids, 1993), 302.

2. See Dale Patrick's review of my book, *Law and Narrative in the Bible* (Ithaca, 1985) in *JBL* 106 (1987), 521–23; John Ramsden, *Man of the Century: Winston Churchill and His Legend since 1945* (New York, 2002), 210. Allegory is a distinct literary genre, literally, "the other utterance in public" different from the one in private. It assumes a supernatural origin for the text that is to be interpreted. See David Daube, *Ancient Hebrew Fables* (Oxford, 1973), 8 [BLL, 701]; also entry "Allegorie" in *Lexicon für Theologie und Kirche* (Freiburg, 1957), 1:346–47.
3. G. B. Gray, *Numbers,* ICC (Edinburgh, 1903), 189–90; Levine, *Numbers 1–20,* 424; Jacob Milgrom, *Numbers,* JPSTC (Philadelphia, 46), 130; and Ashley, *Book of Numbers,* 303.
4. Levine, *Book of Numbers 1–20,* 416.
5. Ashley, *Book of Numbers,* 296.
6. Levine, *Numbers 1–20,* 422.
7. Thomas Hobbes, *Leviathan,* ed. Richard Tuck (Cambridge, Eng., 1996), 42.

CHAPTER 8. THE RITUAL OF THE RED HEIFER (NUMBERS 19)

1. David Daube provides a detailed analysis of the episode in *Studies in Biblical Law* (Cambridge, England, 1947), 191–200 [BLL, 241–49].
2. Ibid., 195 [BLL, 244]; Robert Alter, *Genesis: Translation and Commentary* (New York, 1996), 128–29.
3. Similar meals were the fare of the Spartan warriors, and blood drawn from their horses the means of survival of the armies of Genghis Khan. In the *Odyssey* the winner of the contest between the two beggars is to receive goat sausages, and the disguised Odysseus eventually tastes one, which is "bubbling with fat and blood" (*Od.* 18.55, 140).
4. See K. A. Matthews, *Genesis 11:27–50:26,* NAC 1 (Nashville, 1996), 389. We might recall Dean Burgan's line about Petra (Edomite terrain): "Match me such a marvel/ save in eastern clime/ a rose red city/ half as old as time."
5. See Daube, *Studies,* 193–97 [BLL, 244–47]. Victor P. Hamilton, *Book of Genesis 18–50,* NICOT (Grand Rapids, 1995), 186, cites Daube's solution to Jacob's cheating Esau but is mistaken in thinking that Daube weakens his argument by postulating an etymological link between 'adom (red) and dam (blood). He does not. The link can be by sound alone. Drawing on Akkadian sources, Baruch Levine does argue for a link in meaning between the two words, *Numbers 1–20,* AB 4A (New York, 1993), 460.
6. Levine, *Numbers 1–20,* 470; G. B. Gray, *Numbers,* ICC (Edinburgh, 1903), 250. On the problem of placement, Gray states, "The present chapter, like c. 15, though it clearly belongs to P, has no intimate connection either with what precedes (c. 16–18—the revolt of Korah) or with what follows (c. 20—the arrival at Kadesh)," 241.

7. There is a similar reference to the fraternal tie in Amos 1:11; cp. Deut 2:4. See N. H. Snaith, *Leviticus and Numbers*, CB (London, 1967), 277; Eryl Davies, *Numbers*, NCBC (Grand Rapids, 1995), 209.
8. Gray, *Numbers*, 384.
9. Jacob Milgrom, *Leviticus 1–16*, AB 3A (New York, 1991), 711.
10. On the meaning of *parah*, see Levine, *Numbers 1–20*, 461.
11. Milgrom's statement that Lev 22:21 has the "identical construction" is inaccurate. *Numbers*, JPSTC (Philadelphia, 1990), 158.
12. For examples of wordplays in Numbers, see Timothy Ashley, *The Book of Numbers*, NICOT (Grand Rapids, 1993), 340, 521 (play upon the name Levi, and on the words for spear and stomach), and Levine, *Numbers 1–20*, 422 (a play upon *'edut*). On the role of myths and etymologies in rituals, see Geoffrey Miller, "The Legal Function of Ritual," CKLR 80 (2005), 1202.
13. Gordon Wenham, *Numbers: An Introduction and Commentary*, TOTC (Leicester, 1981), 146; Gray, *Numbers*, 250; Leonard Elliot Binns, *The Book of Numbers* (London, 1927), 127.
14. Lawrence Wright, Letter from Jerusalem, "Forcing the End," *The New Yorker*, July 20, 1998, 42, reports on an American cattle breeder who is attempting to produce a heifer that is wholly red so that some contemporary Jews and Christians can produce the ashes from it in order to usher in the Messianic era (according to their understanding of the biblical ritual).
15. Martin Noth, *Numbers*, OTL (Philadelphia, 1968), 140; Milgrom, *Numbers*, 158; also William K. Gilders, "Why Does Eleazar Sprinkle the Red Cow Blood? Making Sense of a Biblical Ritual," JHS 6 (2006), 2.
16. Gray, *Numbers*, 253; Binns, *The Book of Numbers*, 127; Milgrom, *Numbers*, 440 (see also 158); also *Leviticus 1–16*, 835.
17. Noth, *Numbers*, 140; Milgrom, *Numbers*, 438–41; ABD 3:115. See the criticism of their position by Davies, *Numbers*, 197, 199–200; Albert Baumgarten sees no link with the parallel rituals Milgrom cites in ancient Near Eastern sources. He finds "patently implausible" Milgrom's argument that the ashes constitute a ritual detergent that will absorb the impurities to which they will be applied, "The Paradox of the Red Heifer," VT 43 (1993), 444; see also Gilders's criticism of Milgrom's understanding of Eleazar's action with the blood, "Why Does Eleazar Sprinkle the Red Cow Blood?" 9.
18. See Calum Carmichael, "The Origin of the Scapegoat Ritual," VT 50 (2000), 167–82.
19. Eilberg-Schwartz, *The Savage in Judaism* (Bloomington, Ind., 1984), 188.
20. ABD 3:115.
21. Miller, "The Legal Function of Ritual," 1189.
22. Milgrom, *Numbers*, 443, taking up from Gray, *Numbers*, 244–45; Noth, *Numbers*, 141; S. Wefing, "Beobachtungen zum Ritual der roten Kuh (Num. 19 1–10a)," ZAW 93 (1981), 341–64; Roland de Vaux, *Ancient Israel* (New York, 1961), 2:461; and Paul Mpungu Muzinga, *La pratique des Rituels de Nombres 19 pendant la période hellénistique et romaine* (Pendé, France, 2008), 45.

23. Davies, *Numbers*, 193.
24. De Vaux, *Ancient Israel*, 2:462.
25. Levine, *Numbers 1–20*, 464–65.
26. On the reference to the Red Heifer ritual in Ezek 36:25, see Moshe Greenberg, *Ezekiel*, AB 22A (New York, 1997), 730, 738, and Walther Zimmerli, *Ezekiel*, trans. James Martin (Philadelphia, 1983), 2:25–48, 243, 248–49.
27. On rituals with acts that are analogous to those they are designed to counter, see Claude Lévi-Strauss, *The Raw and the Cooked* (New York, 1969), 335–36; also David P. Wright, *The Disposal of Impurity: Elimination Rites in the Bible and in Hittite and Mesopotamian Literature*, SBLDS 101 (Atlanta, 1987), 39–43. On the rainbow, see Moshe Weinfeld, *Deuteronomy and the Deuteronomic School* (Oxford, 1972), 205, 206.
28. A. O. Bell, ed., *The Diary of Virginia Woolf* (London, 1978), 167 (17 February 1922).

CHAPTER 9. SPEECH ACTS (NUMBERS 20–24)

1. Kadesh is in Edom, and it is likely that the rock is red because of the terrain—so the water may have come from red rock. The situation is reminiscent of Esau's "red, red" request, which changed his name to Edom, the "Red One." Common vocabulary can sometimes indicate continuity of presentation, in this instance, from Genesis to Numbers. Thus Timothy Ashley notes that the idiom in Num 20:24 about Aaron being gathered to his kinsfolk at death is the same one used in Gen 25:8 (Abraham), 17 (Ishmael); 35:29 (Isaac); and 49:33 (Jacob), *The Book of Numbers*, NICOT (Grand Rapids, 1993), 379, 393.
2. Walter Weyrauch, "Taboo and Magic in Law," SLR 25 (1973), 798 (discussing the conceptual rigidity of black-letter law in contemporary American legal culture, its effectiveness and practical importance because of its magical components).
3. In her accompanying note to Num 20:1–13, Nili Fox emphasizes this difference, JSB, 323.
4. See Calum Carmichael, *Women, Law, and the Genesis Traditions* (Edinburgh, 1979), 57–65, on Judah; *The Spirit of Biblical Law* (Athens, Ga., 1996), 87–88, 143–49, on the Sabbath commands and on Saul. On how conflicting layers of tradition are preserved, see Marc Brettler, *How to Read the Bible* (Philadelphia, 2005), 35–36. An excellent study of the topic of doublets is Aulikki Nahkola, *Double Narratives in the Old Testament: The Foundations of Method in Biblical Criticism*, BZAW, 290 (Berlin, 2001).
5. On Balak's attempt to curse Israel and the comparison with Isaac's blessing, see G. B. Gray, *Numbers*, ICC (Edinburgh, 1903), 327, 328.
6. "At the very least it seems capricious for God to tell Balaam to go on his way in v. 20 and then to become angry with Balaam because he was going in v. 22," Ashley, *Book of Numbers*, 454; see also Jacob Milgrom, *Numbers*, JPSTC (Philadelphia, 46), 189; and Gray, *Numbers*, 332. We might also recall the account in Exod 4:24–26 of how Yahweh, having just chosen Moses as leader of the Israelites, sought to kill him.

7. Gray, *Numbers*, 318.
8. On Balaam as an Aramean, and on the topic of Balaam's negative portrayal, see Gray, *Numbers*, 315, 320–21; also on the later identification of Balaam with Laban (Targum Jon. On Num 22:5; *b. Sanh* 105b), 321; also Pinchas Kahn, "Balaam Is Laban," *JBQ* 35 (2007), 222–30. On the phraseology of Num 24:25, "And Balak went his way," as reminiscent of Gen 32:1 "And Jacob went his way," Gray, 379.

CHAPTER 10. SEXUAL AND RELIGIOUS SEDUCTION (NUMBERS 25–31)

1. On speculation about the tribe's actual history, see Roland de Vaux, *Ancient Israel* (New York, 1961), 1:7, 2:370.
2. Philip Budd lists the many critics, *Numbers*, WBC 5 (Waco, 1984), 321.
3. Gordon Wenham, *Numbers: An Introduction and Commentary*, TOTC (Leicester, 1981), *Numbers*, 191.
4. Jacob Milgrom, *Numbers*, JPSTC (Philadelphia, 46), 219.
5. See David Daube, "Unjust Enrichment: A Might-have-been" *RJ* 9 (1990), 295–96 [*BLL*, 558–59].
6. See Calum Carmichael, *Law and Narrative in the Bible* (Ithaca, 1985), 270–76.
7. See Daube, "Error and Accident in the Bible," *RIDA* 2 (1949)," 212–13 [*BLL*, 373–74] and *Appeasement or Resistance, and Other Essays on New Testament Judaism* (Berkeley, 1987), 105–10 [*BLL*, 109–12].
8. David Daube, *Studies in Biblical Law* (Cambridge, 1947), 205–13 [*BLL*, 253–59].
9. Baruch Levine, *Numbers 1–20*, AB 4A (New York, 1993), 427–28.
10. Levine, *Numbers 1–20*, 428.
11. David Cotter, *Genesis, Berit Olam, Studies in Hebrew Narrative and Poetry* (Collegeville, Minn., 2003), 238.
12. *JSB*, 65.
13. G. B. Gray notes that the use of *ṭaph* for "little ones" in Num 31:9, 17, 18, 32:16, 24, 26 is "exceeding uncommon, if indeed ever found" in another P source (PG) he identifies. The term occurs in Gen 34:29 in regard to the children of the Hivites, *Numbers*, ICC (Edinburgh, 1903), 421.
14. N. M. Sarna, *Genesis*, JPSTC (Philadelphia, 1989), 233.
15. Shechem sees Dinah, "takes her, lies with her, and humbles ['*innah*] her" (Gen 34:2). It is almost certainly seduction (Shechem "speaks tenderly to her"), not rape, as so commonly claimed. Hebrew '*innah* is a legal term referring to the offense of a man taking a woman without the proper formalities. In Deut 22:24, where there is the humbling of a betrothed woman, the woman has consented to intercourse. See Calum Carmichael, *Sex and Religion in the Bible* (New Haven, 2010), 57–58. One rule inspired by negative judgment of Dinah's behavior is the proverbial-type injunction not to plow with an ox and an ass.

CHAPTER 11. REUBEN'S LEGACY (NUMBERS 32–36)

1. Calum Carmichael, *Law, Legend, and Incest in the Bible* (Ithaca, 1997), 38–41.
2. Adriane Leveen, *Memory and Tradition in the Book of Numbers* (Cambridge, Mass., 2007), 42.
3. David Cotter, *Genesis, Berit Olam, Studies in Hebrew Narrative and Poetry* (Collegeville, Minn., 2003), 261.
4. The commentary by Jacob on Judah in Gen 49:6–12 is wholly negative, with irony the key to its meaning. Joseph, not Reuben and not Judah, is given primacy in the family as Genesis 48 and 48:22–26 clearly spell out (cp. 1 Chron 5:1, the right of the firstborn goes to Joseph). On the condemnatory nature of the saying about Judah, see E. M. Good, "The 'Blessing' on Judah, Gen. 49:8–12," *JBL* 82 (1963), 427–32; Calum Carmichael, "Some Sayings in Genesis 49," *JBL* 88 (1969), 438–44.
5. See *Jewish Antiquities* (London, 1930), trans. H. St. J. Thackerey, 4:167.
6. My student Austin Blum of the Cornell Law School pointed out this exclusion.
7. Ron Pirson, *The Lord of the Dreams: A Semantic and Literary Analysis of Genesis 37–50*, JSOTSS 355 (Sheffield, 2002), 73.
8. Hans Jochen Boecker, *Law and the Administration of Justice in the Old Testament and Ancient East* (Minneapolis, 1980), 36.
9. Pamela Barmash, *Homicide in the Biblical World* (Cambridge, Eng., 2005), 101. Her adoption of Moshe Greenberg's solution in "The Biblical Conception of Asylum," *Studies in the Bible and Jewish Thought* (Philadelphia, 1995), 45 (that the accidental killer is automatically guilty and therefore has to spend prison time) is not convincing.
10. Jacob Milgrom, *Numbers*, JPSTC (Philadelphia, 46), 292.
11. *A Dictionary of Modern Legal Usage*, 2d ed., ed. Brian Garner (Oxford, 1995), 901.
12. See Walter Weyrauch, "The Experience of Lawlessness," *New Criminal Law Review* 10 (2007), 432 n. 41.
13. Leveen, *Memory and Tradition*, 180. On scholars who conclude that Numbers 36 is a supplement or an appendix, see Philip Budd, *Numbers*, WBC 5 (Waco, 1984), 388–89, who agrees with the scholars cited by him.
14. On the rare use of the passive form of *tsawa*, "was commanded," in Num 36:2 and Gen 45:19, see G. B. Gray, *Numbers*, ICC (Edinburgh, 1903), 477, 478. The Spartan kings decided the disposition in marriage of a woman who was her father's sole heir (Herodotus 6.57). On the Ancient Near Eastern situation, see Timothy Ashley, *The Book of Numbers*, NICOT (Grand Rapids, 1993), 543.
15. Eryl Davies, *Numbers*, NCBC (Grand Rapids, 1995), 369. Working with notions about the sources P and D, Milgrom thinks that there are philological grounds for postulating Numbers 36 as a later addition to an earlier version of the Book of Numbers, *Numbers*, 511. He cites the use of the term *šebet*, "tribe," instead of what he expects in a priestly document, namely, the term *maṭṭeh*. The former term, I would point out, is used about the twelve tribes of Israel in Gen 49:28 (detailing the sons of Jacob with Joseph singled out as the primary son). Milgrom also cites the use of *dabaq*, "to cleave to," as anomalous in Num 36:7, 9 (marital unions affecting loyalty to a tribe) but not in

D. We find it, however, in Gen 2:24 and Gen 34:3 in the more concrete sense of a man cleaving to a woman sexually. In other words, in evaluating the vocabulary of Numbers, we have to look at all the texts in Genesis–2 Kings and not feel constrained by the straightjacket imposed by scholarly theories about different source materials in the Pentateuch.

16. See chapter 6 and, for details, see Calum Carmichael, *Illuminating Leviticus: A Study of Its Laws and Institutions in the Light of Biblical Narratives* (Baltimore, 2006), 122–31.

Index of references

BIBLICAL SOURCES

Genesis
1, 18, 85
1:27, 28, 186
2:24, 194
6, 69
6:1–4, 64
6:4, 65, 68
9:3, 108
9:3–6, 11
9:4, 108, 114
9:6, 19
9:13, 118
12, 11
12:1–3, 27
13:14–18, 14:13–24, 19
15:1, 55
15:13, 27
17:1, 8, 55
19, 18
20, 11
20:3–7, 73
20:12, 159
21, 11
23, 19
24:3, 37, 156
25, 20, 22, 91, 92, 99, 105, 106, 109, 110, 112, 113, 115, 117, 118, 120, 121, 122, 124
25–32, 120
25–36, 162
25–38, 141
25–50, 7, 20
25:8, 191
25:9, 19
25:17, 191
25:19–34, 100, 101
25:20–34, 103
25:21–23, 19
25:25, 105, 110
25:27, 104, 110, 114
25:28, 104, 112
25:32, 115
25:34, 118, 123
26:35, 163
27, 4, 105, 124, 126, 130, 132
27–50, 120
27:20, 4
27:27–29, 124
27:28–29, 130
27:29, 130, 162
27:33, 124, 126
27:34–41, 130
27:36, 105

27:40, 130, 162
27:41, 130
27:46, 156
27:46–28:1, 163
28, 20, 91, 121, 127
28–31, 120
28–35, 135–36, 147
28:1, 156
28:1–15, 149
28:6, 8, 156
28:12–15, 73
28:13, 55
28:14, 133
28:20, 120, 128
28:20–22, 8, 127, 136, 147, 148, 149, 150
28:22, 92, 99, 100
29, 1, 126
29:21–30, 159
30:16, 156
31, 130, 152, 155
31:10–13, 73
31:13, 130
31:19, 155
31:24, 73, 134
31:29, 134
31:32, 8, 20, 136, 148, 150, 151, 152, 153
31:34, 7, 155
31:43, 44, 154
31:44–54, 152
31:50, 154
32, 7, 8, 20, 120, 130
32–33, 121, 129, 130
32:1, 192
32:11, 133
32:13, 132, 133
32:14–22, 132
32:16–21, 24, 25, 29, 30, 131
33, 120, 130, 133
33:10, 131
33:14, 133, 136,
33:16, 134
33:18–20, 157
33:20, 20, 138, 146

34, 1, 6, 11, 13, 20, 120, 133, 135, 136, 137, 138, 139, 140, 142, 143, 144, 145, 146, 147, 148, 149, 155, 156, 157
34–35:4, 139
34:1, 137, 155, 156
34:3, 194
34:5, 138
34:25–30, 136, 140
34:28, 157
34:29, 136, 138, 154, 157, 192
34:30, 8, 138, 140, 142, 144
34:31, 138
35, 11, 20, 120, 138, 140, 142, 144, 145, 146, 149, 163
35–37, 163
35–45, 160
35–50, 159
35:1, 20, 127, 138, 148, 149
35:1–3, 146, 157
35:1–4, 155
35:1–7, 136, 147
35:2, 138, 155, 157
35:2–4, 136, 154
35:3, 138
35:4, 157, 158
35:5, 142
35:7, 8, 20, 146, 148, 149
35:9–20, 136, 148
35:11, 55, 149–50, 156, 159
35:12, 55
35:14, 8, 148
35:15, 8
35:16–20, 149
35:22, 162, 163
35:22–29, 163
35:22–36:43, 160, 161
35:27–29, 19
35:29, 191
36, 20, 120, 162, 164
36:1–5, 163
36:6–8, 162
36:8, 161
36:31–43, 32, 133

36:35, 138
37, 11, 19, 55, 57, 58, 61, 63, 69, 70, 71, 78, 81, 83, 85, 86, 91, 92, 94, 95, 100, 126, 141, 160, 164, 165, 168, 171, 172, 176
37–45, 160, 174
37–50, 10, 18, 45, 54, 57, 60, 61, 62, 77, 120
37:1, 59, 77
37:2, 63, 169
37:3, 87
37:5–8, 72, 87
37:6, 74
37:6–8, 65
37:7, 73, 80
37:8, 84, 87
37:9, 62, 85
37:10, 70, 77, 80
37:12–14, 171
37:18, 20, 21, 165, 167
37:26, 172
37:26–28, 26–35, 126
37:27, 172
37:30, 170
37:31–33, 64
38, 24, 25, 27, 28, 30, 32, 36, 40, 50, 52, 55, 57, 58, 62, 97, 126, 185
38:1, 50–51, 58
38:2, 52
38:11, 50, 51
38:15, 37
38:15–26, 159
38:21, 35
38:26, 30, 50
38:29, 27, 42
38:30, 27
39, 86
39:1, 58
41–47, 21, 55, 61
41–45, 55, 59
41:16, 23
41:36, 46
41:40–44, 62
41:44, 55
41:45, 23

41:47–49, 61
41:57, 62, 76
42, 55, 63
42–45, 63
42:6, 9, 65, 69, 75, 80
42:12, 9
42:22, 171
42:28, 74
42:30, 65
42:33, 96
43:1–14, 63
43:9, 47
43:14, 46
43:18, 47, 95
43:22, 47
43:23, 48
43:26, 69, 75, 76, 80
44, 63
44:1–17, 97
44:18, 21
44:33, 126
45:3, 4, 74
45:8, 80
45:10, 56, 95
45:19, 193
46:4, 117
46:8–24, 141
46:10, 139
46:27, 141
46:32, 34, 56
47, 54, 55
47:6, 56
47:22, 22, 23
47:23–26, 16
47:24, 17, 49
48, 54, 56, 164, 193
48:22–26, 193
49, 35, 184
49:3, 4, 54, 162
49:5, 139
49:5–7, 140
49:6, 6, 193
49:6–12, 193

49:12, 35
49:28, 193
49:33, 191
50, 22, 55, 57, 173
50:1, 117
50:1–13, 19
50:10–13, 183
50:13, 19
50:15–20, 173
50:15–21, 57
50:19, 74
50:20, 70, 74
50:24, 19

Exodus

1:5, 141
1:8, 20, 57
4:22, 56
4:24–26, 191
5:1, 3, 16
5:7, 188
5:10, 21, 22–23, 6:16, 20, 16
12, 58, 109
13, 109
13:9, 16, 88
14:8, 80
14:14, 97
15:3, 97, 118
15:25, 123
17, 125
17:1–7, 124, 129
20:7, 4
20:8–11, 125
20:15, 4
21–23, 2, 11
21:28–32, 172
22:7–13, 51
22:16, 17, 13
25–29, 3
31:1–11, 12–17, 85
31:13–17, 84
31:17, 85
32, 95, 125

32:26–29, 171
35:3, 83, 188
40:35, 3

Leviticus

1–3, 1–15, 3
6:2 (5:21), 46
6:2–7 (5:20–26), 44–53
6:5, 53
8–9, 3
8:9, 185
9:23, 3
10, 15
11:24–28, 117
12:2, 184
15:19, 20, 7
15:19–24, 6
16, 113, 114
18, 159
18:3, 15, 60, 70, 160, 177
18:11, 12, 159
18:14, 16
18:15, 32, 159
18:16, 32
18:18, 159
18:24–30, 160
19:11–12, 2–4
20, 159
20:12, 32, 159
20:17, 19, 20, 159
20:21, 32
20:23, 160
21:12, 185
22:21, 190
22:4–6, 117
24:5–9, 77
24:14, 82
25, 10, 57, 70, 71
25–27, 16
25:2–13, 10
25:13, 177
25:42, 60
26:3–5, 16

27, 16
27:16, 19, 17

Numbers
1, 21, 22, 141, 142
1–4, 15, 21, 23
1–25, 141
1:47–53, 22
2, 22, 24
3, 22, 24, 25
3:1, 18
3:1–10, 22
3:4, 15
3:11–13, 23, 52, 105
3:40–51, 23, 105
3:44–4:49, 25
4, 22, 23, 24
4:17–20, 23, 24
5, 23, 24, 26, 27, 29, 32, 42, 54, 57, 69, 185
5–6, 28, 68
5:5, 186
5:5–10, 26, 44, 50
5:5–6:27, 25, 41
5:6–10, 44, 49, 53
5:7, 51
5:8, 50
5:12, 32
5:12–31, 29
5:18, 38
5:28, 27
5:30, 31, 32
6, 23, 24, 26, 27, 34, 37, 40, 42, 54, 57, 69
6:2, 34
6:2–21, 26, 33
6:3, 36
6:5, 37, 38, 39
6:11, 38
6:19, 39
6:24–27, 42
7, 24, 54, 56, 57, 105
7–8, 54, 55
7–14, 7:2, 11, 12, 54
7:48–59, 56

8, 22, 24, 56, 57, 105
8:17, 18, 19, 57
9, 24, 55, 57, 58, 59
9:10, 58
9:14, 58, 59
9:23, 21
10, 24, 59
10–11, 55, 59
11, 20, 55, 61
11–14, 60, 61
11:1, 82
11:4–6, 12, 60
11:16–30, 61
11:18, 18–32, 60
11:28, 29, 62
12, 55, 61, 62
12:2, 3, 62
12:6–7, 74
12:8, 62
13, 63, 64, 65, 69, 161
13–14, 55, 63
13:2, 19
13:19, 56
13:22, 19
13:27, 56
13:32, 63, 69
13:33, 64, 65
14, 64, 65, 66, 69, 70, 142
14:3, 60, 66
14:4, 60
14:5, 65
14:9, 77
14:15, 16, 66
14:30, 62
14:33, 64
14:34, 66
14:36, 37, 69
14:40–45, 44, 66
15, 19, 65, 68, 69, 70, 71, 89, 90, 101, 177, 187
15:1–16, 68, 71, 72
15:1–21, 76
15:2–21, 73

15:3, 82
15:4, 72
15:14–16, 78
15:17–21, 68, 71, 72, 73
15:17–36, 82
15:19, 77
15:22–31, 68, 71, 78, 79
15:23, 79
15:24, 187
15:27, 79
15:30, 80, 83
15:31, 80, 81, 82, 83
15:32–36, 71, 81, 82, 85, 97
15:37–41, 71, 86, 87, 88
15:38, 87
15:40, 96
15:41, 88
16, 70, 83, 84, 89, 90, 92, 94, 95, 100, 116, 145
16–18, 22, 91, 94, 97, 105
16:3, 94
16:5, 14, 15, 95
16:28, 96
16:29, 30, 89
16:32, 77
17, 95, 96, 100, 116
17:1–15 [16:36–50], 93
17:8, 96
17:8–10, 85
18, 92, 98, 99, 100, 101, 106, 108
18:1, 100
18:20, 99
18:32, 100
19, 19, 22, 101, 103, 106, 108, 109, 110, 114, 117, 118, 119, 121, 123, 157
19:1–22, 106
19:2, 110, 115
19:4, 114
19:9, 112, 113
19:10, 117
19:14–16, 114
19:17, 113
20, 118, 120, 121, 122, 123, 124, 125, 127, 128, 129

20–24, 120, 135
20–36, 120
20:1, 153
20:1–13, 122, 146, 191
20:8, 122, 123
20:10, 11, 122
20:12, 123, 153
20:14, 109, 127
20:14–16, 20, 21
20:14–21, 124
20:14–29, 117
20:24, 191
20:24–28, 153
21, 19, 121, 127, 128, 129
21–36, 127
21:3, 5, 5–9, 128
22, 132
22–24, 7, 20, 43, 121, 124, 129, 130, 133, 134
22:1, 133
22:3, 132
22:5, 192
22:6, 131
22:8, 131, 132
22:9, 134
22:13, 131
22:17–18, 132
22:18, 124
22:19, 134
22:20, 130, 134
22:21–35, 131
22:22, 130, 131
22:22–24:25, 131
22:25, 31, 132
23:3, 131
23:7, 133
23:9, 133, 136
23:10, 133
23:13, 124
23:23, 131
23:25, 130
24:7, 8, 43
24:9, 130

24:14, 134
24:17–25, 130
24:25, 134, 192
25, 11, 18, 20, 133, 135, 136, 137, 138, 139, 140, 148, 154, 156
25–27, 143
25–31, 135, 136
25:1, 133, 134, 136, 156
25:1–3, 1–7, 138
25:1–13, 156
25:2, 138, 155
25:3, 155
25:4, 139
25:5–8, 156
25:6, 6–8, 137
25:14, 139
25:16–18, 138
25:18, 140, 165
26, 105, 141, 142
26–27, 136, 140
26–30, 140
26–36, 141
26:10, 77
26:19–22, 25
26:53–56, 141
26:59, 16, 159
26:63–65, 141
26:64, 65, 141, 142
27, 8, 11, 136, 142, 143, 145, 149, 174, 175, 176
27:1–11, 143, 144
27:3, 145
27:12–23, 146
27:13, 153
27:14, 146
27:21, 147
28, 8, 20, 136, 147, 148, 149
28:7, 14, 148
29, 8, 20, 136, 147, 148, 149
29:18, 24, 27, 30, 33, 34, 37, 38, 148
29:39, 148, 150
30, 20, 136, 148, 150, 152, 153, 154

30:2, 149, 150, 152, 153
30:2–17, 8
30:3–5, 154
30:3–16, 153
30:6–8, 154
30:16, 8, 152
31, 11, 20, 136, 137, 139, 140, 154, 155, 156, 157, 162, 163
31:2, 153
31:7, 155
31:8, 156
31:9, 192
31:15–18, 156
31:16, 134, 155
31:17, 18, 192
31:21–24, 157
31:29, 30, 157
31:49, 49–54, 157
31:50, 54, 158
32, 161, 162, 164
32–34, 159, 160, 161
32–36, 159, 160, 163, 176
32:1, 4, 162
32:8, 161
32:16, 24, 26, 192
33, 163
33–34, 151, 164
33:1–49, 19
33:3, 80
34, 163
34:21, 151
35, 159, 160, 164, 165, 168, 170, 171, 172, 174
35:9–34, 10–34, 165
35:12, 169
35:16–18, 16–21, 20, 21, 22, 23, 167
35:24, 169
35:25, 170
35:26–28, 173
35:30, 167
35:33, 19, 169
36, 11, 141, 147, 160, 164, 174, 175, 176, 177, 193

36:1, 176, 177
36:1–12, 177
36:2, 193
36:5, 175, 177
36:7, 193
36:8, 177
36:9, 193
36:12, 177

Deuteronomy

2:4, 190
4:15–19, 85
5:11, 4
5:12–15, 125
5:19, 4
7:1–3, 6
8:2, 16, 66
12–26, 2, 12
12:23, 114
15:19, 115
17:14–20, 21:15–17, 109
22:10, 6
22:12, 86, 88
22:13–21, 86
22:23–27, 29
22:24, 192
22:28, 29, 13
23:5, 134
24:1–4, 83
24:16, 144
24:19–22, 75
32:21, 82
33:8–11, 171

Joshua

17:2, 7, 20:7, 171
24:10, 134
24:32, 171

Judges

13:1–7, 34
13:2–5, 16:1, 17:6, 18:1, 21:25, 41

Ruth

4:7, 37, 118
4:12, 37
4:18–22, 42

1 Samuel

1:1–11, 34
1:11, 13, 15, 16, 41
15, 127
15:8, 43
18, 1
25, 36
28, 127
31, 126

2 Samuel

1, 126
8:12, 12:31, 43
13:23–28, 36–37

2 Kings

3:20–22, 105
14:1–14, 1
17:35, 65

1 Chronicles

5:1, 54, 193

Nehemiah

13:2, 134

Job

28:7, 104

Psalms

106:19, 125

Proverbs

9, 38
23:29, 35

Ecclesiastes

7:13, 9:11, 67

Canticles
2:5, 36, 185

Isaiah
7:1–17, 63
16:7, 36
34:5–7, 63:1–6, 105

Jeremiah
7:18, 36, 188
44:19, 36

Ezekiel
35:5, 5–6, 16–21, 117
36:25, 117, 191

Daniel
2, 75, 76
2:11, 76
2:31–35, 75, 76
2:46, 76
4, 75, 76
4:10–17, 76

Hosea
3:1, 36, 185
4:11, 35
5:3–14, 63
8:6, 125

Amos
1:11, 190
2:7, 9, 11–12, 36

Habakkuk
3:9, 11, 118

Zephaniah
2:1, 83

Matthew
17:25, 26, 186
19:24–27, 183

1 Corinthians
10:14–23, 22, 82

TARGUMS

On Numbers (Jonathan)
22:5, 192

APOCRYPHA AND
PSEUDEPIGRAPHA

Jubilees
34:18, 19, 113

Sirach
38:5, 123

Testament of Judah
12:2, 3, 35, 36

PHILO

De specialibus legibus
4.31, 46

TALMUDIC SOURCES

Mishnah
Berakoth
5:5, 131
Nazir
2:7, 36

Tosephta
Pesachim
1:27, 183

Babylonian Talmud
Berakoth
34b, 131
Erubin
64b, 183

Kiddushin
23b, 22
41b, 131
Menahot
44a, 86
Nedarim
35b, 22
Sanhedrin
105b, 192
Yoma
19a, 22

Jerusalem Talmud
Abodah Zarah
40a, 183

MIDRASHIM AND OTHER JEWISH SOURCES

Genesis Rabba
31:32, 153
34:1, 156

Leviticus Rabba
27:2, 183

Numbers Rabba
19:3, 106

Pesiqta de Rab Kahana
4:7, 106

ANCIENT LEGAL SOURCES

Code of Hammurabi
131, 132, 26

Hittite Laws
1–5, 172

Middle Assyrian Laws
A10, B2, 172

CLASSICAL AUTHORS

Homer
Odyssey
18:55, 140, 189

Herodotus
6.57, 193

EARLY CHRISTIAN AUTHORS

Theodoret of Cyr
Historia ecclesiastica
3.5, 185

Subject Index

Aaron's benediction, 41–43
Adjudication: impartiality, 147, 164, 169, 171, 172; status dependent, 82, 84, 89, 97–98, 169
Agency, 131
Agnation, 144
Allegory, 91
Amnesty, 173–74
Ancestors: founding nation, 4, 6, 7, 8, 20, 21, 22, 53, 64, 65, 87, 105–6, 115, 118, 124, 127, 140, 148, 150, 159, 160, 172, 173, 176, 178; opposition to, 1, 18 (*see also* Imitation par opposition); recall, 40, 106, 113, 157 (*see also* Memory)
Animal-human distinction, 104, 132
Aphrodisiac, 185
Assimilation, 56
Avenger of blood, 168–70
Azazel, 114

Beginnings: in Genesis, 7–8, 20, 24, 27, 40, 42, 54, 69, 71, 87, 91, 100–102, 108, 117–18, 119, 133, 135, 136, 141, 147, 148; law codes, 11–12; significance, 74, 83. *See also* Ancestors
Betrayal, 32, 49
Betrothal, 29, 192

Birthright loss: Esau's, 4–5, 9–10, 19, 22, 91, 99–101, 103–5, 111–12, 113, 115, 118, 120–24, 127, 151, 157, 162; Reuben's, 159–63
Bitter water, 26, 28–29, 31
Blasphemy, 65, 82
Blood: animal, 87, 112; eating, 91, 99, 101–2, 104, 105, 107, 108, 111–15, 118, 122, 123, 157, 189; Joseph's coat, 9, 59, 126, 168–69; land, 19, 117, 169; magic, 118; menstrual, 7, 34, 40; person's, 165–66, 169, 170, 171–73; sanctuary, 102, 106, 108, 110, 114; wedding night, 86
Bodily parts, 88
Bride-price, 1, 14

Calendar, 20, 148, 149
Charisma, 62
Childbirth, 39, 136, 148–50, 152–53
Cities of asylum, 159, 160, 164–65, 170–71
Clothing, 37–39, 40, 71, 83, 86–88, 96, 105, 106–7, 111, 138, 157, 165, 169. *See also* Blood: Joseph's coat
Coded communication, 6, 84
Confession, 30–32, 49–50
Conscience, 27, 30–31
Contamination. *See* Pollution

Subject Index

Corpse, 38, 40, 58–59, 64, 106, 107, 108, 110, 114, 115–17
Creation, 1, 18, 83–85, 89, 126, 188
Curse, 27, 28, 29, 31, 42, 124, 129–31, 135, 153, 191

Day of Atonement, 58, 113–14, 118
Dead: wronged, 50–51
Death: direct divine action, 15, 24, 25, 39, 42, 52, 89, 97; repelling, 19, 101, 107–15, 118; sentence, 23, 29–30, 77, 81–82, 84, 85, 86, 89, 152, 166, 169, 172; suicide, 126–27; wilderness, 66
Decalogue, 11
Deposit, 45–46, 51, 184
Dinah's fate, 137–38
Divination, 97, 129, 135, 136, 155
Divine beings, 20, 23, 34, 64–65, 68, 69, 79, 80, 85, 90, 95, 97, 121, 125–26, 129–32
Divinity: claim to, 9, 16, 60, 61–62, 69, 70, 74, 77, 83, 84, 88, 90, 94, 96, 188
Drunkenness, 35–37, 41, 75, 126

Enrichment: unjust, 144, 174–77
Equity, 175
Error, 105, 110, 169
Etiology, 139
Exclusiveness, 55, 61, 74, 138
Exorcism, 40, 116

Fable: thistle and cedar, 1–2,
Fathers and sons, 7, 8, 9, 36, 50, 56, 57, 80, 135, 140–43, 144, 145, 147, 149, 161, 163, 168, 193
Favoritism, 9, 87, 90–91, 100, 101, 169, 171
Fetus, 31
Fiction, 13, 52, 109, 114, 115
Firstborn: status, 22, 23, 24, 91, 92, 94, 99, 100, 116, 117, 139. *See also* Birthright loss
Forgiveness, 45, 57, 64, 78, 154, 173–74
Formalism, 54, 82, 169, 192

Gender, 34
Gifts, 17, 56, 73, 98–99, 132, 174
God: apologizing for, 67; duty bound, 60; failure to use name, 123, 146; misuse of name, 2, 4, 45, 47, 48, 53, 123; morality and omnipotence, 66; rebelling against, 80–81, 84, 123, 146; reliance second-best, 51; reputation, 67, 123, 146; ruler like Pharaoh, 15, 16, 21, 22, 23, 55–57, 60; temple's sovereign, 186; testing God, 129; testing man, 66–67
Golden Calf, 85, 95, 125, 171
Greed, 34, 52

Hair: Esau, 4, 103, 104, 110, 126, 132; Nazirite, 33, 37, 38, 39, 185; suspected adulteress, 31, 38, 39
Heraclitus of Ephesus, 10
Historical development, 3–6, 13, 44–45, 48, 49, 51, 73, 139
History writing, 3, 5, 7, 8–9, 10, 12, 13, 15, 21, 91, 134, 139, 159, 178
Homicide, 159, 160, 164–68, 171, 174, 176
Household gods, 1, 7, 8, 20, 136, 148, 150, 151, 152, 153, 155
Hubris, 82, 84

Idolatry, 11, 20, 36, 76, 138, 139, 165, 188. *See also* Joseph
Illusion, 112, 114, 119
Imitation par opposition, 9–10, 15, 37, 38, 39, 56, 78, 91, 101, 110, 111, 112, 118, 177
Incest, 16, 30, 31, 32, 159, 160, 161, 162
Intermarriage, 6, 133
International order, 140
Invented tradition, 40, 114, 117, 119, 139
Irony, 177, 193
Israelite identity, 57, 116, 136–40, 145, 155, 163
Israelite infighting, 54, 57, 69–70, 89, 100, 164
Israelite law: actual history, 4, 6, 13, 17, 45, 48, 53, 60, 115, 117, 119, 168, 169, 171, 172

Israelite religion, 4, 26, 117
Israelite sacrificial system, 73

Jealousy: divine, 82; human, 28–29, 62, 88; religious-political, 139–40
Joseph: anti-type to Moses, 18, 95; dreams, like Daniel's, 75; not from God, 73, 74, 80, 187; Egyptian policies, 10, 16, 49, 57, 60, 70–71, 177; idolatrous, 9, 19, 61–62, 70–79, 81, 83, 85, 90; loss of inheritance, 11, 147, 160, 174, 176–78; marriage, 62; priestly powers, 23; scholarly assessment, 2
Josephus, 163
Jubilee, 10, 57, 70–71, 174, 177–78

Language: power, 123–24, 146
Laws: and narratives, 2, 4, 5–7, 10–14, 17, 20, 45, 81, 84, 88, 110, 117, 125, 176, 182; hypothetical, 17, 49, 52, 117, 172; indeterminate, 175; overliteral meaning, 47, 105, 151, 153; placement of collections, 11–13; similar, 13–14, 44–45
Legal advocacy, 12
Legal constitution, 17
Legal instrument, 51, 105, 154
Legal process, 140
Levirate custom, 29–32, 35–40, 51–52
Levites: like Egyptian priests, 22–23; impartiality, 144, 171; status, 25, 56–57, 97, 99–100, 139, 157
Licentiousness, 35–38, 86
Literary convention, 10, 11, 20–21, 109, 119, 176
Lost object, 45, 47
Lovemaking, 35–36, 156
Lying, 2, 4

Magic, 85, 106, 113, 115–16, 118, 124, 191
Marriage: David's, 1; Jacob's, 1, 9–10, 149, 152; Joseph's, 62; Moses', 62; renovated, 83; sacred character, 32; unacceptable, 1–2, 133, 136, 137, 138

Meat, 108, 110–15, 118
Memory, 28, 30–31, 39, 58, 59, 64, 71, 88, 93, 106, 108, 116, 157–58. *See also* Ancestors: recall
Menstruation, 6–7, 34, 40, 150, 152
Mental element, 79–80
Metaphor, 77
Migratory history, 7, 59, 120, 130, 135, 141, 159, 163,
Milieu: influence, 10, 11, 78, 160
Miracles, 60–61, 96–97, 123, 125, 129, 132
Miscarriage, 27
Moderation: Jacob's, 6
Montesquieu, 3
Mourning, 38, 39

Narratives: construction, 9–10; double retribution, 126; doublets, 125–27; replication and reworking, 19, 20, 130, 140, 161

Oaths, 46, 47, 51, 53, 100, 105, 118, 120, 122, 123, 136, 148, 150–54
Ordeal, 26, 184
Origins. *See* Beginnings

Passion, 29, 140
Passover, 57–59, 108–9, 118
Patriarchs. *See* Ancestors
Personification, 77
Pollution: blood, 118, 166, 169; booty, 157; carrying out ritual, 112; death, 102, 106–8, 110, 114–17; water, 123
Priests: highest authority, 147–48; high priest's death, 173; relationship to deity, 95–100; special tithe, 108; use of blood, 108, 110, 114
Primary history, 1, 5
Procreation, 132–33, 184, 186
Prophetic insight: past and future, 15, 182
Prostitution, 29, 32, 35–41, 52, 53, 86, 138
Proverbs, 6, 192

Psychological impact, 31, 76
Public sinning, 123
Punishment: communal, 145; double, 125–27; extreme, 66, 89; individual, 144; light, 48; mirroring, 29, 30, 35, 36, 64; puzzling, 121

Qadištu-woman, 39

Ransom, 166, 171–73
Rape, 192
Religion: definition, 97
Rite: archaic, 117; exorcism, 116; foreign, 117; forms, 118; funerary, 117; official, 97; riddance, 106, 108
Ritual: drama, 101, 108, 115–16, 118
Robbery, 47

Sabbatical cycle, 10, 57, 70–71
Sacred fire, 82–83, 157, 188
Sacred order, 19, 22, 25, 82, 83, 97, 100–101, 105, 108, 118, 122, 123, 145, 148, 173
Scribal activity, 4, 5, 10, 11, 12, 84, 113, 117, 125
Seduction: religious and sexual, 35–36, 135–37, 154–56, 163; sexual, 13–14, 18, 29, 37, 38, 52, 120, 143, 192
Service to foreign king, 75, 83
Sibling rivalry, 61–62, 94–95, 100, 124, 141, 164
Signs, 31, 37, 38, 40, 59, 85, 88, 93, 97, 110, 114, 118, 173–74
Silence, 51, 109, 144, 163, 168, 184
Simeonites, 135, 137, 139–40, 156

Slaves: blameworthy, 60; renewal of slavery, 60, 64; status, 145, 176
Storytelling, 2, 9, 11, 12, 27, 29, 41, 73, 81, 86, 134, 178. *See also* Ritual
Superstition, 87, 97
Survivors, 62–63
Syllogism, 186

Temple tax, 182, 186
Theft, 2–5, 95, 105, 151, 152
Theocracy, 145
Time, delay, 115, 154
Trust: in deity, 61, 62, 65–66, 123, 128, 142; human, 23, 24, 27, 32, 44, 49–53

Unwanted salvation, 131, 134
Urim, 146–47

Violence: approval, 139–40

Wellhausen method, 2–5, 13, 44–45, 48, 50–51, 53, 125, 129, 140, 175, 178, 189, 193, 194
Wine, 33–37, 41
Women's oaths and vows, 8, 20, 26, 28, 33, 37, 39, 40, 136, 152–55
Woolf, Virginia, 119
Wordplays, 35, 105, 110–11, 184, 190
Wrongful looking, 9

Zeal, 138–40, 142, 155, 156, 157, 163
Zelophehad's daughters, 7, 143–45, 149, 174–77